OVER THERE

OVER THERE

The Story of America's First Great
Overseas Crusade

FRANK FREIDEL

BURFORD BOOKS

Printed in the United States of America

10 9 8 7 6 5 4 3 2 1

Library of Congress Cataloging-in-Publication Data
Freidel, Frank Burt.
    Over there : the American experience in World War I /
Frank Freidel.
        p.   cm.
    ISBN 1-58080-106-4
    1. World War, 1914–1918—United States.   2. World War,
1914–1918—Campaigns—Western Front.   I. Title.
D570.F74   2002
940.4'8173—dc21
                                                    2002151687

Contents

INTRODUCTION

In 1917 and 1918 some two million Americans crossed the Atlantic to participate in the first great crusade in Europe. It was a profound experience for these young men: the first mass American discovery of Europe and of the realities of warfare in the twentieth century. The experience was as diverse as the backgrounds of the men themselves and their varying encounters. It molded their future thoughts and lives in many ways and thus helped shape the direction of the American nation. The purpose of this account of some of them is to suggest what the war meant to them all and what it may signify in the American heritage.

For many of these young men, the Declaration of War in April 1917 was the call to an unpleasant task. Some already knew that as many men had died at the fortress of Verdun as on all the battlefields of the Civil War, and that this modern conflict was more notable for wretched huddling in the mud and frightful death than for high idealism.

Long before American entrance, a few, dreaming chivalric
dreams, had volunteered to serve with the French or the British.
Even after a year and a half of combat, the young poet Alan
Seeger could write a friend:

"We go up to the attack tommorow. This will probably be
the biggest thing yet. . . . I am glad to be going in [the] first
wave. If you are in this thing at all it is best to be in to the limit.
And this is the supreme experience."

It was Seeger's last letter.

Many others enlisted as soon as the United States became
involved. One father wrote of his sons: "Brought up on the
Battle of Gettysburg and frequently reminded that a test of
patriotism comes sharply in some form to every generation, it
was to be expected that the three Brown boys . . . would go to
war against the Germans."

In the months after April 1917 the National Guardsmen
were mobilized, and through Selective Service an army num-
bering in the millions was built. Most of those who went overseas had fun and thrills, but also underwent the discomfort of
being billeted in French barns, training in the mud and cold,
and then serving in trenches still more uncomfortable.

At the front there was the roar of the barrages: "Now talk
about noise, there can never be as much noise concentrated in
such small space again I believe." There was cumulative
fatigue, hunger, and thirst, compounded by living for weeks in
clothes often wet and almost always lice-ridden. There was
the stench of dysentery and death. Sometimes death was present in peaceful form: "Now and then we saw a figure clad in
olive drab on the ground, some so closely simulated sleep that
were it not for the frost on their clothing and hair one would
think it was only a Yank asleep." Usually death was frightful.
A brave officer who been through too much told Dr. Harvey
Cushing in October 1918:

"The chief trouble now is the dreams—not exactly dreams
either, but right in the middle of an ordinary conversation the
head of a Boche that I have bayoneted, with its horrible gurgle
and grimace comes sharply into view. . . . Yes, it was unpleasant

amputating those men's legs, and we had to sharpen a knife from a man's kit for it, but what could one do otherwise? . . . But the worst of all are the dying faces that come to me of the men of the command—the men I could not bear to see die—men whose letters I had censored, so I knew all about them and their homes and worries and dependents."

While struggling for survival Americans were little disposed to give much though to war aims. Lieutenant Howard B. O'Brien, who in the 1920s published anonymously a sensitive diary, *Wine, Women and War,* wrote home from behind the lines in 1918:

"The gilt chips off the glamor of soldiering pretty quick over here. Mail call and the quality of the mess become of deeper interest than the future of the world or who wears the crown of Courland. . . .

"Consciously or not, we are here to fight for democracy even if we make ribald remarks when you mention it. But, frankly, we don't give much of a damn for the future of the Balkans, or trade routes to Kamchatka; and while 'bringing the Kaiser to his knees' is a sonorous phrase, it is to many of us at least, neither specific enough, nor satisfying if it were—for when poor old deluded Wilhelm has agreed to everything and bit the dust . . . there still remains the German people to dispose of and a world future concerning which, alas, too few people have tangible ideas."

Lieutenant O'Brien wrote while the war was going on. Then came the Armistice and months of wait before going home, months marked by more discomfort and endless maneuvering and drilling—all of which, with the fighting over, seemed pointless to the soldiers. At last they returned, received heroes' welcomes, and settled back into civilian life. Their crusade was over.

What had it meant to them? Some of the most articulate interpreted their experiences and emotions in novels; John Dos Passos, Ernest Hemingway, and a host of gifted writers emerged as spokesmen for the warring generation. Others, less celebrated as literary figures, deserve to be heard also, through their

diaries, letters, and the regimental histories they hastily com-
piled during the waiting months of 1918–1919. These others
also have much to say, writing sometimes crudely, sometimes
with stylistic skill, and often with a compelling eloquence. This
is their book.

1

"THE WORLD MUST BE MADE SAFE FOR DEMOCRACY"

On a gloomy day in the summer of 1918, an artilleryman, Coningsby Dawson, sat in his shelter on the edge of a Canadian trench on the Western Front amid rain, mud, and melancholy, wondering when if ever the war would be over. "Not soon," he and the men of his company all agreed. "I believe that, and yet I hope," he wrote home:

"Along all the roads of France, in all the trenches, in every gunpit you can hear one song being sung by the *poilus* and Tommies. They sing it while they load their guns, they whistle it as they march up the line, they hum it while they munch their bully-beef and hardtack. You hear it on the regimental bands and grinding out from gramophones in hidden dugouts:

Over there. Over there
Send the word, send the word over there,
That the Yanks are coming—

"Men repeat that ragtime promise as tho it were a prayer, The Yanks are coming. We could have won without the Yanks—we're sure of that. Still, we're glad they're coming and we walk jauntily. We may die before the promise is sufficiently fulfilled to tell. What does that matter? The Yanks are coming. We shall not have died in vain. They will reap the peace for the world which our blood has sown."

The First World War, seemingly so endless, had broken out in the summer of 1914, and after the sweeping advance of the Germans toward Paris had been broken in the First Battle of the Marne it had developed in the west into a grim war of attrition as each side held off the other in trenches and strongpoints, a siege and countersiege from Switzerland to the North Sea. And as each side mounted massive offensives to try to break through the other, or in turn threw its reserves into stemming the enemy advances, the blood of a whole generation of Englishmen, Frenchmen, and Germans was poured out from Flanders to Verdun. Each summer, wrote the artilleryman, the British troops had told themselves they had spent their last winter in France, "but always and always there has been another."

With appalled fascination neutral America had followed from afar the first two and a half years of the great siege—but had remained neutral. Then at 8:30 on the evening of April 2, 1917, President Woodrow Wilson solemnly appeared before the Congress of the United States, which he had summoned to meet in special session. The American people well knew why he was there—to assert that the recent course of the Imperial German government had been in fact nothing less than war, and that the United States should formally accept the status of belligerent that the German government had thrust upon it. The President did more than make this request and enumerate the German provocations that led to it. In words of eloquent idealism, he set forth the positive goals for which the United States should fight:

"It is a fearful thing to lead this great peaceful people into war, into the most terrible and disastrous of all wars, civilization itself seeming to be in the balance. But the right is more precious than peace, and we shall fight for the things which we have always carried nearest our hearts—for democracy . . . for the rights and liberties of small nations, for a universal domination of right. . . . To such a task we can dedicate our lives and our fortunes, everything that we are and everything that we have, with the pride of those who know that the day has come when America is privileged to spend her blood and her might for the principles that gave her birth and happiness and the peace which she has treasured."

One sentence above all, people remembered from Wilson's war message: "The world must be made safe for democracy."

In this noble fashion, President Wilson summoned the youth of America into the most bloody of all wars in human history up to this time. Before the Armistice, millions of men entered the armed forces, some never leaving the United States, some serving on the seas, and nearly two million reaching France. Some went as crusaders, some as adventurers, and some because they had no other choice. Of those who fought, 81,000 never returned. Of the multitude that came back, some were still idealistic and some disillusioned, but few there were who remained untouched by their experiences. They had indeed helped reap the peace, and though they had survived, paid heavily for the harvest.

The events that led to American entrance into the war were easy enough to trace. While through their trench warfare on the Western Front the French and English troops on the one side and the German on the other had in effect been besieging each other, the British and Germans had been engaged in a parallel blockade on the high seas. The British Navy, of superior strength, had kept the Imperial German Navy bottled in the North Sea, and operating in keeping with traditional rules of naval warfare for the most part, prevented neutral nations overseas from supplying Germany with munitions and foodstuffs. Early in 1915 Germany began to retaliate. Its submarines, contrary to international law, began to sink ships bound for England without warning, and in May of that year, to the horror of Americans, torpedoed the great passenger liner the *Lusitania*,

Marching through London on the way to France, August 1917

German cavalry leaving Berlin, August 1914

Sinking of the tanker Illinois, March 18, 1917

drowning 1,198 people. Ultimately President Wilson, holding the Germans to "strict accountability," obtained a pledge that submarine commanders would stop surprise sinkings. The German government kept its word until the beginning of 1917, when the military leaders in control took the calculated gamble of resuming unrestricted submarine warfare even though they expected the resumption would bring an American declaration of war. They estimated that the submarines could starve England into submission before the United States could muster decisive strength.

Thus it was that President Wilson, who as late as January 1917 had hoped for an equitable "peace among equals"—a "peace without victory"—reluctantly decided that he must ask Congress to declare war against Germany. He and a large part of the American people had come to believe that the cause of Germany was an unrighteous one, a belief heightened by an intercepted message from the German Foreign Minister, Arthur Zimmerman, proposing that in the event America went to war, Mexico join with Germany and win back her lost territory north of the border. On March 18, Wilson learned that German submarines had sunk three American ships, among them the oil tanker *Illinois*, steaming down the English Channel in ballast, bound homeward to Texas, a large pair of American flags and the initials "U.S.A." painted on its side. It was not sunk without warning, but rather stopped by a German submarine, boarded, plundered, and destroyed by setting off bombs in the oil compartments. Three days later the President decided upon war and called a special session of Congress.

When Congress voted a war resolution on April 6, 1917, the nation had little idea what this momentous step involved. The United States seemed to be entering the war because of the rather narrow reason that Germany had violated its neutral rights. Only in ensuing months did the American people come to be indoctrinated with Wilson's noble aims—and also with a passionate hatred of Imperial Germany. Throughout the war blaring bands, flying flags, and unlimited patriotic oratory whipped the fighting spirit of civilian America to a fever pitch.

President Wilson marching in a Liberty Loan parade

Assistant Secretary Franklin D. Roosevelt, Secretary of the Navy Josephus Daniels, and the bureau chiefs

No one in April 1917 envisaged how enormous the American contribution would have to be in terms of either men or supplies. The general assumption was that the Allies needed more food, material of war, and loans, but that they possessed sufficient manpower. This was to be a struggle for freedom of the seas in which it was thought the Navy would do most of the fighting. The Navy Department under Secretary Josephus Daniels and Assistant Secretary Franklin D. Roosevelt was relatively well prepared, but had been restrained by President Wilson until the actual declaration of war. It made an indelible impression upon Roosevelt that President Wilson, acting out of conscience, would not permit the Navy to go farther.

"I was Acting Secretary of the Navy and it was the first week in March. . . . I went to see the President and I said, 'President Wilson, may I request your permission to bring the Fleet back from Guantanamo, to send it to the Navy Yards and have it cleaned and fitted for war and be ready to take part in the War if we get in?' And the President said, 'I am very sorry, Mr. Roosevelt, I cannot allow it.' But I pleaded and he gave me no reason and said, 'No, I do not wish it brought north.' So, belonging to the Navy, I said, 'Aye, aye, sir.' And started to leave the room. He stopped me at the door and said, 'Come back.' He said, 'I am going to tell you something I cannot tell to the public. I owe you an explanation. I don't want to do anything . . . by way of war preparations, that would allow the definitive historian in later days to say that the United States had committed an unfriendly act against the Central Powers.' "

The Navy almost instantly dispatched a large part of its destroyers to Europe, but the role of the Army did not become clear for some days. Most people thought there would be no more than a token American Expeditionary Force, made up of regulars and volunteers. Theodore Roosevelt, aging and ill, sought to obtain permission to enlist a division to take to France in the same fashion that he had once led the Rough Rider regiment to Cuba. Only when the French and British missions arrived late in April did it become apparent that the Allies were desperate for fresh men to hurl against the German armies. One indication of how little expectation there was that the United States would undertake a great mobilization was the long, slow debate in Congress that spring, after war had been declared, over whether soldiers should be drafted into the Army. "In the estimation of Missourians," asserted Speaker of the House Champ Clark, "there is precious little difference between a con-script and a convict." In the end the Selective Service Act was passed and a great American war-making machine slowly came into being.

"It is not an army that we must shape and train for war; it is a nation," declared President Wilson in proclaiming that men in their twenties must register for the draft on June 5, 1917. "The nation needs all men: but it needs each man not in the field that will most pleasure him, but in the endeavor that will best serve the common good. Thus, though a sharp-shooter pleases to operate a trip-hammer for the forging of great guns, and an expert machinist desires to march with the flag, the nation is being served only when the sharp-shooter marches and the machinist remains at his levers. . . . It is in no sense a conscrip-tion of the unwilling: it is, rather, selection from a nation which has volunteered in mass."

On the appointed day, 9,660,000 men registered. Secretary of War Newton D. Baker on the morning of July 20 presided over the drawing of a "great national lottery" to decide the order in which they should be called into service. Blindfolded, he reached into a glass jar containing 10,500 numbers in cap-sules—the largest number in any registration district—and pulled out number 258. In each district throughout the United States, the man holding that number was the first to be called.

2

THE SCHOOL OF SOLDIERY

The burden of creating an army at short notice, falls most heavily upon the recruit," one of their number, Private Harry R. Richmond, observed while attending a training camp in New Mexico. "He must be whipped into action. The method of training therefore, now employed, in the various camps and particularly at Camp Cody is very intensive. The rookie is expected to learn now in three weeks, what his fellow soldiers acquired a year ago in three months. We are drilled nearly 7 or 8 hours per day, and the astonishing thing is that we are mastering the school of soldiery surprisingly well."

At the time that Private Richmond wrote, in June 1918, he was one of a million and a half men in training in army camps and naval training stations throughout the United States. A year earlier, the War Department possessed barracks sufficient to house only the Regular Army and was erecting tents in southern camps to put all of the National Guard under canvas by August 1, 1917. That summer work began on sixteen cantonments to house the National Army of draftees. Each arose on eight to twelve thousand acres of land with a good water supply, near a railroad. To construct sufficient barracks within sixty days seemed a staggering task; there had been no such large-scale government undertaking since the digging of the Panama Canal. Hastily the War Department devised a standard plan for a two-story structure, of the sort thereafter so familiar, large enough to hold a company of troops. Workmen cut arriving trainloads of lumber into predesigned duplicate parts, and on a mass-production basis the barracks went up. One morning the frame arose; two days later the building was finished. By mid-September, thousands of buildings and tents were ready and draftees began to arrive even before there were sufficient uniforms and equipment for them. By similar speed-up mass-production methods the Army hoped to transform civilians into well-trained soldiers ready for the front lines, not in the three years that European armies had expended upon peacetime conscripts, but in a matter of months.

The arriving recruits found the camps an impressive sight. One draftee called the "detention camp" for newly enlisted men near Camp Funston "a tent city of soldiers." Another, Wayne Heter, wrote from Camp Kearny, California:

"One side of the camp is a solid rectangle of khaki and white tents which are occupied by the Infantry. The opposite side is a rectangle of tents with a parallel rectangle occupied by corrals, stables, field guns, wagons, and other equipment necessary to the members of the adjoining rectangle, who are artillerymen, cavalrymen, engineers, signal corps, and the men of the remount station. It is a big busy city, minus the vice and the street corner loafers."

There was little time for loafing once the new men reached the camps. After a few days training at Camp Travis, Texas, Rex H. Thurston wrote:

"When we got off the train which stopped right in the camp, we were chased up to a barracks where we were examined for contagious diseases and also had a mouth examination.

We were then taken up to dinner. It was about eleven o'clock and we had postponed our breakfast.

"Each county was then separated and marched into the receiving station and waited until our county was called, and then fell into line as our names were called off in alphabetical order. Each man was given a large envelope in which he placed all his money and valuables, and then sealed it. In marching by a desk we delivered these envelopes to the party sitting there and he placed our name on it. We were then passed into a room where we stripped and wrapped our clothes in a paper. Our names were taken and placed on the packages. These are sent home by the government. From then on it was all action. We passed through a shower bath and then went in single file to doctor after doctor, a pasteboard around our necks and each one had something to write on it. Our finger prints were taken, all scars recorded and they began to hand out clothes. By the time a man gets around to shoes he is dressed from head to foot, and is also carrying a large bag full of clothes and blankets. We then sign up for everything, our pedigree is taken and we go on and are inoculated in the right arm and vaccinated on the left arm, and are marched out the front door dressed like soldiers but feeling a long way from being one.

"We were then placed in the barracks we now occupy and have been in quarantine ever since. . . . Life in camp is full of surprises. We get up in the morning at 5:45 and must be dressed by 5:50, so you see a man has to make every move count. We then assemble in front of the barracks for reveille. Breakfast at six, which generally consists of some kind of fruit, oranges or bananas, some breakfast food, eggs, potatoes and coffee. At 6:45 we are called out for drill, which continues until 11:45. At twenty seconds before twelve the big siren on the fire station blows till twelve sharp and every soldier and officer in camp stands at attention for those twenty seconds. This is in honor of the boys who have fallen at the front.

"Dinner at twelve-fifteen which consists of meat, potatoes and beans or peas, pudding and either cake or pie, and wheat bread or biscuits. We have ice water to drink for dinner.

"After dinner we attend lectures on army rules, articles of war, war material and everything pertaining to the army, and at recess singing practice, and in spare time we clean our rifles which require a great deal of cleaning to pass inspection.

"We were drilled on all movements in marching without rifles and are now learning it all over again with the rifle, and a man sure finds out how awkward he is when he starts it. We are being drilled a little harder every day, but haven't had any long hikes yet.

"At 5:30 we are called out for retreat. This is when the flag is lowered. The roll is called, arms inspected and every man is supposed to be slicked up, shoes shined, clothes clean, and he must be shaved. This is one thing they insist on in the army— everything must be clean, barracks, porch and grounds. Every once in a while we have to get out and pick up all the cigarette butts, matches and all trash scattered in the yard."

Beginning trainees in the Navy underwent parallel experiences. "The first few weeks after a recruit is landed on Goat Island (or Yerba Buena Island) he is totally lost," Fred E. Curtis wrote from San Francisco. "It is as tho he were dropped from the clouds into a new world. The clothes, sleeping accommodations, language and regularity of daily work are all totally different from civilian life. The recruit is very apt to be discouraged, altho very few of them admit it. When they first land at the main dock of the island a petty officer takes them in charge. He sees that their civilian clothes are disposed of . . . and that they get their new outfit of regulation clothing. This clothing is all towed in a bag (called a sea bag), except one suit, which they wear.

"The next step in the making of a sailor is when he is sent to the upper part of the island, called 'Detention Barracks.' Here he loses all of his hair, it being clipped off close, and in the course of the three weeks detention he is vaccinated against smallpox and typhoid fever, has his teeth re-examined, and a chart made of his mouth, showing all fillings, crowns and false work. The fundamentals of naval training and regulations are instilled into his mind. He is taught how to keep clean at all times, salute officers, and drill. When the three weeks are up they (usually a company of about a hundred) come down to the main barracks, where they are given opportunity to enter the various school for special training. There is a gunners' school, coxswain's school, signal school, radio school, yeoman school, cooks' and bakers' school, hospital school and commissioned officers school. I was first in the coxswain's school, pending the start of the next commissioned officers' school. Now, as you know, I am in the latter one."

The low point for most recruits was the vaccinations. When Eldred Trezise entered "Detention Barracks" at the Great Lakes Naval Training Station as one of a group of 154, "Everyone was afraid of the shots and the ones who already had theirs made it even worse for us while waiting for ours by telling us how it would hurt and all that bunk. By the time our turn came we were nearly sick already.

"A whole company would march by a doctor and some helpers in single file, and as we went by he would stick us with a long needle on the right arm. Of course we had a little patch of iodine there, but one fellow in front of me was so frightened that he forgot to move on after being stuck, and when the doctor turned around he stuck the first brown spot that he saw with the result that the man got a double dose and nearly fainted. He began to fall and someone gave him a push to help him the rest of the way down. He lay on the floor, with everyone laughing at him, but the ones who already had theirs. I got mine next and did not feel like laughing much, but sat on the floor with the rest of the bunch. Gee, I felt punk and all the rest did, too, judging by the way they looked.

"We made up for that, tho, after our detention was up. It was right after pay day."

Following his basic training, Trezise spent five months in coxswains' school and emerged a petty officer ready for sea duty. He regarded the training camp with a veteran's pride: "Great Lakes is a city of 30,000, with 29 power houses, and 27,000 men in training. The largest band in the world, 700 pieces and 200 bugles, with John Philip Sousa to lead them, is here." As for war,

"Sherman might have been right, but we all think he was wrong when it comes to navy life. I weighed in at 138, but I put the scales to 174 at Waukegan last Saturday, so you see how it affects me. . . . We don't know where we are going, but the band plays, 'Over There' every day, and they can't send us any too soon."

In the Army and Navy alike, most men liked the food in the training camps, although there were a good many jokes about eating navy beans and peeling onions. Southern men had to adjust to a diet much different than they had known at home. An Alabama soldier writing to his family from Camp Upton, Long Island, lamented, "I would give any thing if I was there to eat peanuts and sop molasses with those good hot biscuits and butter. I'm not leaving out that good cold sweet milk either."

Many a man who had never touched a pot or pan in civilian life found himself working in a kitchen or ladling a chow line. "I am on mess duty now," one declared, "and it is sure some job to feed between five hundred and a thousand men at one sitting—some job for a boiler maker." But policing of kitchens, as well as policing of other sorts, was, as Corporal William C. Walker pointed out, part of a soldier's experiences:

"In our first camp at Denver, one of the big disappointments was learning that kitchen police does not consist of guarding the kitchen, but of peeling spuds and washing pots and pans, and that stable police do not watch the stables but serve more as a manicurist of mules. And you know that army mule is not the most gentle animal on earth.

"When we hit Camp Green at Charlotte, we thought we were going to have a few months of training in a nice warm southern camp, but we only stayed there about two weeks. However, in that short time we learned to eat yams and to bootleg Coca Cola on Sunday. Here we also lost our horses which . . . makes Camp Green a pleasant spot in my memory."

Men from the city were almost unanimous in their failure to appreciate the army mule. "You should have seen me currying a gooseleg mule," wrote John Crowe, an artilleryman, from Camp Zachary Taylor, Kentucky. "He kicked me on the arm but not being satisfied with that tried to bite my head off. However he

Private T. P. Loughlin of the 69th Infantry saying farewell to his family

Herbert Gould leading singing at Great Lakes Naval Training Station

Peeling onions at Camp Kearny, California

only succeeded in getting my hat. . . . I think there's going to be a lot of fun when they undertake to teach a lot of us town boys to ride a bucking mule." Another commented, "If I've got to die for my country, I want to die gloriously on the field of battle. I'd hate to have my brains kicked out by a mule."

And then there were inspections. "To paraphrase a certain well known sentence, army life is just one inspection after another," C. W. Stubbs complained facetiously. "We've had three so far this week and there are still several hours till next week. We had our regular weekly cleanup inspection this morning. Everything has to be washed or polished according to its nature. I'm always scared till its over that I have overlooked some speck or that a fly will walk on something.

"I'm learning another trade. I'm getting quite expert as a laundress. It's very simple. First you get a tub, washboard and a cake of soap. Then you strip off all your clothes and throw 'em in the tub. Then you pull on a suit of overalls, go out behind the bathhouse, turn the hose into the tub and go to it. Some times you ought to wash your overalls too. After about an hour of elbow grease and perspiration you hold the result up to the sunlight. If you have worked hard and been fortunate the result will pass the next inspection."

In contrast, most of the men seemed to enjoy much of their training with weapons, even bayonets. "It's funny how a fellow will lose his fear of the cold steel," Trezise pointed out. "I think it is confidence in his ability to put it where he wants it in bayonet practice that is responsible. The hand is quicker than the eye, and with one swing of the rifle you can put in three strokes, quick as a wink, and any one of which will put a man out. If you miss the first one there are two more coming to you and they are both there ready for use. If you miss all three, jump and try it all over again. Get him first, or he'll get you, and the war will be lost as far as you are concerned." At Camp Humphreys, Virginia, wrote Frank Sweeney, "They have dummy Huns hanging from large cross beams and are taught the best method of approach and the proper jabs to get him before he gets us. Sometimes the men enter into this game so heartily that they break their bayonets pulling them out of the dummy Huns."

The rifle range gave men an opportunity to gain status. "We shoot to qualify for marksmen," Ernest Arterburn explained. "There are thirty shots fired, and if all are bull's-eye, a fellow can make 200 points, but it takes only 150 to qualify. I made that and also the sharpshooters' course, and tried for expert, but it was snowing when I tried, so I could hardly see the target."

More mathematics were required on the artillery range. Stubbs, who had known a little about surveying, found his skill handy in locating gun positions from maps, but was ready to joke about his new work: "The captain had been asking one or another of the men how they would find the ranges to different targets. Finally, pointing out a brindle steer off in the sage, he asked turning to the first sergeant, 'Sergeant suppose we should concentrate the fire of the entire battery on that bull, what would happen?' 'Hamburger,' replied the sergeant." Not everyone took artillery training so lightly. A new lieutenant, freshly commissioned from the officers' training camp at Fort Riley, Kansas, was sent to the Artillery School at Fort Sill, Oklahoma. He rather indignantly replied to an inquiry from his parents, "No, this is not 'another training camp for men who were not proficient,' but almost the reverse, as it has only been lately that any one lower than a major or possibly a captain, could go to it. . . . It costs the government $10,000 to send each man through here. So you see I'm worth a wee bit don't you?"

Robert Underwood congratulated himself upon being in the most interesting branch of the service, the Signal Corps, at Fort Leavenworth, Kansas:

"The men here have constructed a complete trench system in miniature, the trenches being only a few inches deep, and have wired the whole system just like it is done on the fighting front. There are small telegraph poles with fine wire stretched on them, tiny houses to represent headquarters and small wireless towers, in fact everything complete, just as it is in France. We are to study the wiring and general system of communication in order to give us a lineup as it is carried out in actual practice. It is an absorbing study."

Along with a full regimen of work, the Army and Navy supplied ample recreation for the trainees. Secretary of War Baker had labored during 1916 when troops had been stationed along the Mexican border, seeking to eliminate prostitution in the vicinity of the camps; he tried during the war to bar the soldiers from brothels and saloons, and to provide wholesome leisure-time activities through the Y.M.C.A. and similar organizations.

"They take good care of us here," George Van Doren wrote from Camp Cody. "They are very strict, but I would rather they would be that way than not. We went to church this morning at the stadium. That is a big outdoor meeting place. The stage is under cover and is quite large, likely about seventy-five feet long and twenty feet wide. The seats are all around the front of the stadium, and there are sufficient for about 7,000 men, I should judge.

"I will have plenty of reading matter as the Y.M.C.A. has a good library where I can get lots of books and magazines. There are one or two good bands around here but we don't hear much of them, but there is always some one playing some kind of an instrument, or singing, or both. We never see anything very exciting, no more so than at the ranch. There was a goat came into our company street yesterday, and it made as much excitement as I have seen since I have been here.

"We can buy candy, ice cream, popcorn and pies at the canteen, but I don't go in for it much. . . .

"I surely have wished that I could see you folks, but I can't; so, there! . . . when I do you won't need to be ashamed of me. The men here are rather tough as to talk, but they are most of them men. We have good officers and instructors and as yet no chance to go to town. When we do, some of the men will get into trouble, I suppose, but I hope not."

Most men were less melancholy, yet did stay out of trouble in the cities. "The one thing that made this camp bearable," wrote one soldier, who had been living in a tent in the snow, "was the friendly and hospitable treatment we received from the people of Long Island and New York. We also had a bit of the big city and exploring that wild trail called Broadway." And then

Gas bomb attack during night maneuver, Camp Kearny, California

Sailors on parade, Great Lakes Naval Training Station, Illinois

there were the admiring feminine glances one received if one were in the service. "This part of the country is all right and even girls are not so pretty as they are out there, they are very flirty, anyway, They never did that to me before, so I guess it is the uniform."

By the end of the training period the morale of most soldiers was good and they were physically hard enough to endure long hikes and exhausting maneuvers without ill effects. One infantryman, C. M. Vandeventer, after describing nine days of cross-country marching and sham battles, concluded, "I do believe if I am here another year I could outwalk a horse and carry a hundred pounds besides." This hardihood would be essential in France.

3

WAGING WAR
ON THE ATLANTIC

The gigantic American mobilization under way in the spring of 1917 would be of no avail if Emperor William II and his military advisers could make good their gamble and block the sea-lanes of the Atlantic. On the night of January 9 at the final conference, Admiral Henning von Holtzendorff had pledged success:

"Everyone stood around a large table, on which the Kaiser, pale and excited, leaned his hand. Holtzendorff spoke first, and, from the standpoint of the navy, both well and above all in confidence of victory. England will lie on the ground in at most six months, before a single American has set foot on the continent; the American danger does not disturb him at all." Field Marshal Paul von Hindenburg followed with less sanguine assent. The previous day he had told Admiral von Holtzendorff, "We are counting on the possibility of war with the United States, and have made all preparations to meet it. Things can not be worse than they are now." Chancellor Theobald von Bethmann-Hollweg in a lengthy statement wearily gave way. "The Kaiser followed his statements with every sign of impatience and opposition and declared in closing that the unrestricted U-boat war was therefore decided."

Immediately in April 1917 the United States Navy picked up Admiral von Holtzendorff's gauntlet. How serious the challenge was became apparent when the British released their statistics to the Americans. Shortly before the United States entered the war, Secretary of the Navy Josephus Daniels ordered Admiral William S. Sims, President of the Navy War College, and of all the admirals the most friendly with the British, to sail to London to establish liaison with the Admiralty. What Sims learned from Admiral Sir John Jellicoe was even more horrifying than the Navy Department had guessed. The Germans were sinking ships at the rate of 900,000 tons per month. Jellicoe frankly predicted, "They will win, unless we can stop these losses—and stop them soon."

But the conservative Board of Admiralty had no new plans for cutting the losses, save to augment their own forces with American destroyers as quickly as possible. Through the second quarter of 1917, of every four vessels that headed across the Atlantic to England or France, only three safely returned to American ports. If this rate of sinkings continued into October, pessimists predicted, the Allies would not possess sufficient shipping to continue the war. President Wilson, Secretary of the Navy Daniels, and the younger American naval officers were determined that new methods must be employed against submarines. "As you and I agree the other day," Wilson complained to Daniels on July 2, 1917, "the British Admiralty had done absolutely nothing constructive in the use of their navy and I think it is time we were making and insisting upon plans of our own, even if we render some of the more conservative of our own naval advisers uncomfortable."

The Admiralty, feeling as always that the first line of defense of the British Isles was the Grand Fleet, were using most of their smaller vessels to screen it as it maintained a vigil in the

North Sea against the Imperial German Navy. Since the indecisive Battle of Jutland in 1916, the German Navy had been confined to the ineffectual feints; later a squadron of five or six American battleships aided the British in the duty of keeping it bottled. Many of the remaining British small vessels were employed in maintaining a screen across the English Channel to protect the supply lines to France. A few of the rest were on anti-submarine patrol.

Above all, the task of the United States Navy in the war, as the younger officers instantly recognized, was to clear the sea lanes of submarines and guard the "bridge of ships" carrying men and supplies to Europe. This, they agreed, could best be accomplished through convoys. The Admiralty, fearing for the safety of the Grand Fleet and the channel crossing, firmly opposed the establishment of convoy systems as a means of bringing merchant ships and troop transports safely across the Atlantic. Admiral Sims, strongly backed by the Navy Department, insisted upon establishing convoys, and under pressure the Admiralty gave way. In the early summer of 1917 convoying began, and by August was being employed on a large scale.

Because the naval war was to be directed against submarines, the Navy Department suspended the building of battleships and planned construction of 250 destroyers and 400 submarine chasers of 110-foot length. Scientists developed rudimentary detection devices, the forerunner of the sonar of the Second World War and thereafter, and munitions experts designed effective depth charges. Most of the new ships were not yet off the ways at the time the war came to an end, but the Navy by then was employing 200,000 men and 834 vessels either in convoying or in European patrols, and had grown overall to encompass 533,000 men and some 2,000 ships.

The naval establishment in Europe that had begun so simply with the dispatch of Admiral Sims came to stretch as far south as Gibraltar and as far to the east as the island of Corfu in Greece, at the mouth of the Adriatic. Destroyers were based at Queenstown, Brest, Gibraltar, and in lesser numbers at several other ports.

Duty for the few men who were fortunate enough to be on
Admiral Sims's staff at the Naval Headquarters in London was
both exciting and pleasant. Thomas E. Dehoney, who in civilian life had figured livestock rates for the Santa Fe Railroad in
Kansas City, was delighted to find himself a naval radio opera-
tor in London. "You cannot appreciate how really interesting
this radio game is," he wrote. "Berlin sends German propaganda
by the hour—a steady stream . . . stations in Spain, France,
England and, last but not least, America are at our finger tips."
But the beef in London was not that of Kansas City. "Meat, ah!
How I long for a piece of hamburg steak with garlic! Meat-
coupons are so highly cherished that they are included in the
estate and descend to the heir upon the death of the holder."
And there were other shortages too. "Matches are so infrequent
that when I hesitate on the corner and strike a match to light
the inevitable cigaret, twenty grown men rush up madly and
exclaim, 'Hold the light, please.' I have to wear asbestos gloves
to keep from scorching my finger-tips."

Men on sea duty knew few such comforts. At night they
could not smoke at all on the decks, since the flare of a match
could be seen for a long distance, and even the glow of a cigarette was dangerous.

The first Navy vessels to see wartime service were a division
of destroyers dispatched to Queenstown, Ireland, to serve with
the British. After a stormy nine-day crossing, the commander of
the six buffeted vessels, Joseph K. Taussig, reported to Admiral
Lewis Bayly on May 4, 1917. How soon, Admiral Bayly
inquired, would the destroyers be ready for service at sea. "We
are ready now, sir," Taussig replied. "That is, as soon as we finish refueling."

In time, 34 destroyers came to be based at Queenstown,
going out from the base on convoy duty or patrol. In November
1917 two destroyers from Queenstown, the *Fanning* and
Nicholson, forced the surrender of the German submarine U-58.
Duty on the destroyers even in the summertime could be
unpleasant in rough seas as crockery flew about the wardroom.
One could sleep only by bracing oneself in a bunk, and one's

arms and legs became tired from constant holding on to lines or ladders. In the winter far worse storms and bitter cold added to the discomfort. The winter of 1917–1918 was one of phenomenal bitterness on the North Atlantic, and destroyers and cruisers at times steamed into port loking more like icebergs than ships. At sea there was not only the danger from submarines but also that of foundering in the heavy swell, and there was always the uncertainty whether the firing of deck guns and dropping of depth charges were being directed against flotsam and buoys or real targets. Nor was there often much certainty whether a submarine had been destroyed. Happily, sailors were optimists, quick to interpret an oil slick and bit of debris as yet another U-boat sent to the bottom. One such winter cruise in December 1917 was described by William Duke, Jr. :

"We got caught in a gale that prevented our return to port, and had to fly before it for three days, finally reaching Vigo, Spain. . . . I lived ten hours at a pace that counted for ten years, the most tense moment of my life being when, while the seas were breaking over us and we were crawling about the deck holding fast to everything that seemed to fit, looking for a hatch cover that had become unfastened, we suddenly discovered that six mines [depth charges] had become unloosed and were lurching about, butting the bulwarks with every roll of the ship. These mines are controlled by the paying out of wire, and when a certain amount becomes uncoiled they automatically explode. As no man knew just how much wire had become unmeshed we all had to work fast heaving them overboard, and they went 'pop, pop, pop,' as quickly as champagne corks at the French Ball, and how we ever escaped blowing off our own stern is still regarded as a marvel by us all." They rushed ten miles to the spot where a submarine was attacking a sailing vessel; as they approached, the submarine submerged. "We were soon amid the rushing of the turbulent water that is caused by a huge 'sub' directly after submerging. We let go one of our mines from the stern quarter, set to explode at eighty feet. . . . We were soon rewarded by seeing the color of the water change in the immediate vicinity of the explosion." At eleven o'clock that same evening, "the lookout on the bridge discovered another monster lying on the surface, for all the world like some huge wale taking the air . . . while quickly jamming the helm over, the officer of the deck ordered the starboard battery to take a shot. The shot may not have taken effect, as the 'sub' was then in the act of submerging, but as we steamed directly over her wake and let go four mines of different sizes in as many seconds we were soon assured that we had done for another."

When they went ashore at Queenstown (subsequently renamed Cobh) the sailors were usually confined to the base, where they could visit the enlisted men's club. The Irish at near-by Cork were still chafing under British rule and carried over some of their animus to the Americans. Admiral Bayly explained to Assistant Secretary of the Navy Roosevelt when he inspected the base that Bayly avoided trouble by refusing to allow sailors to visit Cork. Years later when he was President, Roosevelt reminisced:

"They tried the experiment of sending about two hundred of our people to Cork . . . and the young ladies invariably preferred the American boys and, of course, the young gentlemen of Cork didn't like that with the result that they staged a raid on our seamen. There being about a thousand civilians, they drove our men back to the train and they came back with a good many broken heads. Liberty from that time was suspended until the Mayor of Cork gave assurance that the town people would behave better next time.

"However, when I went this inspection, as I remember, on the U.S.S. _Melville_, a machine ship, we came to one of the machine bays about amidships, and Captain [Joel R. P.] Pringle looked over in a corner and found a large canvas covering something and turned to a chief petty officer, a very large redheaded man by the name of Flanigan and said, 'What's under that?' Flanigan saluted and said, 'I'll look sir.' He went over and lifted up the canvas and there was the finest assortment of brass knuckles and pieces of lead pipe that you ever saw. Captain Pringle said to Flanigan, 'What's that for?' Flanigan with a grin said: 'Captain, sir, that's for the next liberty trip to Cork, damn these Irish.' "

The crew of the German submarine U-58 as seen from the deck of the U.S.S. Fanning, November 1917

In a storm on the North Atlantic

As was to be expected with good sea stories, Roosevelt's was stretched somewhat. Tom V. Taylor, who served on the U.S.S. *Sampson*, gave a very different picture of shore leave in Ireland: "One of my ship-mates and I, took two little Irish 'Queens' to a show last night, and as we were both broke, we had to borrow the money from their mother. Some class to us, eh? It was a supposed vaudeville, 'For Her Mother's Sake,' a very sad play, and the little girls would cry when it came to the sad parts. However we had a fine time."

Duty on the coal-burning battleships and cruisers that in November 1917 joined the British Grand Fleet in its vigil against the German fleet was considerably more comfortable than patrol or convoy duty, but with less opportunity for excitement whether imagined or real. There was little possibility that the German warships, outnumbered two to one, would reappear, but admiral Hugh Rodman, commander of the American squadron, could console himself that the duty was important:

"It was the policy of the Grand Fleet to go after the enemy every time he showed his nose outside his lines of defense, no matter when or where. Whether he appeared with single ships, divisions, or his whole fleet, out we went after him, by day or night, in rain or shine (and in the months of winter there was mighty little daylight and much less shine), blow high, blow low—and chased him to his hole."

The one bit of excitement came when King George V, dressed in his admiral's uniform, inspected one of the American battleships, and shoveled a small amount of coal into one of the furnaces. Each piece of coal had been carefully scrubbed in advance.

Another sort of duty in which there was considerable hardship with little excitement or glory was aboard minelayers operating out of Invergordon, Scotland, laying a barrage of mines across the North Sea to Norway, under the supervision of Commander R. R. Belknap. This was a distinctly American project, undertaken despite the disapproval both of the British Admiralty and Admiral Sims in London. By the time of the Armistice, 70,000 mines had been laid, and they had trapped at least eight submarines. But the barrage had not been finished, and was not a decisive factor in combating submarines.

"We made twelve trips out with mines," wrote Paul E. Taylor, who served on the U.S.S. *Housantonic*, "—the first were laid June 8th and the last October 26th. . . . That was the most exciting trip we had, too, because right when we wanted to lay mines it was rough, and the North Sea can be blamed rough when it wants to be: so we had to just cruise around out there in the storm for over twenty-four fours, waiting for it to calm down.

"That may all sound nice but when you consider we had over 8,500 mines on and each mine had 300 pounds of T.N.T. in it, you'll realize what it would have meant if a little salt water had got to the vital part of a mine. . . .

"The old tub was having all she could do to hold her own in the storm, but we were between two of our own mine fields and if we'd kept going into the storm (the best way to go) we'd have struck some of our own particular brand of punishment. We had to take it on our side and believe me, we did some rolling. Only once, tho, did we roll so far we didn't expect to come back. We just laid on our side and quivered a few seconds; but we came back all right.

"The funny part of it was, we couldn't take it seriously. It was real laughable to see things sliding from one side to the other. Some of the fellows were pretty sick and wouldn't have cared what happened, but I never felt better in my life than on that trip. . . . The next day it calmed down and we dropped our little black pills in the briny and beat it back for port."

Life on a submarine chaser in the Mediterranean was no less hazardous, but considerably more exciting. John Jordan boasted afterward of his service on chaser No. 225, which had been based at the Greek island of Corfu. "While aboard the chaser I had many thrilling experiences including fires, also the battle of Durazzo which took place Oct. 2nd [1918]. This battle was fought by the Americans, English and Italians. There were fifty ships took part of which eleven were American chasers, there were also fifty airplanes of the French and Italian. . . .

"We were convoying ships and patroling the Mediterranean, Adriatic and Ionian seas. This was particularly flaunt
work especially when we could sight a German or Austrian submarine. In the unit of chasers I was in we have the honor of getting the first German submarine in the Adriatic and found the
submarine base on the coast of Spain. The day we found this
base I never shall forget, it sure was some experience to see
those Germans beat it and we after them.

"Words can't express the life on the chaser . . . they are small
but mighty. They are 110 feet long and ten foot beam, are driv-
en by three Standard motors, they ride worse than a horse or
mule and rock and roll like a cradle."

Life was even more uncomfortable aboard the relatively
crude and fragile American submarines. They were employed in
the treacherous and difficult work of trying to track down
German submarines, and operated from Berehaven, Bantry Bay,
Ireland, and Ponta Delgada, Azores.

Above all, men and ships were engaged in the vital task of
escorting transports and merchantmen past the lurking submarines to the European harbors. Therein were to be found
much of the danger and excitement of the Navy's participation
in the war.

4

THE BIG TRIP

We're all ready for the big trip," wrote Sergeant Neil W. Kimball from Camp Upton, Long Island. "All my possessions, a full equipment for fighting, eating sleeping, and even playing, is rolled up in a cumbersome roll of some eighty or ninety pounds, ready to be loaded on my back when the whistle blows. A year's training and we're ready to go in for the big thing—the real thing. . . . I don't mean that the boys are a lot of fire eaters anxious to hear the cannons roar, but I know there is not a man in the outfit who would take a safe berth in the home guard, or even a discharge, if it was offered to him tonight. And yet, there is little of that 'I'll bring back the kaiser's helmet' stuff. Every man knows the seriousness of the job he is going up against, the filth and the dirty and the hardship they are going to bump into on the other side. . . .

"We've been here at the embarkation camp a week and have seen several outfits come in from their training camp and several other outfits go down to the transports. One of the latter was a regiment of Negroes—drafted men—just a few days up from a Southern training camp. Their lips were a shivering purple as they marched out at 4:30 in the morning in a cold, drizzling rain, their chests thrown out as well as possible with a ninety-pound weight pulling them down, as their band struck up 'The Memphis Blues' as only a Negro band can play it. The same serious look was on their faces as you see on the faces of the boys sitting around the platoon room now. But there was a flashing of ivory and a suppressed 'Yah' as some early riser yelled 'Pick one off for me.'"

For many of the men from the West, the long train ride east to the camps where they awaited embarkation was in itself memorable. Riding across the South, C. W. Stubbs struck up conversations with girls wherever the train stopped. By the time they reached Montgomery, Alabama, which was hot and muggy, he had been three days on the train and felt desperately in need of a bath. "I inquired again about liberty. 'You've got forty minutes,' replied the sergeant. I did a rapid mental calculation and flew. Ten minutes to find a barber shop and strip, ten minutes for a bath, ten to dress and ten to get back to the train. . . . I was back on the train cool and clean with five minutes to spare. I lit a Red Cross cigaret and just leaned back enjoying the luxury of the feeling. I'm learning one thing in the army, anyway, and that is to grab every opportunity on the fly. . . . From Washington on the people were unusually enthusiastic. From doors and windows, from factories and at crossings we were cheered and waved on our way. At one place we passed some railroad shops. All the locomotives screamed a welcome. At another place a large canvas sign hung across a building with 'God bless you, boys.'

"We were now on the last leg of our journey and traveled at a good rate with the short stops. Cities and little two-by-four states were going by so fast we could hardly keep track of our location. The Red Cross met us at every stop with post cards, cigarets and something to eat. . . . At five o'clock that afternoon we came to our final halt—Camp Dix. . . . We were just five days on the road. . . . Yes, it was a great trip. I waved to all the girls from El Paso to Camp Dix."

For most men, the trip across the Atlantic was less interesting but happily uneventful. From Newport News, New York, or even Montreal, they sailed out on large, fast transports or sometimes on slow, old tubs, part of them on American ships and part on British, and in fair weather and foul. The Americans did not care much for the food on the British ships. "We don't like their blooming tea or their blamed pet cats," a signal corps man wrote. "They said it was rabbit, but we used our own opinion. We had tasted rabbits in the states and we knew." A rather typical convoy was the one in which Private Sessler Walker crossed:

"We sailed from Hoboken, New Jersey on a large transport, carrying about two thousand troops I presume and a great quantity of equipment and supplies. We joined the balance of our convoy of ships including seven large troop boats, 2 battleship cruisers and four small swift torpedo boats or subchaser that were just lying just out of port waiting on us. . . . We sailed quite a ways southward, close to the Virginia coast and there picked up about four more ships loaded with soldiers and three small sub-chaser which had come out from Newport News to accompany us across. Then we had quite a convoy, 11 ships, 2 battleships cruisers and 7 torpedo boats which were very small and weak looking by the side of our large transports for any protection. But they were powerful and had great speed."

Life quickly settled into an uncomfortable routine on the transports. It was "just one continual round of 'move on,'" reported Neil K. Kimball, with the added complication of seasickness:

"When I think of Mr. Hoover's slogan, 'Food Will Win the War,' I feel powerfully discouraged for all that is lost. . . .

"Just to give you a little idea of what the life of a democracy saver on the rolling main is, I'll try to outline a day's program:

"6:00 A.M.—You fall out of your hammock and engage in a grand scramble to get completely uniformed before all the clothes are gone. . . .

"6:05—Free for all with wrapped puttees. After several bad starts you finally get your leg partially bandaged, to find that your neighbor has been bandaging his leg with the other end of the same puttee.

"6:15—You go to the upper deck and count noses (or more properly speaking, bows). You are relieved and surprised to find that the entire fleet has weathered the night O.K. . . .

"6:45—Breakfast is announced and you hasten to the rail to admire the view.

"7:15 until 12 noon is given over to leaving whatever place you happen to be in at the moment you are told 'You can't stay here!'. . . .

"5:15—Boat drill. You gaze with dismay on the rafts labeled 'To carry twenty men' and begin to realize what an ultra-conservative Sherman was.

"7:45 to 8:00—Acrobatic stunts by soldiers endeavoring to swing into hammocks without losing blankets, life preservers or tempers. . . .

"Somehow or other, it gives the rear rank bucks a guilty joy to know that bars and stripes are no protection against mal-de-mere. And, as Chet says, another evidence of the democracy of our army is that it doesn't matter whether an officer or soldier goes overboard—the ship won't stop in either case."

Most of the men amused themselves on the decks watching boxing and wrestling matches or playing cards. They seemed to take seasickness as part of the adventure. "Well I was some sick the third day out and I surely thought I would throw up my shoe soles, but soon recovered and enjoyed the balance of the trip," wrote Private William Gentry. Some did suffer from prolonged rough passages. "I tried to eat three meals in two weeks," wrote Thomas G. Edwards. "I have eaten as much in one day as I had on our entire voyage. Upon our arrival in England I noticed that my clothes were all too big. I needed a shave, my knees were weak and I was hungry."

The danger of submarines made the trip exciting, but most of the troops seemed confident that the camouflage, zigzagging, and above all the protection of the accompanying destroyers and cruisers would keep them from harm. "Never in my life have I seen a happier crowd of men than those on board when our convoy was sighted," wrote Gentry. "Honest Mack, it looked like Barnum & Baileys parade coming across the water." Another remembered, "We met some more destroyers and then we were seemingly in a hive of bees, these destroyers darted in and about us and sure did take good care of us it made a person wish almost that a Hun would put in his appearance, he couldn't have lasted long."

Daily boat drills, warnings against smoking after dark, and the admonition to sleep in one's clothes in the danger zone kept the soldiers alerted. "No lights were allowed on deck," said William C. Walker, "and it was as much as your life was worth if you attempted to come up with a lighted cigarette." Another wrote, "A good many of the boys were fined pretty heavy for not wearing their life preservers at all times."

Sometimes periscopes, or what appeared to be periscopes, emerged near the ships. One transport captain remarked afterward that his lookouts on the first voyage spotted enough periscopes to form a picket fence across the Atlantic. The temptation to exaggerate adventures with submarines when writing home must have been great, but many a description was obvious in its candor. "We had two submarine scares on the way over, and as luck would have it both of them turned out to be false alarms," Gentry told a friend back home. "The first was when an alarm clock went off and the bugler gave abandon ship call. . . . The next time . . . was when one of the fellows reported a periscope off the port bow, the gun crew shot several times and the supposed . . . periscope turned out to be a bale of hay." Clyde A. Crawford wrote: "Just as chow was over we heard the guns on an American collier, which followed us, cut loose. . . . After arriving at my life boat station I looked up for the cause of this said firing but I could see nothing at all. Whether it was a sub or not remains for the log book of the collier to show."

Corporal Walker, crossing on the *Baltic*, saw a shocking sight on February 5, 1918: "Just after dark Eddie and I were sitting up on deck when we felt the ship quiver and then start out like a race-horse. . . . The *Tuscania*, a large camouflaged ship which had been sailing a few hundred yards behind us on the trip, sent up a signal rocket and then all her lights came on and in a few minutes went off again and we realized that she had been torpedoed and was going to the bottom. We first thought one would think that we should have stayed behind and helped to rescue the boys that were being sunk, but that is not the way of war, and we left her behind as fast as possible."

The *Tuscania*, a British ship, was in sight of Northern Ireland that afternoon, and most of the soldiers were watching the boxing matches, happy that their trip was almost over. Everett Harphan was sitting in the headquarters office waiting for mess:

"At 5:45 an awful explosion, which sounded like a near-by clap of thunder, shook the great liner from bow to stern as if she was a toy. Almost instantly the lights went out, which told us the ship was struck in the engine-room and there was no chance to beach her.

"There was quite a scramble to get on deck, myself in the midst; but for the number on board (about 2500) there was very good order. By the time I got outside the ship had begun to list heavily to starboard, and it looked as if we should all be lost; but presently she began to right herself again, altho it was evident she was sinking. The men started lowering the life-boats immediately, and one or two were wrecked or capsized upon being launched, which made the men to come later more careful. I worked at the life-boats for nearly two hours, and when we did pull away from the ship she was about ready to founder. . . .

"Never shall I forget the wash of waters upon her upper decks, with the crashing of rigging and masts, all brilliantly illuminated by the lights from the auxiliary motor. We drifted about in a boat tossed like a chip in ice-cold water up to our knees, all dipping constantly to keep afloat. The spray and foam dashed over us almost constantly, and it seemed we would freeze in the wind."

Fortunately, very few of the men aboard the *Tuscania* were lost, and it was the only Europe-bound transport to be sunk. The *Von Steuben* in June 1918 narrowly missed being torpedoed while homeward bound. One of the firemen, Byron L. Groesbeck, wrote home:

"It was Wednesday afternoon and we were steaming along at seventeen knots. The calm of an ocean, which rippled like a great basin of oil, and of sky which was guiltless of a cloud, was broken only by the throb of our engines and the spindrift of the great prow of the *Von Steuben*.

"Suddenly came a warning from the lookout in the foretop that six life-boats were in sight of the port bow, about 1,000 yards away. The captain, who is ever on the alert, ordered the gun crews to their stations. The deck at once became the scene of preparations. There was no confusion. Every man knew his place, and the guns were manned and all made ready for possible action within a minute. Almost at the same instant the foretop reported a submarine and the lookout in the chart house reported the wake of a torpedo coming directly for us.

"Orders came thick and fast, but without hesitation or confusion. The port engine was reversed, and the steersman put the wheel hard aport, which turned the ship sharply. At the general alarm we came on deck and it made us hold our breath as the great oblong engine of death skimmed by, missing our bow by a bare twenty feet. A record of the thoughts and emotions that gripped the hearts of the men as the torpedo passed would be interesting."

Vice Admiral Albert Gleaves, commander of convoy operations, later commented, "Here was a case where three brains acted quickly and in coordination, the lookout, Louis Selzer, the Captain, Yates Stirling, Jr., and the Helmsman. The slightest mistake on the part of any one of the three would have resulted in the loss of the ship."

No mistake on the part of captain or crew played any part in the fate of the *President Lincoln*. It sailed from Brest on May 29, 1918, as one of a convoy of four troopships escorted by destroyers. About sundown of the next day, when the convoy had passed through the most dangerous waters, the destroyers left to pick up an incoming convoy. Incoming troopships were most heavily guarded, and returning ones had to bear greater

Men of the 105th Field Artillery boarding the transport Mercury, *Newport News, Virginia, June 30, 1918*

Some men never left the United States. Guarding a shipyard, December 1917.

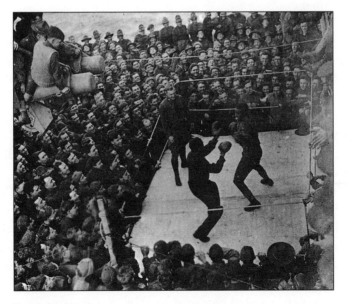

Prizefight aboard a transport

risks. In this instance disaster befell, for in the night the German submarine U-90 sighted the slow-moving convoy, and sailing ahead of it, waited submerged the next morning until it appeared. Singling out the *President Lincoln,* the largest of the ships, the submarine fired three torpedoes toward it. The look-outs spotted the torpedo wakes but the Officer of the Deck could not throw over the helm in time. Two torpedoes struck simultaneously below the bridge, and the third torpedo hit 120 feet from the stern. The ship settled rapidly while the crew in an orderly fashion launched rafts and lifeboats filled with sick men being returned to the United States, and themselves slid down life ropes into the water and swam to boats.

"When it come my turn to abandon ship," Chief Yeoman Leonard McCallum recalled, "I slid down a line and sort of stepped onto a raft upon which there were five other lads. We started to paddle away from her side but were forced back against her twice. Officers were singing out for all to get away quickly as possible on account of the suction. That didn't both-er the crew much because as some of them tried to paddle away, they'd yell, 'Liberty party shoving off, etc.' it all seemed more like a picnic.

"When we felt that we were a safe distance away from the ship we turned to take a last look at her and what a fascinating sight she was. Our flag was flying, the gun crews were firing, the steam was hissing and above it all, sounding like the death cries of some big old animal, could be heard the mournful shriek of the siren. She seemed to be sinking very slowly, when sud-denly there was a loud explosion, her big stack was forced back on the water and with a mighty roar the *President Lincoln* disap-peared stern first under the waves."

In about two hours the U-boat appeared among the rafts and boats, trying to find the commander, Captain P. W. Foote, but Foote had disguised himself in a khaki shirt and sailor's white hat. The men assured the submarine comander that Foote had gone down with the ship. Noticing Lieutenant Isaacs in his officer's blouse, the commander ordered him aboard the U-boat and after a time sailed eastward.

As soon as Captain Foote was sure the submarine was gone, he ordered the twelve lifeboats tied in a line and had each take aboard as many men as they could from the rafts. "When we felt that the submarine had disappeared for the last time our spirits arose," said McCallum. "We expected to be picked up by the destroyers the next day, anyway, so why worry. . . . At about 9:00 it became real dark, and at ten-minute intervals Coston signals were lit in each life boat. The boys started to sing all the popular songs such as 'Good-by, Broadway; Hello, France,' 'Over There' and 'Keep the Home Fires Burning.' . . . Shortly after midnight a quick pale yellow gleam quivered a short distance away from us, and the next moment the destroyer *Warrington* was in our midst. It was the most welcome sight we ever saw."

Through the night, the men were hauled aboard from their rolling boats onto the *Warrington* and the *Smith*. It was slow and risky work, as the destroyers had to remain on the alert for submarines, which (as often happened) might be using the lifeboats as bait for new victims. At 4:00 in the morning, the destroyers headed back toward Brest, 440 miles away, with the rescued men. Only 26 were lost out of 785 that had been aboard.

At eight the next morning, the *Smith* suddenly cut across the bow of the *Warrington* at top steed and dropped depth charges on a submarine it had spotted. That same afternoon, Lieutenant Isaacs, prisoner on the U-90, found out firsthand what it was like to be attacked by American destroyers. "We quickly submerged and a few minutes afterwards we felt depth bombs exploding all about us," he wrote in his official report months later. "Twenty-two bombs were counted in four minutes; five of them were very close, or seemed so to me, for they shook the vessel from stern to stern. To escape them we were making our best speed, zigzagging, and apparently doubling back on our course. The Petty Officer at the microphones, listening to the propellers of the destroyers, reported continuously whether they were getting close or farther away to the Captain, who was in the conning tower. Soon they could no longer be heard, but we remained submerged at a depth of sixty meters for about one hour longer." At the end of the cruise, Lieutenant Isaacs was delivered to naval officials at Wilhelmshaven and sent on to prison camps where he devoted himself to trying to escape. In mid-October he succeeded in making his way to Switzerland, and a few days later reported in detail to Admiral Sims in London all that he had learned firsthand about the operation of U-boats.

The crew and passengers of the *Mount Vernon*, a transport homeward bound from Brest in September 1918, had somewhat different adventures. They were steaming along at about twenty knots some 250 miles at sea. "I was in the mess hall eating breakfast at the time," Robert Young, one of the seamen, wrote that night. "We had cream of wheat for breakfast and I was reaching for a spoonful when cream of wheat, table and all came up to meet me. The deck vibrated so hard that we could hardly keep our feet. Before I go any further I may as well tell you that I suddenly lost all appetite for food. Everyone knew what had happened when we heard the explosion and felt the ship shake. There was little excitement shown at first but they were men all the way through and it soon passed; then everyone went to their station."

Major Robert C. Rutledge, who was in charge of the 350 troops aboard, described the attack:

"I heard one of the forward guns on our ship fire, and looked out of my stateroom window just in time to see the shot strike the water. . . . Not ten seconds later the torpedo hit us. The sub had come up . . . between us and the *Agamemnon* and fired from a point opposite our bow. . . . The *Agamemnon* chased head at full speed, and we turned around and began the race against 'Davy Jones' for shore."

The *Mount Vernon* had been hit by a torpedo that blew a nineteen-foot hole in its side, and flooded half the boiler rooms; happily the watertight bulkheads held, and although the ship settled ten feet it still maintained its buoyancy by a margin of two or three feet. It had been accompanied by an extraordinary number of destroyers—six of them—at the time of the attack, and the destroyers immediately began dropping depth charges to prevent the submarine from again attacking, and hid the *Mount Vernon* with a smoke screen. Captain D. E. Dismukes tried through extraordinary efforts to head the vessel back to Brest faster than a sumarine could travel, so that he could avoid being attacked in the night. Major Rutledge praised the courage of the stokers:

"There were only eight boilers left and they had to be crowded to the limit to keep the ship going. The stokers are called the 'black gang,' and ordinarily work only four hours at a time because of the severity of their work. It is exceedingly hard and requires a lot of endurance. As soon as we were hit, all of the 'black gang' who were not on duty went below at once voluntarily to help stoke. They all wanted to work, knowing that if the ship went down they wouldn't have the slightest chance, but would be drowned like rats."

There was work for the soldiers aboard, too: "It was necessary to bail the water with buckets. . . . I ordered every man available to join the bucket line. We soon had the buckets moving rapidly, and managed to keep the water down to some extent. Soon after the bucket line was formed somebody started a song, and the whole line took it up and sang while they worked. They kept that up as long as they were bailing, and sang every popular song that has been heard of in the last five years.

"About four o'clock in the afternoon, the ship went over a little further on her left side, and things began to look pretty dubious. . . . We limped into port in the outer harbor of Brest about 2:30 A.M."

It was only an exceptional few of the American Expeditionary Forces who underwent experiences like these on the seas. Altogether, by the time of the Armistice, over two million soldiers had been transported in 1,142 troopship sailings—nearly a million in United States ships—and almost none encountered any hazard worse than *mal de mer*. The troops were sometimes inclined, therefore, to think the sailors had had it soft during the war. "Some of the soldiers may say that the navy was not in much danger," William Thyret, Quartermaster on the

U.S.S. *Narrangansett*, wrote rather indignantly just after the Armistice. His was one of four American ships that ferried troops from Southampton to Havre, and in 21 round trips they had sighted no enemy submarine. That made the return trips, when they were without convoy, nonetheless risky. "It isn't anything nice to cross a channel where they say the submarines are pretty thick, without having a gun aboard or anything else to defend yourself." And there had been engine breakdowns, and one collision. "If it had been a rough sea that night we sure would have been out of luck. We had 2,800 lives in our hands that night. We made port all right."

The soldiers on the *Narragansett* that trip, and all the others on all the other transports, had been glad enough to make port too. The Navy achieved miracles in the face of the pessimistic predictions of the spring of 1917, not only bringing huge armies to France but also an average of four tons of supplies and equipment for each soldier. Submarine sinking declined from the nearly 900,000 tons of April 1917 to only 112,000 tons in October 1918. A large measure of the task was undertaken by the British Navy, which provided 70 percent of the escorting ships compared with 27 percent by the United States. Somehow the United States and its allies had assembled a "bridge of ships," and the two great Navies so effectively guarded it that they won the Atlantic battle. This was the essential prelude to winning the great battles on the Western Front.

5

"LAFAYETTE, WE ARE HERE!"

A hearty welcome awaited the arriving troops when they reached the European shores. To the French and British people, nearly exhausted by the long years of attrition, these fresh young men brought promise not only of an end to the war, but an end through victory. The tumultuous reception Parisians gave on July 4, 1917, to a battalion of the 16th Infantry, the first troops from the United States to parade through the city, was echoed a few weeks later when the first Yanks marched through London, and in diminishing scale was repeated in months to come in countless French cities and hamlets.

The Independence Day ceremonies began at a great French national shrine, outside the tomb of Napoleon, in the Court of Honor at Les Invalides. The President of the Republic, Raymond Poincare, presented flags to General John J. Pershing, towering beside him. Then to the blare of a band, a French battalion marched forth, followed by the column of tall, robust, but all too obviously raw Americans, parading across Paris to the Picpus Cemetery where Lafayette was buried. Pershing later recounted:

"On the march ... the battalion was joined by a great crowd, many women forcing their way into the ranks and swinging along arm in arm with the men. With wreaths about their necks and bouquets in their hats and rifles, the column looked like a moving flower garden. With only a semblance of military formation, the animated throng pushed its way through avenues of people to the martial strains of the French band and the still more thrilling music of cheering voices."

At the cemetery, Pershing made a few extemporaneous remarks, but had designated an old Army friend who was serving on his staff, Colonel C. E. Stanton, to deliver an address. And it was Stanton who uttered the stirring words that caught the imagination of both the French and American nations: "Lafayette, we are here!"

At the time that the battalion paraded through Paris, there were only some fourteen thousand American troops in France, and it would require huge armies—perhaps two million men— to top the balance against Germany. Of the urgent need to throw enormous forces into combat Pershing was well aware. On July 9, he sent a lengthy confidential report to Secretary of War Baker, pointing out how low the morale of the French people had become, explaining that their general dissatisfaction had led to replacement of the French Commander-in-Chief. The new Commander, General Henri Philippe Petain, the hero of Verdun, had conferred with Pershing at the home of a mutual friend:

"At this meeting, he told me frankly that affairs were not going well in France, and that unless the Government and the people would stand by the army and assist at home ... he felt that something bordering on revolution might result. Such an outcome, he said, would permit the Germans to dictate the terms of peace instead of the Allies. He, of course, feels that our entering the war has brought courage to the nation, but, realizing as he does that we shall not be in a position to render any material assistance before next spring, he thinks that, in addition to that, some outside pressure might be brought that would check political intrigue among government officials and prevent a further loss of confidence among the people at large."

General Pershing personally was slightly more optimistic:

"My own opinion is that the army, as it stands to-day, can hold until spring against any probable effort of the enemy, but that poverty and discontent, magnified by the socialistic press, especially should the Government continue to back up the army, may so dishearten the people and the army that the latter will lose its morale and disaster follow."

With this sense of urgency, General Pershing set about the complex task of building, supplying, and training the American Expeditionary Forces. He hoped that by June 1918 they would number a million men—and he insisted through long months of argument as it was coming into being that it must operate ultimately as a separate army along its own sectors rather than being fed piecemeal as replacements for depleted French and British regiments. Fortunately for Pershing, he was a man of strong will who had received full powers from President Wilson when he had been appointed Commander-in-Chief, and who continued to enjoy the confidence of both the President and Secretary of War. On the one hand Pershing contended strongly with the Allied Powers to maintain the integrity of American troop units; on the other he resisted the efforts of the Chief of Staff and bureau chiefs in Washington to supervise operations in the field and supply programs in France.

At the end of the summer of 1917, Pershing established his General Headquarters far away from Paris, in Chaumont, a hilltop town in Lorraine, not far from the area where the arriving American troops were training, and the adjacent to the sectors in the front lines that they were expected soon to fill. There the G.H.Q. remained until July 1919. From his desk in Chaumont and even more in his far-ranging tours in his staff car emblazoned with four stars, Pershing built, molded, and sent into action the growing American Expeditionary Forces. Through

1917, as convoy after convoy landed green troops, the task was one of organizing and training in preparation for the fighting ahead.

The battalion that marched through Paris on July 4, 1917, had landed at St. Nazaire when the first convoy arrived at the end of June. Admiral Gleaves noted:

"The arrival of so many transports within so short a space of time caused great congestion in St. Nazaire's small harbor. All the troopships carried cargo and large quantities of troop equipment and stores. The unloading of all vessels and quick preparations for the return voyage presented a perplexing problem with the poor facilities available and the shortage of labor.

"Five hundred negro stevedores had been brought from the United States by the Army to discharge ships, but they were found altogether unequal to handle such a large number of vessels. The Marine Regiment, which had been carried in the *Henderson, De Kalb* and *Hancock*, relieved the situation somewhat by turning to and discharging their own vessels.

"The sea wall was a scene of great activity as the docks, cranes, and railroads endeavored to absorb several hundred per cent more than their usual capacity. From the ships' holds were discharged boxes of provisions, ammunition, locomotives, baled hay, horses, automobile trucks, gasoline and other Army impedimenta. French stevedores, American sailors and marines, negroes and German prisoners worked side by side. . . .

"The population gathered along the quays looked on in whispering wonderment at the young khaki-clad strangers who had appeared, almost over night, from over the seas. There was no cheering, no patriotic demonstration, only the respectful silence of the women and children, the old men and the broken soldiers."

At the height of the movement of troops through St. Nazaire, as many as fifteen thousand men at a time were disembarking there. Three thousand Negro stevedores were brought from the United States to try to unload vessels in the cramped harbor. The jam of ships was so bad that often troops had to remain aboard transports for several days before they landed, and there were instances when cargoes deep in the holds actually made another round trip to the United States before they were unloaded. A few miles up the Loire River from St. Nazaire, the S.O.S. was rushing the construction of a new modern port with adequate rail facilities. Meanwhile troops were being buffeted through St. Nazaire. In increasing numbers they disembarked at Brest, which in time eclipsed St. Nazaire. Forty percent of the troops landed first at Liverpool or other English ports and then crossed the channel to France.

Whenever they first arrived, they were happy indeed after their long, hazardous, and often rough crossing of the Atlantic. Private Main D. Bagby commented, "Columbus himself could not have been more pleased to see land than we were." William Gentry wrote, "The entrance to the harbor where we landed was the most beautiful sight that I have ever seen. When a few hours from port several aeroplanes were sighted high in the air. A great crowd lined the dock walls and gave us a hearty welcome. We were held on board for several days after arriving. One morning we were ordered to shave, wash our leggings, and roll our packs, and in the same afternoon we were marched off the ship and loaded onto our 'special train.' "

Corporal Barney Tovin of the 43rd Artillery remembered:

"On the twelfth day we sighted land and the next morning, which was the thirteenth day, we were outside of Brest. Our boat being too large to dock, we had to wait until they could get a smaller one to take us from the transport to shore. All that day the 'water rats,' as the French children who live in seaport towns are called, came out to the transports in little rowboats and sailboats, which they maneuvered themselves, and all the troops threw money at them which they all scrambled to get. We had lots of sport with them.

"At three o'clock a boat, which was formerly in ferry service on the English Channel, pulled up against our transport and our whole regiment was piled on. Our band was on the deck and as we came to the shore they played 'The Star Spangled Banner' and the 'Marseillaise,' the French national air, while all within hearing stood at attention and saluted.

"We then went ashore and lined up for our hike to our camp, which was about five miles distant. When we got outside of the dock there were thousands of French peasants cheering and waving flags. We marched through the center of the town and on to the outskirts where our camp was. . . .

"When we reached the camp there were no barracks or tents or shelter, so we were marched out onto the field and ordered to pitch our pup tents. Some of the boys put up the field stoves and our cooks got to work. Bacon and hard tack never tasted better since I was introduced to it."

The great complaint of the troops that landed in England was that they were forced to subsist on the British rations, which were far from their liking. W. E. Thomas of the 89th Division wrote his friends back home:

"We landed at Liverpool June 24th; had a nice hike of about three miles to Knotty Ash, where the British had a camp called a rest camp, but the only rest we had was our stomachs; we got some cheese and tea while there a few days. We could not get away from the camp, guarded with fixed bayonets; if we all had been the worst kind of criminals they would not have watched us closer. Finally we left there and hiked to the stock yards and loaded on what they called a passenger train. . . . We left there arriving at South Hampton. . . . We had another hike of three or four miles to another rest camp out to the commons, only staying over night, leaving early for the dock, and we crossed the channel to Cherbourg, France. Another hike of about three miles to a British rest camp. We now had formed our own ideas of a British rest camp. We were the first American troops to arrive there, as they had just got things agoing, but forgot the grub, at least it looked that way."

Colonel Johnson Hagood, who later served as Chief of Staff of the S.O.S., was even more sour in his comments on British accommodations and rations. His regiment, the 7th, crossed the channel from Southampton aboard a dirty, sidewheel channel steamer misnamed *La Marguerite* and disembarked at Le Havre:

"As each soldier marched proudly down the gangplank he was once more issued rations. This time not in bulk but loose,

A torpedoed ship going down. Men are sliding down the ropes, and at left one has just splashed into the water.

"The column looked like moving flower garden."

General John J. Pershing at his desk at Chaumont

without even so much as a piece of wrapping paper. This was not the familiar American travel ration of canned tomatoes, salmon—'gold fish'—and beans, but the British ration of biscuits, cheese, and tea. Each man already had his rifle, ammunition, full pack, overcoat, barrack bag containing six months' individual reserve supplies, and a piece of company property. Some had suitcases and live pets. What to do with the cheese was the question. Some put it under their arms as a Frenchman carries a loaf of bread. Some broke it up and stuffed it into their pockets. Some put it in their hats. And others began to eat it as the simplest way of getting it ashore. But no sooner had the regiment lined up on the dock than the question was settled by an indignant American quartermaster who declared that the British had no right to issue rations on French soil (full charge, of course, being made against the United States) and directed me to return the whole thing, cheese, biscuits, and tea, to the British forthwith. I returned to the ship and offered to give back the cheese, but the British refused to accept it because it had been broken apart and could not be put together again.

"Our next move was to what was known as a 'Rest Camp'—the reason for selecting this name has always been a mystery—Rest Camp No. 3, at Le Havre.

"From this time forward the effort to force rations upon us suddenly ceased and all elements seemed combined to keep us from getting any. We were informed that the Rest Camp ran like clockwork; that we should find our tents ready, our baggage in place, and our meals—as for them it would be as simple as a cafeteria! Every soldier would be issued a meal ticket and all he had to do was go up, get punched, and eat all he wanted. Service was continuous day and night.

"The only trouble about this arrangement was that when we applied for meal tickets the British quartermaster, running true to form, said they were all out, and the Cafeteria man had adopted a slogan somewhat like the one of the Chinese laundry—'No tickee, no shirtee.' . . .

"But you cannot stump an American soldier. The men had money and the company funds were fat. So they all managed to get something to eat in town."

The next day, Hagood's troops entrained for their billets in the interior of France, but during the earlier months of debarkation many of the troops spent dreary days in temporary camps near the ports. Lieutenant Edward D. Siroir and Corporal William McGinnis of the 102nd Field Artillery thus spent ten days in October 1917:

"During our stay at St. Nazaire nothing of real significance took place. It rained incessantly all the time. The mud was almost knee deep. The food situation was not much better than on the boat. We were quartered in Adrian Huts, long, narrow, wooden buildings of very poor material, covered on the outside with tar paper. Inside there was no flooring and we were compelled to sleep on the damp ground. In some cases the men had to pitch pup-tents, because the roofs leaked so badly. There was a foot of water in one of the huts assigned to Battery C. Most of our time at this camp was spent in foot drill. The rest of the time was spent constructing a reservoir for the city of St. Nazaire. . . . Amusements were scare, but the Y.M.C.A. furnished movies and boxing bouts and passes were issued every night to go into the city."

Within St. Nazaire during these early months there were serious pitfalls for the unwary. There many an American boy, protected while he was in training camps in the United States, was first exposed to hard liquor. Not all could write home as did Gary Roberts: "Tell Uncle Caloway he just ought to be here to help the boys drink beer, whine, champane, coniac and lots of other drinks. I have my first to drink yet. And that's not all. I'm not going to. Oh! yes I did have a drink of grape juice yesterday for the first time since I left the States. It doesn't contain any alcohol you know so it won't hurt me."

Full of liquor, the novices were easy to lead to houses of prostitution, where they ran the risk of contracting venereal disease. Premier Georges Clemenceau strongly urged General Pershing to permit the establishment of licensed houses for the A.E.F. Pershing and his staff firmly rejected the proposal, ruling all known houses of prostitution to be off limits to soldiers, and forbidding troops to buy or accept as gifts whiskey, brandy, or champagne. The A.E.F. did establish prophylactic stations, but General Pershing issued a stern order warning that "a soldier who contracts a venereal disease not only suffers permanent injury, but renders himself inefficient as a soldier and becomes an incumbrance to the Army."

The Army had good reason to take vigorous action and maintain strong precautions. Colonel Hugh H. Young, a distinguished urologist from John Hopkins, and his associate, Colonel Edward L. Keyes, reported in 1918:

"We have not received the slightest co-operation form the French authorities. With reference to fighting venereal disease at Saint-Nazaire. In fact, all the efforts, and particularly those of the Mayor, have been most antagonistic. He has tried in every way to get people to say that it would be better to open the houses of prostitution and have the miserable condition of our troops as it was some months ago. The Mayor has tried in every way to get a wedge in so that our men can be allowed all kinds of liberty while in this port. When you think that transports of 12,000 to 15,000 men used to come through this port and stay here as long as ten or fifteen days and that an average of $20 to $30 was spent by each, you can easily see how much the town loses by our methods. . . . To give an idea of how much money the prostitutes made under the old method, one Madame deposited in one bank in one month 75,000 francs [about $15,000].

"If a saloon is caught it is closed for a short time, but it re-opens and goes on just the same. . . .

"I wrote a prescription for 7½ grains of cocaine and sent the worst-looking man we could find to get it. He priced a few articles, then got in a corner and presented the prescription. It was filled without protest."

Temptation also existed in all the interior cities of France. One lieutenant wrote in his diary, "Wandering through dark streets. Ever-present women. So mysterious and seductive in darkness. . . . A fellow's got to hang on to himself here. Not many do."

Even though the French officials were reluctant to cooperate, firm American regulations brought effective results.
Colonel Young cited the seven weeks' record of seven thousand
men, only fifty-six of whom reported for prophylaxes, and only
one of whom caught venereal disease. Lieutenant Colonel
Harry B. Anderson, a southerner serving with the 26th (Yankee)
Division, wrote:

"To start with, France, in spite of four years of war and being
overcrowded with millions of troops of all races, is not an
immoral country. . . . The venereal disease record in this division is practically nil. Of course, we have spent half of our time
in a deserted country and the rest in simple country villages,
inhabited by strait-laced, old-fashioned country people. In the
cities, as in all cities, the daughters of Lilith abound. The streets
in the immoral districts are policed by sentinels, and no
American soldiers are allowed in the neighborhood."

Years later, Colonel Frederick Palmer, who had been Chief
Press Officer for the A.E.F., summed up his impressions:

"Some of our returning soldiers boasted the more of their
amours because these had so slight a basis of experience. As a
matter of fact, many of them, easily the great majority, knew
enforced if not voluntary continence all the time they were in
A.E.F."

6

THE DISCOVERY
OF FRANCE

As the troops entrained for their billets far in the interior, they began their acquaintance with rural France. It was not the France of which they had dreamed, the land of Gay Paree and of the picture postal cards—though from their boxcars some did catch distant glimpses of the Eiffel Tower or the chateaus of the Loire Valley. Rather it was a France of small hamlets and solid farmhouses in which large numbers of them came to be billeted. Some specialists and most later arrivals were sent to camps, and it was on passes good for a few hours that they made the acquaintance of French people, both in villages and cities.

First, and unforgettably, the soldiers encountered the French trains, tiny and inefficient by American standards of that time. "We made a little fun of the English trains," William C. Walker remarked, "but when the boys saw the French box cars marked, 'Hommes 40—Cheveaux 8' you should have heard

them roar. It is something new you may know for a man to be
put in the same class and cars with horses, but at that we had a
very enjoyable ride." Most men did not find the boxcars pleasant. "We not being livestock, were loaded in forty strong,"
Chester Bon Egidy informed his family. "No one could lay down
or even sit down, and I along with the other thirty-nine, did my
sleeping standing up." Dr. William H. Baker, who had enlisted
as a private, joked, "It was great to find a place to sleep. You
either had your foot in somebody's face or somebody had their
foot in your face. . . . If a pretzel manufacturer had a photograph of that bunch trying to sleep he certainly could have
picked out some beautiful designs for his product. We had three
nights and two days of that."

For the troop commanders, the trains were equally unpleasant. Colonel Hagood, having endured the channel crossing in
La Marguerite, marched his regiment to the Le Havre station to
board trains for their secret destination in France.

"What this destination was or how long it would take to get
there no one knew or attempted to guess. It was one of the
secrets we were keeping from the Germans. . . .

"I assigned the one train to each battalion and four of the little box cars to each company; had the men load on their baggage, company property, furniture for the day rooms, etc.; and
then went to the 'Chief de Gare' to learn where we could find
the passenger trains. I was told in polite French, which I did not
understand, that there were no more trains and that if the
Americans filled up the trains with baggage instead of with soldiers, the French were sorry. After two hours' argument, during
which time the Chief de Gare, in true French style, had several
times ordered the train to start and I, in true American style, had
ordered it not to, it was finally agreed that we should let the
baggage go ahead with a few men in charge and that additional trains would be provided for the men. As soon as this arrangement was disclosed to the men, they all rushed forward to go
with the baggage. Some crawled inside. There was no room for
them to sit or stand. Some clung to the outside and some
climbed on top of the cars. When company commanders

ordered the men on top to get off and fall in ranks, they, too, crawled into the box cars on top of the others. After a feeble effort on my part to unscramble the mess, I decided to let it go as it was and we started off, as we supposed, to the front.

"We had no rations except some canned goods the old soldiers had wisely hidden in their baggage before leaving home, and some cheese and biscuits that remained from what the British gave us when we left *La Marguerite*. . . . We were on the train twenty-eight hours. There was no water, there were no sanitary arrangements and no regular stops. Sometimes the train would stop on a siding to let another train pass. Then the men would jump off for various purposes and we would have great difficulty in collecting them again. However, we did not lose a man, and when we arrived at our destination and I made a little talk to the men saying that I was sorry they had had such a—of a time and that I should make it up to them, one old sergeant stepped out and said: 'I hope the Colonel will not worry himself. The men enjoyed it.' "

Captain Arthur Sewall Hyde suffered similar vicissitudes in leading his company of casuals (men not as yet assigned to any unit) to their training area:

"At last, about 8:30 P.M., we arrived at a place and detrained in the pitch-dark, and marched through a picturesque little village amid the cries and cheers of the French peasants. Unfortunately the Captain in charge of the train ordered us to the wrong station, the Colonel did not expect us, and there was some delay in getting billets for all our men. The place we should have gone to was ten miles farther on, and I heard two days later that they waited for us until 11, and wondered where we were. . . . However, I learned a lot . . . about billeting, etc. The men slept in wine cellars dug in the sides of the hills, about 50 to a cavern. We officers were billeted in a little house with an old Frenchman and his wife, who took fine care of us, and we were comfortable. . . ."

As for Hyde's company: "They never gave me a bit of trouble and were a good lot. . . . They were all sorts and kinds: Miners, school-teachers, college-graduates, laborers, mechanics, druggists, electricians, clerks, some ignorant, some educated."

Children waving to the 101st Ammunition Train, 26th Division, Soulosse, April 1918

A pair of American soldiers lunching at the Citroen Munition Plant, August 1918

For men of such different backgrounds to live together required some adjustment. For them to live parceled out among wine cellars, barns, and in peasant households through the French countryside required even more adjustment. Soldiers from rural areas contrasted the French farms with those they had known at home. Corporal Earl O. Coontz wrote home to Deer Trail, Colorado:

"The farmers collect in little villages where they live. . . . Then they farm the adjoining land . . . and don't know what a tractor or engine is. They use the old tread mill type of power. That is the way they thresh their grain. A big horse in this tread mill just keeps walking up hill and runs the mill which runs the little thresher. . . . Our machines could thresh as much in an hour as they thresh in a week, honestly and papa, I wish you could see the way they work their horses. . . . They do all the harrowing with a 1 section wooden harrow, with wooden teeth in it, and sow their ground by hand. But one thing I have noticed more than anything else, is how they save; there is absolutely nothing goes to waste. . . .

"Oh, yes, when you first enter one of the villages you would think they have no stock of any kind, but they have. One roof covers the family, stock—'chickens, hogs, cows, and horses,' all in the same building. . . . Each village has a public wash pond, where the women take their clothes on wheelbarrows down there to wash them. They have a little box affair where they kneel."

Living quarters and barn were usually under the same roof, as Corporal Coontz remarked, and it was usually in the loft of the barn in the hay, cold and dark, with lights strictly prohibited, that the enlisted men found themselves sleeping. The Reverend Francis P. Duffy, chaplain of the 165th Infantry (Father Duffy of what was popularly known as the Irish 69th), in censoring a letter, came upon the remark, "There are three classes of inhabitants in the houses—first, residents; second, cattle; third, soldiers." So it must have seemed to most of the troops. General James G. Harbord, who, together with Captain George Patton, accompanied General Pershing on an inspection of the 1st Division, wrote wryly in his diary on August 1, 1917:

"The billet is a new institution in our army, and no doubt many old soldiers turn a regretful memory to the clean camps of their own land. In this country a 'Town Major' is appointed, and goes to every house in a village and marks on it the number of officers , men and horses the place will accommodate. . . . In the haylofts they cannot smoke or have lights, and there are eternally present the odors of the stable. . . . It is a system that has little to commend it from our standpoint, but tents for a million men cannot be thought of when cotton is needed for hundreds of things . . . when shipping space is valuable. . . . We inspected them with considerable detail, those billets."

Dysentery plagued the soldiers during their first few months in the billets. The Town Majors tried to improve sanitary conditions by removing forcibly the manure piles standing in front of each house or barn, despite the protests of the peasants. But the trouble continued, and the soldiers existed miserably.

Considering the discomfort in which the troops lived, in a strange country with different customs and a tongue difficult to master, the billeted troops got along remarkable well with the peasants. There were misunderstandings not only over the removal of manure piles but also over the commandeering of firewood, but the peasants seemed remarkably warm and hospitable. Although in time many soldiers felt they were being exploited, complaints were few in letters home, and warm sympathy seemed the rule rather than the exception. A Negro in the Medical Corps, Jesse E. Dickson, wrote that he could see how the war had added to the difference between the French people and the home folks. "I don't mean that the country itself is changed, for it still is one of the most beautiful places I have ever seen," he explained, "but you can see in so many different ways how the people are sacrificing every luxury to aid the country. Our country may have a big toll to pay before the war is over, but never as great as . . . France."

At first especially, the efforts of the Americans to make themselves understood were ludicrous. "When we first came most knew no French at all," Lieutenant C. C. Gooding of the Aviation Corps pointed out. "One of our boys was out in the front of a farm house, jumping up and down waving his arms and crowing like a rooster. He wanted to buy a chicken but the French thought he wanted to amuse them. It was surely funny and finally when he went out in the farm and chased a chicken around they got the idea."

George Sullivan found his lack of French a handicap when he went to a barbershop: "Well, the lady barber and I had an awful time. I wanted her to shave me first, before she washed my head but she had a way all her own and then came the shave. It was a very rough ten minutes and I believe I will shave myself after this."

Any Yank who knew a little French was in great demand. Harry W. Ostrander, a lieutenant in the artillery, wrote his sister: "The French think I will learn the language in a couple of years, and the Americans who do not speak it at all regard me as a past master. I get quite a lot of practice making their wants known to the storekeepers, but when one of the boys wants me to express the state of his heart to the pretty demoiselle behind the counter, I have to resign. For one thing, being the third party in such a conversation is a delicate operation in itself. Beside, my friends can think up pretty compliments faster than I can think up translations. Also, as soon as we get the girl fussed and pleased, she goes into high gear and my third speed language can't keep up with her. Of course, being a third party in these conversations isn't always so bad. For instance, a bird at the front sent word by a friend of his to be remembered to a girl in a candy store here. I was pressed into service to render his regards to her, which I did. She did not remember the bird's name and he did not know hers, but he told me where the shop was and that is how I found her. I did not tell her that though. She wanted to know how I was sure she was the right girl and thought perhaps I was mistaken. 'No,' I said, 'I could not be mistaken, for the officer had said the prettiest girl in all of France, so it was very simple.' Of course I got in solid with her right away."

By the end of the war, many of the soldiers not at the front were making at least desultory efforts to learn French. Neil W. Kimball reported to his parents from Brest:

"As I sit here at my home made table (with one short leg) with a flickery candle for a light, I can hear a most heated discussion down around the stove. Now it is going something like this:

" 'I tell you it is tooasweet! Why, here it is right in the book.'

" 'I don't give a damn what the book says.' It's the argumentative corporal this time. 'I know. It's tootsweet. Didn't I hear Evelyn say it no mor'n ten minutes ago when I left her after my bed time vin rooge? She says, 'You comment ici tootsweet,' meaning 'come back pronto, kid; I'm strong for you.'

"And that's the way it goes all evening. Most of the unattached soldiers have collected a red cheeked, wooden shod French lassie and a bilingual dictionary and are making valiant efforts to improve their education in French. And you don't notice any of them playing hookey from their lessons, either.

" 'Now listen to this damn book, will yer?' It's the argumentative corporal again. 'All about the silver handle of the fork and the quill pens of my aunt, but not a thing like "Say, kid, you sure got wonderful orbs" or "Ain't I seen you somewhere before, girlie?"' . . .

"The most discouraging thing is to spend several hours composing a nice little oration in French and to have it wrecked on a reef of shrugging shoulders and 'no comprees.' The argumentative corporal spend two hours the other day learning to ask a petite young grocery clerkess to attend the band concert with him, and when he finally got it out she produced a small package of cheese and said 'Doos franc, pleese.' . . .

"But aren't your sympathies with the soldier who has promised to send his wife hand made lingerie from France? I've seen as high as half a dozen standing sheepishly around the entrance to a mercerie. With a final look at the dictionary, a furtive glance up the street and a pull at the overseas cap they open the door and dive in with flaming cheeks. Oh yes, there are heroes who don't go over the top."

Sometimes it was the French who knew some English. John Valente wrote from Dijon:

"I was talking to a French girl who could speak a little English and I asked her:

" 'What do you think of American boys?'

" 'Oh, zay haf ze grand idea!'

" 'And what do you mean by the grand idea?' I asked.

" 'Oh, zay haf such a way about zem! Zat I can't explain! Zey understand! what you mean so quick like zat! Zey learn like ze flash.' . . .

"About here . . . I told her that they had beaucoup franc . . . and she said, 'Wee! Wee!' . . .

" 'We knew it all the time,' I rejoined, and so our conversation ended."

Valente was more generous when talking about the French people he had met:

"They will take you in their homes with practically no acquaintance, and you are almost boss. Anything you want is yours, and what they give is given from the heart."

Officers, like Lieutenant Donald B. Wurzburg, often formed warm ties with the French families who provided them with billets: "In this village the woman in whose home my trunk is, took out my uniform and cleaned it, and a pair of trousers and mended them, all without my knowledge. She would not take a cent either, but I made her diminutive son a present, which she at once put into a savings-bank. He is four years old, but no larger than a son at two. He wandered in the other day and indicated that he desired a conference with me. I bent down and he whispered a rapid line of infantile French with the local accent, out of which I made that if I had a little candy he could be induced to partake. I managed to secure a tin can of bonbons from the commissary, and he has done nobly. Each time I gave him a piece he first took it to his mother and secured permission to eat it. If she thinks he has had enough and refuses, he never whimpers or protests."

William C. Walker, who learned a few French phrases while he was billeted in a small village, wrote of the hospitable treatment he received:

"A young lawyer from Denver and I started out one Sunday for a little walk in the country and stopped in a house to ask for information and nothing would please them but that we stay for dinner, and before we left we had spent the whole day and very few Sundays I ever spent in a more enjoyable manner. . . .

"They were a typical French family living in a big roomy stone house with its ever-present garden full of all kinds of good things. . . .

"Once inside the house the main thing that attracted our attention was the fireplace that filled one end of the dining room and on which the dinner was cooked. I haven't seen a stove outside of a hotel since I've been in France. We sat there and watched the dinner cook and it had been so long since we had seen a regular family meal that I expect we showed all to plainly our impatience at the inherent French slowness. A nice fat young rooster was trussed on a spindle attached to a clock work affair, and as it slowly broiled there in front of the log fire it made a scene and sent out an aroma that was a treat for a hungry soldier."

Courtship in a French home meant learning new customs, as Dale Packard discovered:

"When you call on a French mademoiselle, the whole family remains present in the room during the entire visit, and when you leave, a kiss is donated by the whole family including mademoiselle. Where I go most often there is only Monsieur, Madame, Mademoiselle and a son who is away in the army so the kissing proposition isn't so bad, but I wish the old gentleman would shave off his moustache. . . .

"I arrive at the house about 7:00 P.M. as I must be in camp again for taps at 9:30. First Madame and Mademoiselle tell about what they have done since I saw them last. They never forget that I am a poor linguist and always try to explain everything in French that I can understand. Then they tell me about the last letter from their son at the front. . . . Then pretty soon Monsieur bring out a bottle which he says contains good wine, but which tastes about like vinegar to me, so I manage to take no more than a sip of it , but I tell the old man that it is fine to escape being considered impolite. Then Mademoiselle who has studied English in school for a year gets out a little French-English dictionary and we study

French and English while Monsieur reads the newspaper and Madame sews.

"When I leave Mademoiselle, whose first name is 'Germaine,' goes out to the garden and brings back some flowers to put in my coat."

Sadness tinged these interchanges between the incoming soldiers and the long-suffering French people. Private Harold A. Goodman, who was serving at Base Hospital Number 27 in a city of 30,000 population, marveled at how few civilian men he saw in the streets, and how many menial tasks were being undertaken by women:

"The white wings in the street have been replaced by women. At any important railroad centre I saw women cleaning boiler tubes and filling the tender with coal. They were dressed in overalls and indeed looked strong enough for the work. Nearly all women are in mourning, very few, however wear veils, just a plain black dress with a turban or large ribbed felt hat."

While Goodman was buying cigars in a tobacco store, a messenger came to tell the proprietress her husband had been killed. "She covered her face and burst into tears. . . . As I turned to leave I heard her baby cry. She clasped it to her breast. Two other small children came running into the store laughing, and full of glee. They saw their mother heart broken. They were just large enough to realize the loss of their father. . . . The next morning I bought more smokes at the same store. Her eyes were still red. She tried hard to smile and greeted me in a cheerful way."

In the end it was the fact that the Americans proved themselves good soldiers, thought Sergeant Linton B. Swift of the 16th Railway Engineers, that caused the French to be enthusiastic and unreservedly friendly:

"To tell the truth, for the first ten months we were over here I felt that we were simply 'on probation.' That, friendly as they were toward us, the French could not accept us whole-heartedly until they understood us better and until we had shown what stuff we were made of. Many of our ways were strange to them.

They, whom we had been thinking of as excitable and rather superficial people, couldn't understand our [noisiness] and brusk ways, which must have sometimes seemed simply irreverence to them, in the face of a nation's grief.

"There is hardly a town without its long roll of dead, its crippled soldiers, and its widows in mourning. And into these towns train-loads of Americans would come—yelling and singing, and hanging out of the windows, while the people looked on in amazement.

"And then—in a country where people on leaving a store turn and say, *Au revoir, messieurs et mesdames,* to every one present— an American who slammed in and out of the place seemed—to say the least—lacking in manners. But they didn't criticize; they just waited. And now ... they have found out the average American is a real man, who may lack some of their own forms of politeness, but who, nevertheless, will insist on carrying an old woman's burden for her; [and] they have discovered, also, that the American is a good fighter."

A West Virginia mother unexpectedly received a letter from France:

"Madame:—

"Doubtless you are going to be very much surprised on receiving this letter for we do not know each other. I know only, that like me, you are the mother of a soldier for I have had the pleasure, quite recently of lodging your son, Capt. Roberts and it is to acomplish the promise that I made him, that I send you a few lines.

"Your son is truly charming Madam, and it is with great pleasure that we have welcomed him at our fireside, where for a few days he has taken the place of my eldest son, also an officer, who fell for France last year.

"Believe me, Madam, that it is with our whole hearts that we welcome your children and receive them, for do they not come to avenge ours, and aid them in liberating our country? ... Among these, your son is one of the best, always ardent in accomplishing his duty and I am truly happy that during the few days which he spent with us, I have been able to give him a little joy. We will not forget either that he has been the first of the Allies who has sat at our fireside and that he has made us know your country. On leaving, your son said to me, 'Write to my mother.' This is his wish realized.

"Goodbye, Madam, receive with all my sympathy the expression of my best thought.

"Madame E. Michant"

7

Supplying the Troops

Enormous supply lines slowly came into being as the American Expeditionary Forces, finding that the French could not provide adequate ports or railroads or camps or warehouses, began building its own on a scale therefore unprecedented. All this involved much manpower; Pershing estimated that of the first million men that arrived in France no more than five hundred thousand would be available for the front lines. Thus it was that hundreds of thousands of men found themselves assigned to the Services of Supply, filling vital needs but seldom seeing active combat. Major General James G. Harbord, who was in command of the S.O.S. in the final months of the war, has paid tribute to the officers and enlisted men who filled its ranks.

"By far the great majority of the officers and men who wore the shoulder insignia of the S.O.S. were fresh from civil pursuits. They came from every walk of American life and from every field of its business. The sacrifice at which they served could be measured by the energy and intelligence which they gave to their duties in the knowledge that the more they gave, the sooner the War would be ended. We were engaged in what was relatively a civil task, compared to combat. Far from the sounds of the drums and the guns; unsought by the glory-hunters; absent when promotions were being distributed; ineligible even at the price of life itself for the medals that reward heroism in action; doomed to spend the rest of their lives explaining why they served in the Services of Supply—their equal in trained intelligence and general fitness for their tasks could not have been found in any other land than the one for which they so truly fought. Such men may not have been within range of the enemy guns but they did more for their country by living for it than they could possibly have done by dying for it."

In General Harbord's view, the model American business-man in the S.O.S. was Charles G. Dawes, who become a Brigadier General and the General Purchasing Agent of the A.E.F. Dawes, who a quarter of a century earlier had been Pershing's closest friend, was a leading banker in Chicago when the United States entered the war; he enlisted as a Major in the 17th Engineers, but in August 1917 Pershing brought him to Paris to head purchasing. Dawes managed somehow to locate and purchase in a western Europe supposedly stripped of mil-itary supplies some ten million tons compared with seven mil-lion tons sent from the United States. Despite his qualities as a purchasing agent, General Dawes did not always look suffi-ciently spruced to suit his friend Pershing. On one occasion Dawes noted in his diary: "He spoke to Harbord and the lat-ter walked across the road to me. As Harbord carefully but-toned up my overcoat, which was opened, including the hooks at the top, he murmured in my ear, 'This is a hell of a job for the Chief of Staff—but the General told me to do it.' Some soldiers told me that in England there was a kodak taken of John with one breast-pocket unbuttoned. For this picture I am going to search that country—to use it for justifiable defensive personal purposes."

Where supply problems were concerned, Dawes was alert and precise even to Pershing's standards. In an explosive memorandum to the Commander-in-Chief, sent in April 1918, he argued vehemently for unified military control over all the Allied supply organizations still operating competitively and redundantly behind the lines. "If we do not have military management and military control," he declared, "we may fail and a German army at the ports may save us the trouble of unloading some of our engineering material from ships, thus devoted, which should have been bringing men and food to have stopped our enemies where they are now." An inter-Allied board for the pooling of supplies did come into being, and Dawes became its American member.

The S.O.S. evolved out of an earlier organization, the L.O.C.: Line of Communications. Through 1917 its troubles were legion. As winter approached, clothing for the troops became scarce because whatever was being produced in the United States was badly needed for the draftees pouring into the encampments there. The A.E.F. were forced to purchase uniform tunics from the British, complete with brass buttons bearing the royal crown. The soldiers' comments on the "King George buttons" were lively and sarcastic. At the same time, sufficient Christmas presents for the troops to fill over a hundred freight cars came dribbling in through January 1918.

Even when the proper supplies reached France, it was exceedingly difficult to get them to the correct divisions. Colonel Johnson Hagood, placed in charge of the advance section of the supply service in the fall of 1917, encountered one frustration after another. The Quartermaster of the 42nd Division received word from the French that 900 horses were on the way, but no forage was available. Hagood was informed by the French that the shipment could not be stopped, so the Quartermaster finally located some forage. Then the horses never arrived. The 26th Division received several packing cases addressed to a Boston department store containing quantities of baby clothes. "Trainloads of wagon bodies arrived in my area with no wheels," Hagood later remembered. "The supplies of

Generals James G. Harbord and Charles G. Dawes

Shoes worn out by soldiers in France, Salvage Depot, Tours, March 10, 1918

the 42nd Division, at Vaucouleurs, were scattered out over a ten-acre field, most of it in the open and in such condition that it could neither be segregated nor used. This division had only six trucks to distribute troops and supplies over a billeting area of about eighteen square miles." In desperation, Colonel Hagood on November 15, 1917, addressed a memorandum to General Pershing's Chief of Staff, General Harbord:

"If the United States does not actually fail, its efficiency is certainly going to be tremendously decreased by the sheer incompetence of its line of communications, beginning in the U.S. and ending at the French front. This incompetence not only applies to the machine as a whole but, we may as well admit, applies to the individual officers and employees, none of whom has had experience in solving such a problem. In this, of course, I include myself.

"I am informed that a ship lay at one of our base ports in France for forty-two days waiting to be unloaded and costing the government in the neighborhood of ten thousand dollars a day. At this end of the line the situation has been properly described . . . as an eye-sore to his division and a disgrace to the United States. One of the brigade commanders told me that his men had gone as long as twelve days without pota-toes, eight days without any vegetable component at all, and that it was a common experience to have no bread. French and Canadian Officers and troops seeing the men in this pitiable condition have come to their rescue and helped them out. At one time ninety per cent of all the transportation of one American division had been borrowed from a French cap-tain, who had secured it by a personal appeal to his own divi-sion commander.

"Not only has the L. of C. failed, so far, to function prop-erly in the supply of our own men but it has so clogged the French railway yards, storehouses and quays in this section as to cause an official complaint to be made to the Com-mander-in-Chief, with the unofficial statement to me that they were being embarrassed in their movement of troops to the Italian front."

The response to these conditions was the creation of a more effective system for sending supplies from the docks to storage depots, to regulation stations, to divisions at the front. Since the overall organization still seemed unworkable, in February 1918 a board under Hagood devised a complete overhaul. The Hagood Board proposed a new "Service of the Rear"—but since ribald soldiers might associate this title with latrine duty, General Pershing substituted the name Services of Supply. Throughout its existence, Hagood was Chief of Staff of the S.O.S. The commanding officer until the end of July 1918 was General Francis J. Kernan. The sudden replacement of Kernan came as a "great shock" to Hagood since he "had rendered most distinguished service." Pershing replaced him with Harbord, a combat general, in part to forestall a War Department plan to install General George W. Goethals, builder of the Panama Canal, in independent command over supplies.

General Kernan was a desk commander of the S.O.S.; Harbord, to Pershing's delight, spent his time in incessant inspections. He immediately ordered a special train, complete with office, dining, and sleeping facilities, and with two automobiles on a flatcar. By night he traveled by train; in the daytime he used the automobiles to visit the widespread facilities of the S.O.S. He thus spent three of four days a week away from his headquarters at Tours.

Immediately upon assuming command General Harbord spent a week with General Pershing, inspecting S.O.S. activities in the ports and its intermediate zone of operations. He later remembered:

"Tours, the S.O.S. Headquarters, already had a military population of nearly twenty-five hundred American officers and nearly forty-five hundred soldiers. There we began by visiting the Central Records Office. . . . Its records . . . contained the vital information concerning each individual in the American Expeditionary Forces. Such records showed his arrival, his assignments, his whereabouts, his health, his mail address, his wounds, his death and all the information on which later his bonus and all future governmental awards were made. It grew from one officer and clerk at Chaumont, and at the time of the Armistice in had at Bourges some six thousand officers and enlisted men, and over five hundred British women.

"These women, familiarly known as W.A.A.C.'s, were of the British Women's Army Auxiliary Corps, and their organization, consisting of thousands, extended from the front line to the base ports. . . ."

General Harbord also had within his empire several hundred uniformed American telephone girls, all of whom were bilingual so that they could handle calls with equal facilities either in English or French. One of them pointed out to her parents in Oregon that although the magazines incessantly hailed the achievements of other American women in France:

"Never a word about the Signal Corps Unit of 250 girls who plug from morning until night, who scream their lungs out to trenches over lines that are tied to trees, to fence-posts, and along the ground. Not that we care. We came over here to do our work and to give quick service and to help the boys a few miles ahead of us to get what they want and what we need to get, the Kaiser."

On his August inspection, Harbord noted:

"The Chief Quartermaster, Brigadier General Harry L. Rogers, . . . assured General Pershing that the quantities of food and clothing on hand were ample to meet contemplated requirements. At various storage depots there were accumulated forty-five million rations, or about forty days' supply for the command. There was a shortage in animals, forage and labor. The French had promised us eighty thousand horses, but that would be only half of our needs. Many of these very animals had been bought in America. . . .

"There were about thirty-two thousand non-American laborers available, of different nationalities, from Italians to Chinese, including prisoners of war. The Labor Bureau, organized under Lieutenant Colonel John Price Jackson as a part of the Dawes activities, was trying to get labor from France, Italy and Spain. There were about fifty thousand American labor and forestry troops, including about a regiment of combatant troops.

"The Motor Transport Corps under Brigadier General Meriwether L. Walker, an officer of Engineers, and a good one, was finding difficulty in obtaining trained mechanics and chauffeurs, notwithstanding the numbers we had thought ourselves able to send to the French at an earlier period. Only about half the number of automobiles and trucks actually needed in the S.O.S. were in stock at the time of our visit. This was a situation which, with all our boasted mass production and leadership in the motor industry, was never remedied. At the date of the Armistice the American Expeditionary Forces were short of the prescribed motor vehicles of all kinds, to the total of fifty-five thousand. . . .

"The Chief Ordnance Officer, then Brigadier General Charles B. Wheeler, reported that ordnance supplies were arriving regularly, but that no field guns had come. . . . He feared that the French would not be able to produce enough for both their needs and ours. The powder and explosive program was up to expectations but, due to shortage in steel, the manufacture of artillery guns which had been left to the French was slowing down.

"St. Pierre-des-Corps, several miles up the Loire from Tours, was a great center of supply personnel and activities. Besides several thousand railroad men quartered at Camp de Grasse, there was an immense Salvage depot there, which actually saved millions of dollars to our country. . . .

"The main storage plant at St. Sulpice was about half completed at the time of our visit and everything looked well. . . . The Commander-in-Chief neglected nothing, and he strode along like a professional pedestrain. He was a hard man to follow. On the other side of the Gironde from the city of Bordeaux and about six miles down the river lay Bassens. . . . We found the freight was piled up on the docks until the engineers were figuring on the possibility of the weight causing the wharves to sideslip into the river. . . .

"The towns of La Rochelle and La Pallice were practically one continuous settlement. . . . The most interesting feature of the place was the car-erecting plant. Our railroad cars came

from the United States. Knocked down and were brought here
to be erected by an engineer regiment composed largely of men
trained in that trade. . . . The plant was a hum of activity, and to
an observer the air seemed full of flying red-hot rivets, thrown
almost the length of a car and caught in something that looked
like a tin funnel. They were erecting sixty cars a day at this time,
but there came a time, as the end of the war drew near and the
need was great, when they did much better. They ran a conspicuous bulletin board and we figured them in the Race to
Berlin, crediting to the several groups the cars erected each day
as so many points, and competition grew very keen. . . .

"We built berths for eight vessels to unload simultaneously
at Montoir. . . . We did the inspection with a flat car and engine.
The Commander-in-Chief used the tail of the flat car for a
speaking platform—telling the S.O.S. boys how important their
work was, and how intimately their toil was entwined with victory at the front. The S.O.S. needed encouragement. . . . At the
Locomotive Repair and Erection Plant just outside St. Nazaire,
which we next visited, he had an audience of the 19th Engineers
who were doing that important work, and about five thousand
stevedores and laborers assembled in the broad square near the
little locked harbor. At the time the locomotives from America
were, like the cars, coming knocked down. A little later they
began coming set up. . . .

"The party proceeded to Blois. . . . At first it had been used
by us as a depot to which officers arriving unattached to units
were sent until they were needed for assignment to organizations or individual duty. Later it became a Classification Depot
for commissioned misfits of all types, and for many excellent
officers released from hospitals who had to be reclassified. . . .
For many an American it was the grave of buried ambitions, the
temporary home of the hopeless.

"After Blois we went to St. Aignan, a replacement depot
known to thousands of doughboys as 'Saint Agony.' . . . Gievres
was our largest supply storage depot. . . . It covered twelve
square miles in area. . . . Its supplies ordinarily went forward
through the Regulating Station at Is-sur-Tille, but it supplied

directly the Divisions which were operating before Paris when it was threatened in July, 1918. . . . During the August in which we were visiting there, a telegram was received one morning at 8:15 ordering exactly 4,596 tons of supplies which were to comprise 1,250,000 cans of tomatoes; 1,000,000 pounds of dry beans. By 6:15 that evening, this demand had been filled and 457 freight cars were loaded with it and on their way to the advance depot at Is-sur-Tille."

The most serious factor with which General Harbord had to contend was the poor morale in the S.O.S. Many of the officers had been failures at the front, reassigned to duties in the rear. "Sometimes it is merely the physical strain to which they are unequal at the front," Harbord noted in his diary; "the loss of sleep, the thought of sending men forward in numbers to die at their orders, with the remainder of the strain, cause a collapse. . . . Many lack the ability to handle men." Others fresh from the United States, both officers and enlisted men, found themselves in unfamiliar work: "Ribbon-counter jumpers are found in stevedore regiments; . . . lawyers appear in engineer units; longshoremen in the forestry regiments; railroad men in labor battalions, etc. etc."

Tens of thousands of Negro soldiers, finding themselves laborers in France, were treated in second-class fashion. Their officers, both commissioned and noncommissioned, were white; morale improved when some Negroes began to receive corporal's and sergeant's stripes. One white officer declared, "The spirit of St. Nazaire is the spirit of the south." At Camp Williams, Is-sur-Tille, an order dated July 3, 1918, and enforced for nine months thereafter, declared: "All colored enlisted men of this command are hereby confined to the limits of the Camp and Depot until further advised." Whites were allowed to visit Is-sur-Tille and surrounding towns; when Negroes defied the order, they were arrested. "On the other hand, the Negro soldiers themselves were not without faults," Charles H. Williams has pointed out. "Some of their difficulties were due to their own ignorance and to customs that they brought into the army from civil life. On plantations and public works some had been used to 'ducking the boss' and slipping away, and attempts to continue this practice in the army sometimes resulted in their being placed in the guardhouse." But on the whole the Negro troops were hardworking and cheerful. John Hope, visiting a woodcutters' camp, wrote: "Lights were seen in the narrow streets and mud deeper than I had ever seen before. In the morning the men got up at 4:45. The sound they made walking through the mud was unlike any noise that I had ever heard. Even at that early hour some were joking, some singing."

Most white troops too worked hard and complained little. Eldon Maxwell of the 319th Engineers, engaged in building a railroad to haul timber, wrote home in good humor, "About all the fighting I have done so far is to fight cooties." Others, near the front, had their share of dangerous experiences, and still others, far behind the lines, could not resist the temptation to embroider fanciful adventures in their letters home. Some took satisfaction in employing their civilian skills under strange French conditions. Private John J. Jordan, formerly of the Denver & Rio Grande, found himself brakeman first on supply trains to the front, then on the Paris-Orleans line. "And what do you know about it?" he wrote his friends. "I've got a woman boss! . . . She gets the dope on the trains, and she tells me what track to head them in on. She can't speak English so I have to worry along with my irregular French." His division had stretched 141 kilometers eastward, and it had taken from 12 to 60 hours to make the run to the front.

For some fortunate men, service in the S.O.S. was a lark. One corporal enthusiastically informed his mother: "Practically the entire staff is going on liberty to-day, and I am left by myself. . . . I am looking out the window watching the ducks play about in the articficial waterways in front of the chateau. . . . This sure is a beautiful place, and it sure gives me pleasure to walk around the grounds on a nice day like this. We are kept fairly busy at the office. We have plenty of time tho to go around and take in the sights. We are going to have a big athletic carnival soon, but I do not think I will be here that day, as I am hoping to get extended liberty about that time to visit a certain big city. . . . I am having the time of my life, and I don't want to go home until it is all over over here."

Despite problems of morale, inefficiency, and shortages, the S.O.S. record in total was so impressive that war correspondents sent home glowing dispatches replete with staggering statistics. General Dawes, in testifying concerning purchasing before a congressional committee in 1921, made comments that well applied as a balance sheet for the S.O.S. as a whole, both in its shortcomings and its achievement:

"Sure we paid. . . . We would have paid horse prices for sheep if sheep could have pulled artillery. . . . It's all right now to say we bought too much vinegar or too many cold chisels, but we saved the civilizations of the world. . . . Hell and Maria, we weren't trying to keep a set of books. We were trying to win a war."

8

GIRDING FOR
BATTLES AHEAD

During a winter of ominous stalemate, from the fall of 1917 into March 1918, General Pershing hurried his troops through a three-month program of training in preparation for the decisive battles in which they must participate. It was a bleak, uncomfortable winter for the Americans, and a depressing one for their battle-weary allies, whose exhilaration over the summer arrival of the first American troops long since had dissipated into a desperate desire to prevent further heavy losses and conserve their dwindling divisions in the relative safety of trenches and redoubts.

The collapse of the Russian front in the fall of 1917, with the opening of peace negotiations by the new Bolshevik regime, enabled Germany to shift divisions to build a frightening numerical superiority on the Western Front. Simultaneously that black autumn, the Austrians dealt a staggering setback to Italy at Caporetto. On December 22, 1917, General Petain issued a gloomy directive to the French forces:

"The Entente will not recover superiority in manpower until the American army is capable of placing in line a certain number of large units: Until then, we must, under penalty of irremediable attrition maintain a waiting attitude, with the idea firmly fixed in mind of resuming as soon as we can, the offensive which alone will bring us ultimate victory."

Pershing, estimating that the Germans and Austrians would be able to mass 250 to 260 divisions against less than 170 Allied divisions, pressured the War Department to send troops more rapidly. "The Allies are very weak and we must come to their relief this year," he warned Secretary Baker, referring to the 1918 plans. "The year after may be too late. It is very doubtful if they can hold on until 1919 unless we give them a lot of support this year."

The British and French, desperate for the men, found shipping to bring them over (which previously they had been unwilling to divert). At the same time they tried incessantly to persuade Pershing that the transport of American troops should be limited for the time being to infantry and machine-gun units, to be rushed as replacements as rapidly as possible throughout the French and British Armies. Pershing with equal stubbornness insisted that the Americans must be dispersed only for front-line training, or in cases of gravest battle emergency. He was firm in his determination, hacked by the iron will of President Wilson, that as soon as possible a separate American force must undertake its own operations on sectors of the Western Front.

In this air of crisis, the troops were trained to Pershing's specification. One requirement of which every man became aware was that even in the mud and cold of the French training areas they must maintain the snap and polish that their Commander-in-Chief regarded as a requisite of high morale. Pershing cabled in September 1917:

"I cannot too strongly impress upon the War Department the absolute necessity of rigid insistence that all men be thoroughly grounded in the school of soldier. Salutes should be rendered by both officers and men in most military manner. . . .

The loyalty, readiness and alertness indicated by strictest adherence to this principle will immensely increase the pride and fighting spirit of our troops. The slovenly, unmilitary, careless habits that have grown up in times of peace in our Army are seriously detrimental to the aggressive attitude that must prevail from highest to lowest in our forces."

Pershing's main specification was that in the training areas both in the United States and in France officers and men must not be lulled into the French notion that preparation for trench warfare was enough; they must master the techniques of open warfare so that they would be ready to attack. Pershing was schooling his men for victory, not stalemate or defeat. General Harbord reminisced some years later:

"Our Commander-in-Chief believed, and time confirmed his judgement, that the War could never be won by troops of both sides remaining in parallel trenches separated by a few hundred yards. Some day someone somewhere would come out of his trenches and start forward, and thus a stalemate would be broken and the War would eventually be won. . . . Mere training in trench warfare would not be enough for our officers when this event happened. This was explained to our French friends at length, many times over, but they took the opposite view. They criticized our theory and were unkind enough to do it to some of our visiting statesmen, as well as through channels to their own Government."

General William L. Sibert, Commanding General of the 1st Division, reported to Pershing in October on his experiences in the Gondrecourt area:

"Training in conjunction with French troops is slow and we have found that after one or two demonstrations by French organizations it is difficult to keep our soldiers interested. The principal assistance we can derive form the French or English will be from officers and specially selected noncommissioned officers of those armies acting as advisors and critics.

"Our officers are not sufficiently familiar with trench warfare conditions to draft good problems and both the officers and men fail to visualize the possible effect of hostile artillery and trench mortar fire. Consequently dispositions of troops, liaison arrangements, et cetera, which seem satisfactory to us frequently meet with severe and absolutely correct criticisms from the French officers observing the exercises. . . .

"French officers prepare a serious of company, battalion, and regimental problems involving all the various phases of trench warfare and give a setting on the centers of resistance which each regiment has prepared (entrenchments, barbed wire, etc.). Our officers take these problems, state them in American fashion if necessary, and proceed to prepare the necessary orders. The problem is then gone over on the map, rehearsed on the ground and corrected, and finally the unit or units concerned carry out the orders on the ground. French officers observe the work of the troops and are called upon in the critique to criticize all mistakes observed. . . . It has been found that the work in the specialties (bayonet, musketry, machine gun, auto rifle, grenade, etc.) develops very much faster than the instruction of the division staff."

The 26th (Yankee) Division was thus trained under realistic conditions, reported Frank P. Sibley of the *Boston Globe*:

"Most impressive of all, actual entrenchments were dug on the plateau south of Neufchateau, towards Noncourt. A complete system of fire trenches, cover and communicating trenches, and support trenches, with wire entanglements, and a noble great *abri* for the command post was dug, all to absolute model. The work was done by successive details of engineers and infantry. It was all valuable practice, and as soon as the trench system was finished, it was put into use.

"It represented a sub-sector held by one battalion. Every day a battalion went into the trenches for terrain exercises in attack and defense problems. Night attacks and defenses, with realistic fire signals, followed. And presently, two battalions a day were working, under the keen criticism of their French teachers. One battalion would make the attack formations, while the other stood on defense.

"Buglers stationed at fifty-yard intervals on the line of the advance, represented the artillery barrage, and their mournful

Instruction in saluting, 329th Infantry, Le Mans

Bayonet training, on guard position, 329th Infantry, Le Mans

tooting of single notes stood for shells. As the line of raiders advanced, first one and then another bugler would fall silent; this course, was the rolling barrage advancing to cover the infantry advance. . . . Sometimes at night, when there was snow on the ground, the scene became very beautiful; but there was always behind the beauty the consciousness that this was merely a rehearsal of what was soon to come in grim, deadly earnest."

Even as a simulation, the training was often earnest enough. Captain Arthur Sewall Hyde, attending a tactical school for officers, wrote his sister:

"This week, we have had exhaustive instruction in gas lectures, gas-mask drills, and actual experience with the wicked stuff. Thursday we were gassed three times, once with tear-gas, once with mustard-gas and once with phosgene—the deadly kind. One sniff would kill a man but I felt secure in my ridiculous-looking mask.

"Yesterday we had an hour's march with the respirators on—we looked like a long column of two-legged pigs with goggles on—under our steel helmets. It was decidedly disagreeable to exercise with the things on—and it was a relief when it was over.

"Yesterday I had some experience in live-bomb throwing and rifle-grenade work, both rather nasty, nervous work. Today, the whole Company was marching across the range to attend some lecture when we heard an explosion in the rifle-grenade range in a ravine 400 yards away—then cries for 'ambulance' and men running toward us over the muddy fields. A runner reaches us and asked for a doctor. Unfortunately there was none. It seems a rifle-grenade hung fire and exploded in the horn, killing instantly a first-lieutenant instructor and wounding a student. Only yesterday afternoon, that same instructor gave me my first lesson in the use of the rifle-grenade, a good-looking sandy-haired boy, named McCoy, who has been over here since September. It has cast quite a gloom over the whole school, but I suppose we out to expect some accidents occasionally—for there is much work going on on the range all the time."

The schooling made relatively little impression upon many
of the enlisted men. It merely fitted them into a routine through
which they could fight and perhaps survive in the front lines.
Along with the battle training, there were lengthy marches to
harden them. What continued to interest them most that winter (that they could write home about) was their food and their
mail. Allen Taylor wrote:

"I have had some practice with a rifle and make a fair score,
but, now that I am getting familiar with it, expect to turn in
some perfects soon. . . .

"I am quite an expert with my mess kit. I have accomplished
the wonderful feat of holding it in my left hand, balancing the
cover on my wrist, with the small finger thru the ring provided
for that purpose, then I hold the canteen cup in the right hand
and attach the necessary tools to the top of my legging and
march past the dispenser of diet, getting my kit full to the brim
of various articles, such as 'slum gravy,' beans, stewed prunes,
onions and coffee. Next I proceed to the barracks or wherever I
choose to eat, juggling the complete outfit in such a manner
that not a single bean is lost.

"I can wash, cook, sweep, scrub, darn, knit, mend, tat and
sew.

"Mail me a copy of Granville's trigonometry to use in connection with the school of instruction, also my book on algebra.
It will give me something to do in my spare time."

E. H. Tostevin of the 164th Infantry wrote:

"Mail had not been received for a couple of weeks. Yesterday
a small percentage of the boys received letters, and today the
flood came. Everyone received three or four letters and packages
containing everything from eats to silk pajamas. . . .

" 'Hey, Don!' I heard one fellow yell. 'Remember Jack
Somebody, of Lisbon. Got a ten-pound boy!'

" 'Gosh! They've got Dokes on the run. Trying him for trea-
son or something in Minnesota,' was the remark of another who
had found a bit of news.

" 'Well, for the love of Pete! Hey, guys, take a look at this!'
exclaimed another. 'Wonder whether she thinks this is a pink

tea,' and he held up a suit of mercerized silk pajamas. Instantly there was an uproar and the soldier wished he had hid them under his blankets or something."

Some officers found their instruction not so different from the university work they had so recently known. Ben Tandy wrote from a British mortar school in France, "I don't mind the life at all, for I am accustomed to attending classes. . . . The 'bloomin' Britishers are quite a jolly crowd in spite of the fact that we always thought it took them a week to catch on to our jokes." Artillery officers attending Saumur, the famous French cavalry school, which had been transformed into a center for artillery training, were impressed with its traditions and instruction. Hilton U. Brown, Jr., gaily wrote home, "We had equitation again this morning which is horseback riding without stirrups. I only fell off twice and the instructor said I was showing great improvement." And he described an examination: "Meester Brown, come to the board and show us by plotting the trajectory of a projectile what influence the weight of a litre of air has on the ballistic coefficient."

At the conclusion of their schooling, many of the officers were rushed off ahead of the enlisted men for a firsthand view of trench warfare. Often it seems, although thrilling and pleasant for the novices, not to have been a particularly realistic introduction to future battle conditions. Lieutenant Paul Remmel wrote home:

"At the close of school, each American left with a British officer (his friend) for a different division which held a different sector in the ever-changing boundary-line of war—the trench. It was my good fortune to visit in company with a fine young English officer, captain Bond, a sector upon which ensued enough excitement for any live American. . . .

"At last after walking around and around, we finally reached the battalion headquarters (it was then 4 P.M. and gradually growing dark), which was quartered, as everything is, in a dugout 45 to 50 feet under the ground. After climbing down the steep steps I came to the dugout, and it was certainly a surprise. The first thing that greeted my eye was a long table, upon which was a cover of spotless linen, with silver placed all around and grouped around were five English officers drinking tea. Oh, these English, you can not beat them. They go to war with a teacup in one hand and a revolver in the other.

"This dugout was an old German one, which consisted of four rooms, a large dining-room, a signal-room, a kitchen, and bedroom. Imagine that if you can all fixed up with huge mirrors, lounging chairs, stoves, lighted candles in brass holders. These men were sitting around calmly drinking tea and whisky while 45 feet overhead the shells were screaming by. I was introduced as the American who was attached for a few days of instruction, and I was made quite welcome; such a welcome I had never had before anywhere. . . .

"As I drank my tea I was plied with questions, for I was the first American officer they had seen. I seemed to be refreshing to them because they were constantly laughing at my answers. Just before dinner I was led by the colonel, the two majors, and the captain up the steps to see the heavy guns belch into the night, sending huge missiles of death into the German lines; also the heavy guns of the Huns would grunt in retaliation."

Many of the officers reaching the trenches received less enthusiastic receptions. Some of them were already disillusioned by the reluctance of the Allied instructors in training camps to prepare Americans for a war of movement. One of these skeptical lieutenants, Chester V. Easum, has reminisced:

"Worse disillusionment in many cases awaited 'casual' officers sent up to the front as observers with French or British troops to 'see how it was done.' It was simply not being done in January and February of 1918. As had become standard operating procedure in both French and British armies, the most effective assault units (then known as shock troops or storm troops) were somewhere in the rear echelons being trained in new assault techniques with new weapons such as tanks. Elite outfits like the Chasseurs d'Alpins boasted that they did not hold trenches; they only took them.

"Those assigned to holding the lines were the inferior troops who were left available for that inglorious and bone-wearying duty after the effective had been repeatedly screened out. Far from being determined to sell their lives or their sectors as dearly as possible, they were primarily interested only in survival, in holding their areas as cheaply as possible by being careful not to provoke 'the Boche.' They were 'fed up.' They had 'had their noses full.' It was highly disconcerting to a newly-arrived American officer to be told by his British host that, if the Germans wanted his part of France, they might as well come and take it. He had had more than enough of it. Or to be reproached by a French officer for having prolonged a lost war by gratuitously intervening in it.

"Probably few if any members of the American Expeditionary Force could have known how desperately eager the Allies still were to win the war without much more American assistance, so as not to have to tolerate American meddling as to terms of peace. It appeared, however, on the eve of the last great German peace offensive (Friedensturm) that they were about to concede defeat before the Americans could get there in sufficient numbers to avert it.

"It should have surprised no one that the German spring offensive struck precisely at the junction of the French and British sectors held by some of their most war-weary and disheartened troops—or that it tore that flabby front wide open."

9

IN THE QUIET SECTORS

I was talking to one of the fellows who was in the trenches this morning," wrote H. W. Ross. "In the quiet sector they were in, they say, the principal aim of both sides seemed to be to keep the peace. A French sentry told one of them: 'If you see a German, don't shoot; you'll only start trouble.' 'Hell,' said the American, 'that's what we're here for.' "

After the arrival of the Americans, the "quiet sectors" did not always remain quiet. Nevertheless service in them was part of the seasoning General Pershing tried to give divisions before thrusting them into major operations. Thus the 1st Division received front-line training with a French army in Lorraine in October 1917, and in January 1918 took over its own sector near Toul. Similarly other divisions were brigaded with the British near the Somme River, with the French at Chemin des Dames, then took over their own sectors, most often in the Vosges. These lines, in beautiful wooded mountains, had been relatively peaceful since the Germans had failed in their drive on Nancy in 1914. The French had constructed strong positions and the terrain was too rugged to make major offensives seem worthwhile. For the Americans they were ideal areas, and just south of the region where Pershing hoped ultimately to launch an American offensive. Consequently, until the outbreak of the German offensives in March 1918 forced changes in plans, almost all troops received some weeks in the front lines in the Vosges. Even thereafter, division after division moved in and out. The sharp fighting that broke out sporadically did not alter the course of the war, but it gave the forces experience under fire, and provided the first casualty lists back home.

Of all the moves the soldiers had made since they had entered the army, the orders to the front were the most exciting. Private Robert T. Herz wrote a friend:

"From now on I expect to have something worth while to write about. We leave within twenty-four hours for the front. Doesn't that sound real thrillin'? Better break it gentle like to the folks. Probably you had not better show them this letter. I'll tell them after we get back to rest billets—wherever that is and whenever we do. . . .

"Everybody is giving things away or throwing them away. We are cutting down our packs, and this afternoon is the final inspection before we leave. I had to throw away four suits of B.V.D.'s, several pairs of socks, a razor, brush, soap, towels, an books, and they will probably tell us this afternoon to get rid of more."

For artillerymen especially, moving to the front was an onerous task, since most of them had been trained in Brittany or the Loire Valley. Somehow field pieces and horses had to be moved into the tiny boxcars. Lieutenant Jack Taylor remarked, "It was some job loading up one of the dinky French trains where one boxcar holds eight horses or forty men, and in both cases they want to be small horses and small men. . . . Besides this we could carry all we could load on our persons and we all resembled Christmas trees when we got loaded up."

Taylor's trip was much shorter than he had expected, for the train took him not to the Vosges but to the British-held area in the Sommes on the northern plains:

"About 2 o'clock we were surprised to receive orders to get ready to detrain at a moment's notice. Of course we were all excited and thrilled, but couldn't let on before the men. . . . At 6 o'clock we were all unloaded, hitched up and ready to pull out. We were upon the ground where old Hindenburg pulled off his famous retreat a year ago this month. And the country looked it. All kinds of barbed wire entanglements, trenches, earthworks, etc.

"We pulled out for camp and it was darker than pitch. I was in charge of the fourth section and to make matters worse something went wrong with the harness of one of the horses and we were delayed twenty minutes. Of course the rest of the battery went right ahead, and there I was in a strange country, dark as pitch, and with no guide. And, believe me, boys, it was a terrible sensation out there in charge of a section and with so many roads branching off on each side that it made me dizzy and I thought of the probability of getting the wrong one and pulling right into 'No Man's Land.' It wasn't so terribly far, as the booming of the guns and the flares of the star shells could be distinctly heard and seen. We speeded up and after what seemed like ages caught up with the main body. We continued on thru shell-torn roads and razed villages until about 10 o'clock we pulled into camp. We were allowed no lights, and you can imagine what a time we had moving into a strange camp in the dead of night, unloading, unhitching and getting everything under cover or camouflaged."

Most of the officers and men who trained beside the British in Flanders were warm in their enthusiasm for them. They were conscious of the staggering losses the British had sustained, and admired their courage, friendliness, and sportsmanship. One morning Lieutenant J. F. Howe stood outside a dugout with British battalion officers, watching a German aviator shoot down a British observation balloon:

"The Boche 'plane, now under a thunder-storm of shell and machine-gun fire, sailed over our lines to his own. Here, a Boche, by pure 'nerve' and good luck, had registered a clean victory. I expected to hear a stream of vituperation from the British officers. Instead there came exclamations of admiration for the 'cheeky' Boche avaitor."

Lieutenant Howe quickly adjusted to the British way of life in the trenches:

"This being a 'lieutenant' is a jolly bit of a job. I've got forty or fifty big husky khaki-clad chaps in my platoon. I'm 'boss' of the job on occasions, and instructor and counselor and friend to 'em all. I answer their questions, explain the maps and trench systems, censor their letters, flatter their girls' pictures, make them keep their heads down below the parapet, keep them away from exposed places, see that they sleep when they should, jolly them when they are cold and 'blue,' make them change their socks, and see that we all get our full share of soup.

"At night we must all be on the alert. Our patrols go out, and so do the German patrols. Night is the danger time from silent raids and from artillery prepared raids. During the day inspections are made and then we sleep (if there is time). Lack of sleep, plus wind and rain, cold and snow, water and mud (always ankle-deep), shell-fire, and casualties make life interesting. No one minds these things except casualties and then the only outward sign is very quiet cursing.

"But there is another side to trench life. We have a good time, and in 'spots' we really have a jolly good time. Better still, I had—we all had—the thrill of doing something worth while, of doing a little in the only thing in the world that counts at present. . . .

"The men were fine. They were unafraid and they stood hardships without complaining. . . . I've seen men laugh with their eyes and nostrils filling with blood. I've seen these men later in the hospitals. I saw them today. One man from my company has an eye and an arm missing. One man—a young man— a hot blooded American, was found with his throat cut after the raid. There was no need of a hospital in this case."

American platoons serving with French units held the French equally in esteem—and the French reciprocated. One French captain forty-five years remembered how young and raw, and strong and gay they were. One of their songs still stuck in his head:

> *If the ocean were whiskey*
> *And I were a duck,*
> *I'd dive to the bottom*
> *And never come up.*

He too remembered patrols, and slit throats, and the horror of it as the playing at war suddenly acquired a different dimension for these young men, so quickly less raw and less gay.

Private Charles A. Snickers of the 104th Infantry, whose division was brigaded with the French in the Chemin des Dames section, wrote his sister:

"I am writing this letter in a big cave about seventy-five feet underground. It has electric lights and good bunks to sleep on. . . . The Germans have occupied this part of France for a long time, and when they were driven out they destroyed everything, even cutting down the vines and fruit trees, so that there is not much of anything left. . . .

"We have been in the front-line trenches and fired our first shots at the Boche. The first night we were there they put over a heavy barrage on us, but our artillery came back and gave them all they were looking for. . . . I was stationed at a listening-post every night, and the first night I imagined that everything out in No Man's Land was a German. Mostly all of the fighting takes place at night, but everybody is on the job and manages to get sleep in the daytime. While not in the front line we are in 'reserve' and 'support' and have to dig trenches and put up barbed-wire entanglements.

"We have a little church in our cave. On Sundays the chaplain holds services there and passes out cigarets to us."

One officer, after several weeks at the front, asserted:

"My own experience in the trenches was that my chief job was to restrain the men from senseless firing. I would hear the sound of an automatic or of rifle-grenades on the right of my sector, say about 9 P.M. Hurrying to that point in the line, I would inquire,

" 'What did you see?'

" 'Nothing, sir.'

" 'Well, what did you fire at?'

" 'I thought I heard a noise in the wire, sir.'

" 'Do you think you can hit a noise in the dark?'

" 'No, sir.'

"Then we send up a flare which illuminated our front and makes it quite clear that no one is in the wire, so the men calm down and things remain quiet. From what I learned of other platoons, I got the idea that things 'happened' in proportion to the nervousness of the commander.

"One man made himself the laughing stock of the battalion by the stories he told of what happened to him. It is quite true that when you have been peering out into the dark for a while the posts in entanglements begin to put on German helmets and to creep toward you."

On those occasions when the shapes turned out to be Germans, the fighting was grim. The first American battle casualties came in the Vosges at Bathelemont before dawn on November 3, 1917. Clyde Grimsley, who suffered the unpleasant distinction of being one of the first Americans captured in the war, later told:

"Our trenches were about 800 yards from the German trenches. We had two outposts of five men each out in No Man's land, but were not informed of the Germans' approach until they were close upon us. Just before daylight our trench was shelled with a barrage and when it lifted the barbed wire entanglements were blown up and the Germans came over more than 200 strong. . . . They had carefully planned for this removal of the barrier by laying pipes under it filled with explosives. When these went off the wire was blown into huge rolls, great flares lit up the scene and we began to realize what we were up against.

Alabama troops in the 167th Infantry messing in front lines near Ancerviller, March 11, 1918

A French and American raiding party of the 168th Infantry going "over the top" with sacks of hand grenades, Badonviller, March 17, 1918

Marine sentry on guard during a gas attack, Post Command, Moscou, March 27, 1918

"The sensation of a large number of shells exploding near one is that of tremendous heat. One feels he is about to burn up. The flare was the signal to raise the barrage. The Germans came in a close mass, bunching up to get around the mass of barbed wire. There were literally mobs of them and they made good targets, especially as they carried flashlights on their belts. We fired as fast as we could and laid out a great many of them; couldn't miss them, they were too close together. Five of us were at the left of the line in a bend in the trench when they started throwing hand grenades. Two of our five were knocked out, one being left in the trench for dead and another wounded in the shoulder was taken along when we were captured. A grenade struck the parapet in front of us and my buddie and I were hit and so stunned by the concussion that we were help-less." Grimsley and eleven others were taken prisoner; three Americans were left behind dead, their heads almost severed from their bodies.

Captain George C. Marshall of the 1st Division staff dashed to the scene of the raid to investigate, and the next day attend-ed the funeral of the three Americans. A French general, Paul E. J. Bordeaux, declaimed: "Corporal Gresham, Private Enright, Private Hay, in the name of France, I thank you. God receive your souls. Farewell!"

In a similar raid at 2:30 on the morning of April 5, 1918, Private Leslie M. Lane, who was carrying chow to men stationed in outposts near Seicheprey, fared better and emerged a hero:

"I was feeling my way in the darkness along through the trench and turned a corner when suddenly I was confronted by a group of soldiers. The leader and I both hollered 'Halt!' simul-taneously. I ducked down in order to get a better view of them against the dark sky. I was asked in French if I would consent to become a prisoner, and thought it was one of our French friends fooling. . . . The questioner then asked me in quite flu-ent English. . . .

"I then stepped forward to see who my questioner might be, and before my eyes stood a Sergeant-Major of the German Army with a party of about fifteen men. Seeing that I was vastly outnumbered, my first thought was to get to the boys at the advance posts out in No Man's Land, and warn them of the danger lurking behind them; but the officer seemed determined that I was not to get away, for he tried to grab me by the solider. Then I knew it was time to act. I quickly drew my pistol, aimed at him and pulled the trigger, but it was locked and failed to work. I then kicked the fellow in a vulnerable spot so furiously that it brought him to his knees and rendered him *hors de combat*.

"The man behind him made a lunge for me. I pulled the trigger again and my pistol went off, hitting the Sergeant-Major between the eyes and dropping him squirmingly to the ground. I had never had a pistol in my hands before and it was only by luck that I unlocked it. The other Hun leaped over the body of the officer and struck me on the head with a raiding club, which had a wooden handle about two feet long, with a ball-end made of some sort of metal, and rendered me unconscious for a few seconds, during which time the remainder of the party scattered in a disorderly manner, thinking, no doubt, that the pistol shot would attract my comrades.

"The Sergeant-Major was lying across my feet. I could feel his body quivering and thought he was trying to get up. I reached to get hold of him so that I could get up first, and in doing so found that he had pulled the pin from a 'potato masher' grenade, which exploded as I grabbed his hand, shattering three fingers on my left hand.

"I lay there bleeding and thought I was surely going to die. . . . I felt sorry that I could not get home to see my mother and sisters before I 'cashed in' and also that I did not have my $10,000 insurance all paid up.

"At the time I met the German raiders, there was a fellow named Cook with me, and I promptly ordered him back to the lines. . . . He told all the guards along the line that I was either killed or captured. As I was groping my way . . . back to the first aid, . . . one of our guards stopped me as I turned a corner. Knowing there were Germans around, and thinking I was killed, he was taking no chances and made a lunge for me with his bayonet. I saw the gleam of the bayonet aimed at my throat, and raised my injured hand to ward off the blow. As I did so, the bayonet further mangled my thumb and forefinger. ... My assailant came up, getting ready to finish me, and I saw he had an American helmet, and said, 'Wait a minute, I'm Lane.' He helped me to my feet and started apologizing to me, but I had no time to listen, as I was bleeding to death and wanted to get to the first aid before it was too late."

Private Lane, who lost his thumb and fingers, was awarded the Distinguished Service Cross and the French Croix de Guerre. "By his quickness of action," the citation read, "he undoubtedly saved the lives of the men in our advanced listening post."

In time, some American regiments it became so dominant in their stretches of No Man's Land that they boasted they could hang their wash to dry on the barbed wire. Major William J. Donovan of the 165th Infantry (earlier, the 69th) wrote his wife in March: "Yesterday in broad daylight some Alabama troops on our right walked over to the German trenches unmolested and unchallenged. They found a German officer and three men in a dugout. The Alabama party was only five. They killed all four Germans and upon their return found one of their own party missing. They went back and found him caught in the German wire. While rescuing him they heard footsteps on the German duckboard. Lying in wait they caught two other Boche, killed them and stripped all of their victims bringing their clothes back. Their only worry was the dirty socks of the last Hun they caught. The Alabama crowd are the greatest crowd I have ever seen. They wander all over the landscape shooting at everything."

Major Donovan himself displayed such conspicuous courage that he was awarded the Croix de Guerre. Less than a week later, General Charles T. Menoher brought Secretary of War Baker to the sector on an inspection. Calling the Secretary's attention to the medal, Menoher declared, "This officer is wearing this without warrant of law or regulations, Mr. Secretary." Baker replied to Donovan, "I give you executive authority to wear that cross. If any one questions your right to wear it, refer him to me."

For artillerymen the weeks in these sectors meant exchanging barrages from time to time with the enemy. Sergeant Elmer F. Straub arrived at the front near Baccarat at the end of February, and wrote in his diary:

"All of our pieces, caissons, and battery wagons were pulled up into a large pine woods. . . . We walked about one-half mile to some cantonments or rather old barns. Lofts had been built in one half of the barn and sleeping places had been partitioned off. These separate places for each man were filled with hay, and after we had unrolled our blanket rolls and made our beds the place took on a rather comfortable aspect. Everything is very well camouflaged, buildings are painted so as to resemble banks of green grass and blend in with the rest of the surroundings. We can hear batteries of French 75s going along the main road toward the front and they say that we are within rifle shot of the front. I am rather disappointed because we can hear only an occasional shot and things do not seem at all lively. . . .

"March 9, 1918:—At 10:30 I went out to the guns and laid them out according to the dope the Captain had figured. I ate noon mess at the guns and at 1:05 we started to fire. We had two hundred rounds to fire by 6:05 in the evening and it was sure done in fine fashion. Our targets were communication trenches, dug-outs and machine gun emplacements. Sgt. Gillespie's section got two direct hits and Bruning said that things were sure torn up. After they had finished firing I came in to the battery echelon, had my mess and went to bed. . . .

"March 17, 1918:—After evening mess and retreat Bill Shine and I started out to see something. On the way we met John Bosson and [Leslie H.] Coleman so the four of us walked as far toward the front of us down in the valley. . . . Then as we were standing in a perfectly open field we heard a whistle and a s-s-s-s-s-s-s and then a bang. I knew just what it was but Bill Shine didn't, and I can only remember seeing Bill's white face with a very scared look on it as I was falling toward the ground to get out of the way of flying fragments. It was Bill's first time to dodge a burst and he didn't know what to do. . . . Believe me from then on Bill knew just what to do. We all crawled into a

wicker work trench nearby and there waited until eight shells
had burst within 100 feet of us."

In August 1918, Battery D of the 129th Field Artillery went
into action in the Gernardmer section under Captain Harry S.
Truman. Years later Truman recalled:

"Our regular battery positions were in the Herrenberg
forests in the Vosges Mountains. Somebody took a notion to
fire three thousand rounds of gas at the Germans. So we had to
move to another position and put the batteries into place to fire
five hundred rounds at seven o'clock. The horses were sent
back. As soon as the last round was fired they were to come
with horses. They were twenty or twenty-five minutes late. I
got on a horse to see what was going on. He fell in a shellhole
and rolled over on me. The German batteries began to fire on
us. The sergeant gave the men by the wrong flank and two of
our guns got stuck in the mud. While we were working to
release them the Germans fired very close to us and this
sergeant hollered, 'Run, boys, they got a bracket on us.' . . .

"I got up and called them everything I knew. . . . Pretty soon
they came sneaking back. . . . The Major and the Colonel wanted me to court-material the sergeant. I didn't but I busted him
and afterwards I had to transfer him to another battery. Later
the war, he stood firm under the fiercest fire."

Most men soon became used to shellfire. Clyde A.
Crawford of the Signal Corps found it irritating rather than
frightening while he was in the Vosges:

"While in this sector the training of all troops in the division
continued with actual work to do, and Fritz across the valley
watching you do it and laughing to think that his artillery would
tear hell out of it for you that evening. We were on this front 42
days and in that time very few shells came over from Fritz during the day, but about 4:30 to7:30 in the evening he would give
us something to think about and look for. I got so I looked forward to his little shell parties with great delight. Never had one
hit closer than ten feet to me, but I have used up nearly a box
of matches lighting the candle in the dugout while Fritz put
over his remembrances. I repaired two different lines under shell

fire and moved on switch board and message center because Fritz got too familiar with his artillery and blew the roof off our heads. Such things must be expected when at war."

Lieutenant John C. Redington of Battery B, 149th Field Artillery, had reason to be less serene:

"This has been a week full of new experiences and we have had a real initiation into the realities of war. The French had occupied this position before us and we have relieved them. They told us it was a tranquil sector, very quiet. For three days we believed them; then something broke loose. Perhaps the Germans knew we had arrived and wanted to see how long we could last.

"Day before yesterday, commencing at 3 A.M., we were called to deliver five barrage-fires. A barrage, as you already know, is a curtain fire thrown over by the 75s just ahead of our own infantry to protect them against German attack or to protect their advance. In these cases it was against German attack on our front lines. . . . My job is to be at the guns, and I had to turn out six times night before last—three alarms, two barrages, and one gas alarm. . . .

"Last night they shelled my former battery, and one of the first lieutenants, Jordan, the man who took my place, was instantly killed, saddening us all. . . . This morning at nine o'clock, or 8:23, to be exact, I was standing at the entrance of the dugout and two 105s, about a four-inch shell, dropt 100 meters back of the battery. They threw twenty-two shells on the gun position, getting two direct hits, one on top of our ammunition dugout. . . . [It took two hours to clean up the debris, then followed an even more intensive barrage of 253 shells, only three of which were direct hits.] One struck on top of the dugout, in which there were six men caved it in completely; and, again, strangely enough, not a man was scratched. All our telephone lines were broken and for about one hour we were out of communication. The men showed splendid spirit and are eager to retaliate. . . .

"They tell us this is the primary school-training for what will follow in a month or so. I never was enthusiastic about higher education."

10

PREPARING FOR WAR IN THE AIR

From the muddy battlefields below, the war in the air was the greatest spectator sport of the American Expeditionary Forces. There were few soldiers, no matter how dull their life in quiet trenches or near the lines, who did not share the excitement of watching aviators duel far above them. Bryan B. Turner, an artilleryman, wrote in July 1918:

"It's the biggest show I ever witnessed; I'll wager it even beats the ones Nero used to put on in the amphitheater at Rome. I have seen several air fights now, and three planes come down in flames, and it's safe to say I'll never forget the first. Five Boche planes fell upon one lone Ally, and despite the odds, he fought—dipping, circling, maneuvering—but one Boche gained position on him and next he was afire, but still he didn't run; rather circled about as though trying for position until— suddenly he tripped and fell; one wing broke away and the plane thus bereft started a spinning nose dive, blazing like a rocket, straight to the ground, while the other wing—still burning—drifted lazily after. I don't know who he was but I'll say he died fighting and against big odds."

The aviators themselves were the knights, the cavalrymen, of the war, bringing to it what little chivalry could be rescued from the bygone day when making war was the favorite occupation of the high born, operating in keeping with a gentleman's code. They provided the war with most of its romantic heroes, to the disgust of some of the earthbound generals. Aviation was only fourteen years old when the United States entered the war, but techniques were improving so rapidly and the total numbers of planes were increasing so geometrically that it was on the way toward becoming a major engine of destruction in total and impersonal war.

Romance aside, the Air Service was a disappointment to the American people during the First World War because it did not, as they hoped, decisively break the stalemate on the Western Front. In the initial weeks after the Declaration of War, the public hoped for too much, was promised far, far too much, and the following year was angered by the fiasco in aircraft production. Although airplanes had been an American invention, manufacturers had lagged far behind those of the warring European nations in development and production.

Congress and the War Department had done little to nurture the infant Air Service, which was at the outset of the war a small part of the Signal Corps. Colonel "Hap" Arnold, one of the pioneer Army fliers, and to his disgust the chief air officer in Washington during the war, wrote later that as of May 1917: "The total strength of the American air arm at that moment was 52 officers and 1100 men, plus about 200 civilian mechanics. Out of a total of 130 so-called pilots, only 26 were really qualified. Altogether, we had 55 airplanes, 51 of them obsolete, 4 obsolescent, and not one of them a combat type."

Yet the Premier of France, at the instigation of the great American air enthusiast Colonel William Mitchell, cabled in May 1917 requesting that the United Sates send to the Western Front to participate in the battles of 1918 no less than 4500 airplanes with accompanying pilots and mechanics. Further, America should manufacture 200 airplanes and 4000 engines per month. Newspapers enthusiastically advocated a huge program; Congress appropriated $639,000,000.

Measured against these grandiose objectives, the American air program of the next eighteen months was a failure; measured against what had come before, it was phenomenal. In 1919 Secretary Baker wrote:

"We were dealing with a miracle. The airplane itself was too wonderful and new, too positive a denial of previous experience, to brook the application of any prudential restraints which wise people would have known how to apply to ordinary industrial and military developments."

Up to the end of the war, the A.E.F. obtained almost no satisfactory planes from the United States, and was almost completely dependent up on the British and especially the French. When General Halsey Dunwoody, head of supply for the Air Service, was asked afterward what France had done, he replied, "This is a picture that is easy to paint. She did it all!" After his return to the United States when he was asked by what authority he had purchased airplanes in Europe, he replied:

"Congress appropriated a sum of one billion dollars for aviation. I spent sixty-five million approximately, and obtained 9,000 aeroplanes, including school planes, and thoroughly equipped the American Aviation. The rest of the billion was spent in the United States and from this expenditure we never had a single plane that was fit to use at a time whn the aviation sorely needed aeroplanes."

Disappointed as they were with the failure to produce phenomenal numbers of aircraft, Americans both at home and in France thrilled to the exploits of the aviators—especially the aces, those who had shot down five or more enemy aircraft or balloons. Secretary Baker wrote with hyperbole: "The age of Elizabeth is famous for her 'sea dogs.' This age, for America, will be famous for our soaring soldiers."

Only from those on the ground at General Pershing's headquarters came a somewhat less enthusiastic view. Major Frederick Palmer wrote some years later:

Advanced outpost of Kansas troops in the 137th Infantry, Amphersbach, Germany, August 29, 1918

Officers of the 129th Field Artillery at Chateau le Chanay, March 1919.
Captain Harry S. Truman is in the second row, fourth from left.

Colonel William Mitchell about to take off with French officer in a Spad

"Every whim of the ace flier was law to the ground force of the flying field, which had Milord's steed ready for him to mount before he rode forth to the tournament of the skies; and his bath and pleasant quarters awaiting him on his return. Yet by the third year of the War the flier had lost some of his glamour at the front. It had been found that the ability to fly was not uncommon; that there was no end of volunteers for aviation, though there seemed never to be enough common soldiers. Mortality among the fliers was not much higher than among the men who went over the top again and again. Aces had their names emblazoned in the communiques, while the surviving officer of a veteran battalion which took its objective was not mentioned. Ascending, well-groomed and well-fed, to death in a plane seemed quite as pleasant as going over the top from filthy trenches, to be mashed up in No Man's Land among putrid corpses."

General Pershing, perhaps sharing these views, in November 1917 recommended that increased rank and pay for men engaged in flying be abolished. He placed men who were not fliers in top command of the Air Service, and their relations with the aviators were not always cordial. The officer in immediate command of combat operations was himself a flier, Colonel Mitchell (later promoted to Brigadier General), who several years earlier had taught himself to fly weekends at his own expense. He was one of the earliest and most zealous evangelists of the new doctrines of air power.

A number of Americans already were serving as combat pilots in the British and especially the French forces. The French Lafayette Escadrille in which, by the end of 1917, 325 Americans had fought was especially famous. Many of these aviators transferred into the United States Air Corps.

From its tiny beginnings the Air Service began spectacular expansion. In the first year after the Declaration of War, 38,770 men applied for flight training. To obtain acceptance they had to undergo physical examinations and interviews and meet strict standards. The Army specified:

"The candidate should be naturally athletic and have a reputation for reliability, punctuality and honesty. He should have a cool head in emergencies, good eye for distance, keen ear for familiar sounds, steady hand and sound body with plenty of reserve; he should be quickwitted, highly intelligent and tractable. Immature, high strung, overconfident, impatient candidates are not desired."

Nearly half the applicants—18,004 of them—were rejected. Those accepted were enrolled for training in the Signal Enlisted Reserve Corps. They received $100 per month salary and 75 cents per day ration allowance (in contrast to the dollar a day of "buck privates" in the infantry). If they survived the training they received officers' commissions.

Following Canadian and British examples, the War Department established "ground schools" at several universities. These put the "flying cadets" through intensive courses, eliminating less suitable candidates. Next the cadets took their beginning training in the air at a number of flying fields rapidly established in the United States. Some went immediately to British and French schools or to Foggia, Italy, for their flying instruction.

The A.E.F. established several training fields in France to provide advanced and specialized instruction. (The largest field, at Issoudun, offered primary training as well.) Gradually a workable system evolved; about 2000 pilots a month took elementary training in the United States and final training in France. The Issodun establishment became the larest in the world, comprising fourteen airfields, 84 hangars, and innumerable warehouses, shops, and barracks.

Sergeant Prescott, visiting one of the fields, probably Issoudun, wrote home:

"We were walking on a typical American board walk. The buzz of a sawmill, the steady throb of a power-house engine, the knocking of busy carpenters, the whir of airplanes flying in battle groups and singly, the German prisoners road-building, as were part of the great aviation camp on which the finishing touches are now being rushed forward.

"We turned to the right, and passed more barracks. Ahead of us loomed the steel frame of an American water tower, and beside the raod stood an American steam-roller. Beyond were hangars and more hangars. At every turn were signs of American energy."

Both the Army and Navy established a number of assembly plants and repair centers. The largest was the Air Service center at Romorantin. Glenn Trewett wrote home:

"I have been working in a factory or assembly plant for airplanes. All the Liberty plants or 'De Haviland 4's,' as they are called, were sent here in much the same condition as we used to get Fords and our job was to put them in condition to go to the front. . . . I might also say that for the first month and a half we were engaged in putting up buildings and clearing ground for a flying field. So you see I have gained some experience as a structural iron worker and woodsman. But while we have had to work pretty hard sometimes, I can honestly say that I have liked it and am glad that I have had the opportunity to take a very small part perhaps in the fight for civilization and liberty."

An auto repairman from Walden, Colorado, Sergeant L. W. Felter, found much to do at the First Air Depot, the advanced headquarters of the Air Service, at Colombey-les-Belles. He wrote a friend:

"We arrived here on July 16th, [1918] and were put to work repairing airoplanes, driving trucks, etc. I went into the erection and repair department as a rigger, but was put to work installing engines in the ships. Didn't stay at it long, however, as I started doing the soldering, brazing, welding (oxyacet) etc.; anything, in fact, that come along. When we outgrew our hangar and moved into a double one we built a shack outside for my special use. Had a forge and anvil, oxy-acet outfit, two benches and lots of small tools (hammers, chistles, files, wrenches, screwdrivers, hand drill, etc.). That was the start. I also had one helper.

"About this time the Toul sector opened up with a drive that shook the Huns some. From then the American army kept in action and so did we. When the armistice was finally signed I had four men helping to do what I did alone at first. The camp in the mean time had grown from about seven hundred to near thirty-five hundred, so you can imagine the size outfit we make."

When Assistant Secretary of the Navy Franklin D. Roosevelt inspected the Navy's main base and assembly center at Pauillac, he congratulated the three thousand enlisted men on their construction of the base, but was indignant over the defects in the seaplanes shipped there for assembly. "During the past three months," he cabled Secretary of the Navy Daniels, "seaplanes have been shipped to France in such numbers as to congest the ports greatly, yet not a single one of these planes today is equipped to fly in service, and only eight can fly at all."

Most of the cadets, whether they were training at Kelly Field, Texas, at Issoudun, France, or elsewhere, were excited over their work. Kramer Table, who had gone to France to drive an ambulance or truck, managed to get into the Air Corps, and in high spirits on May 22, 1918 wrote his mother:

"Up until a week or so ago I've been in an aviation concentration camp waiting for the crowded conditions of the American flying schools over here to be relieved. Everything now seems to be going along fine. The American schools are turning out any number of flyers and the French took a few cadets in their schools to train them, and I am very glad to say that I was one of the boys to go to a French school. Here one could not ask for better conditions. All we do is eat, sleep and fly. The French feed us, quarter us and give us our training, in fact we are almost the same as French soldiers except that the U.S. Army keeps an eye on us and sees that we do as the French want us to do, and gets us a few things that French cannot. . . .

"Here is our daily schedule: 3:45–5:00 A.M., coffee and go to the field; 5:00–9:00 A.M., flying; 9:00 A.M.–4:30 P.M., sleep, except dinner at 11:00; 4:30 P.M., back to the field and fly until nearly 9:00 P.M.; 9:15 P.M. supper.

"We cannot fly in the middle of the day because the heat causes treacherous winds and we take as few chances as possible while learning.

"After watching so many aviators fly when I was in the Camion service and hearing them tell how easy it was, I supposed it would be a snap to fly one of these birds, but I've surely been kidding myself along. Your first time up with your hands on the controls shows you just what a cinch you haven't got. However, it comes to you gradually, but there is an awful lot more to learn than one would think. We all expect to finish here in about two months and will then receive our brevets. From here we go to an advanced school to take our acrobatics, such as the loop, wing slips, nose dive, fast spirals, leaf drop, etc. When we finish there we are ready for the front, except for a little machine gun work. We may be all finished in three months, but I think it will be more like four."

Solo flying, especially above the clouds, was exhilarating for the cadets. Briggs Kilburn Adams, in training for the Royal Flying Corps, wrote his mother from Camp Borden, Ontario, October 16, 1917:

"This afternoon the sky was full of those great broken masses of thick puffy white clouds with sky appearing so clear and deep blue between them. I climbed up between some until I was on top a thousand feet, then I flew along for an hour or more with the wheels just touching their upper surface. I could almost imagine they were turning. It seemed like riding in a mythical chariot of the gods, racing along this vast, infinitely white field stretching off endlessly in every direction. The clear, open sky above veritably is heaven as we imagined it in childhood. . . . The celestial illusion was perfect, and it was hard to come away from it—really quite a tug."

By the time the novice aviator was learning acrobatics, he had achieved a considerable degree of nonchalance and was looked upon with some awe by earthbound soldiers. Sergeant Prescott breakfasted with one such airman at a training field in France:

"All at once someone began to play the piano. . . . around a big Franklin stove a friend kept time to a fox-trot with his soldiers.

"Two hours later I saw him above the acrobatic field, as it is called, doing a tailspin and a wing-slip. And as I looked up at him thousands of feet in the air, his machine in the faint winter sunlight, with the round disks of color at either end of the lower wings, appeared like some gigantic dragon-fly darting hither and thither to catch a foe. When he came down to earth again he lit a cigaret and began to dance to the same tune he had hummed at the canteen."

There was sufficient reason for men on the ground to respect these aviators even while they were training. The hazards of flight were innumerable, and many were killed in acrobatics, and even in routine activities. Forced landings were commonplace. Lieutenant Hamilton Coolidge wrote his sister on December 1, 1917, that he had been "on one of the most amusing trips I ever made," a cross-country training flight from Issoudun to Tours. He lost his way, landed at Angers, and spent two days there, grounded by the weather, and trying to purchase from pharmacists enough castor oil to lubricate his engine. Finally, in bad weather, he headed back toward Tours:

"Five minutes after my start my motor began to cough alarmingly, but I was able to turn back and make the field all right before the old thing died. The trouble, broken spark plug wire, was easy to fix, and I would have though nothing more of the incident as I gaily started out again, had it not been for the realization that I had used up ten minutes' wroth of precious castor oil. . . . Forty, forty-five, fifty minutes passed, and still no signs of Tour. . . . A solid wall of fog lay ahead, making a plunge into the unknown beyond a risky matter at best. At just that moment I happened to glance at my oil gauge, and it was empty! . . . There was nothing to do but come down. I desperately looked for an open field, chose the only one that didn't seem to be surrounded with hedges, and came sailing down in a way that the little Nieuport has of coming down,—pretty average fast. . . . I cut my switch and was all set to settle neatly on the ground, when bing! The top of my right wing hit a tiny sapling I hadn't noticed, and I made three whirlwind gyrations amid a sickening crackle of framework. When I came to rest, the remains of my poor machine were in a perpendicular position, with your young brother, unscathed, still strapped to the seat. I never even had time to get scared till after it was all over, and then there wasn't any point."

Colonel Mitchell had an unpleasant experience on October 23, 1917, when he flew over the Allied lines as a guest of the French in a Breguet two-seater. The pilot, reputedly the best in his squadron, came in against a strong side wind and turned over the plane. Mitchell was unhurt but vowed not to let another pilot fly him again.

The most incredible adventure came to Lieutenant Gardiner H. Fiske one day while he was flying as an observer in training maneuvers. The pilot, Lieutenant Samuel P. Mandell, wrote:

"I had the thrill of my life yesterday. We were flying formation in these great big busses and the machine I had had, two camera guns on it, one for the pilot and one for the observer. Old F[iske] was standing up on the seat in back shooting away with his camera gun at a scout machine that was flying around us. At the same time I dove to get a shot at him with my gun. I heard a sort of a crash behind, and after I had straightened out looked around to see what it was. Lo and Behold, a man in a leather coat holding onto the tail of my machine. I could hardly believe my eyes, but F[iske] had fallen out of his cockpit when his gun broke loose from its fastenings and I had nosed over. The first thought that came to me was: Will he have strength enough to hold on till I get down to the ground? I put the machine in the gentlest glide I could and started for home, as I could not land where I was up on the mountain-tops. . . . F[iske] all the time was lying with his body across the fuselage right next to the vertical stabilizer on the tail. As I watched him over my shoulder, he gradually wound his way up the fuselage. He got a-straddle of it and gradually slid up, caught hold of the tourelle, and dove head first into his seat. About ten years' weight came off my shoulders by this time. . . .

"F[iske] to-day is reposing in bed, having been excused from all formations. He will never come any nearer death at the front, and nothing can ever scare me any more than this did."

Several air cadets at Foggia were less fortunate. Major William O. Ryan had to write their parents that on January 20,

1918, they had been killed in "one of those almost impossible and wholly unavoidable accidents." To the mother of William H. Cheney he explained:

"He was piloting a machine with Lieutenant Oliver B. Sherwood as observer, and flying over the training field. At the same time another machine, piloted by Aviation Cadet George A. Beach, was also in the air. A very low cloud of fog blew over the training field and closed around your son's machine. He immediately turned to get out of the fog, and as the machine emerged it struck the machine of Cadet Beach, who was also endeavoring to avoid the fog. Both machines fell to the ground, a distance of about one hundred and fifty feet. The funeral was held from the Italian Military Hospital in Foggia at two o'clock on the afternoon of the twenty-first and was attended by troops and officers of the American, Italian, French, and English Armies. All three men were buried with full military honors."

They were the first American soldiers to die in Italy. All the stores in Foggia closed in mourning; the populace crowded the streets, and many Italian women wept.

11

THE GERMANS LAUNCH THEIR GREAT OFFENSIVES

At the end of March 1918 hell broke loose. All winter, the Allies had been aware of their weakness and had looked forward with apprehension to the German spring offensives. German infantrymen outnumbered the Allies on the Western Front by 1,569,000 to 1,245,000. It was the last strategic moment when, by an all-out series of drives, the Germans might win the war. The desperate Allies somehow must hold on until, presumably in 1919, the Americans could redress the balance.

So it was that the Germans, who had been on the defensive in the west since 1916, massed their divisions in Picardy where the British and French lines joined, and on March 21 launched the first of their violent final attacks to try to win the war. After a heavy artillery barrage through fog, sixty-four German divisions trained in new techniques of attack smashed against the weak hinge, pushing back to the Allies, inferior in numbers and habituated to the protection of trenches. In five days they drove 37 miles toward the rail center of Amiens, threatening to separate completely the British from the French. Some Parisians began to flee southward, and for the first time since the Battle of the Marne, the French government considered the possibility of moving to Bordeaux.

The peril was so great that it frightened the Allies into establishing a supreme command. The Italian route at Caporetto the previous fall had forced creation of a Supreme War Council; the spring disasters led to the appointment of General Ferdinand Foch as Commander-in-Chief of the Allied armies.

Before the Germans were checked on the Somme, Pershing had offered to a worried but determined Petain the disposition of the six American divisions thus far available in France, but Petain suggested only that the most seasoned, the 1st Division, be moved to Picardy. On March 28, General Pershing met at the front with General Petain, Premier Clemenceau, and General Foch. To Foch he declared in French:

"I come to tell you that the American people would consider it a great honor that our troops should be engaged in the present battle. I ask this of you in my name and theirs. There is no question at this moment except fighting. Infantry, artillery, aviation, all that we have is yours. Do with it was you choose. Other forces are coming as numerous shall be necessary.

"I am here for the express purpose of telling you that the Americans will be proud to be engaged in the greatest battle of history."

The sledgehammer blows of the Germans did lead to a drastic increase in the rushing of American troops to France. When the German drives began there were still less than 300,000 soldiers in the A.E.F., and 85,000 of them had arrived per month. By July 1, Pershing had his first million men. Meanwhile, Americans, as fast as they could be trained, had to do their part in helping blunt the German blows.

A few American troops stationed with the British were caught up in the fighting in Flanders. Indeed, the first

Americans to see combat service had, curiously enough, been the 11th and 12th Engineers, Railway, attached to the British who were engaged in railroad building at the time of the Cambrai battle in November 1917. Several companies had been hastily armed and held in reserve when the Germans unexpectedly attacked Gouzeaucourt, where they were at work. Similarly, scattered Americans became involved in the great battles beginning in March 1918.

The 14th Engineers, stationed between Arras and Amiens on the British front, were handling supplies when the drive began. Frederic M. Jackson remembered:

"The British told us we'd better not wait for our luggage, but colonel Wooten was a little stubborn and said he wasn't going to leave his coal pile to help the Germans to keep warm. I remember I was one of about twenty men assigned to shovel the coal (about fifty tons as nearly as I recall, used for the railroad) into narrow gauge cars; the last of it went into the last car as dawn was breaking; and I'll never forget the thrill of climbing into the rear end of that last car, swinging my heels contentedly against it, and watching the British infantrymen stream past in forced retreat, and seeing the round helmets of the Germans coming up into the morning sky like thousands of queer wolves and rushing down upon me—and knowing that my train was gathering speed and they couldn't catch me."

Two bridge-building companies in the 6th Engineers fought along with an array of British troops commandeered from a variety of services in what was called after the British general in their command "Carey's Force." Companies D and B had been building large steel bridges across the Somme at Peronne; they had to stand by the bridges for several days while the retreating troops streamed across, then when the last artillery had passed, blew them up. Thereupon the engineers took up arms under General Carey.

The British, managing to stem the first German offensive short of the key railroad center, Amiens, were battered in April by an attack along a twelve-mile front on the Lys River in Flanders. Field Marshal Sir Douglas Haig on April 12 issued a

Special Order of the Day to his troops in which he did not try to disguise the seriousness of the battle:

"Words fail me to express the admiration which I feel for the splendid resistance offered by all ranks of our Army under the most trying circumstances.

"Many amongst us now are tired. To those I would say that victory will belong to the side which holds out the longest.

"The French Army is moving rapidly and in great force to our support.

"There is no other cause open to us but to fight it out. Every position must be held to the last man; there must be no retirement. With our backs on the wall, and believing in the justice of our cause, each one of us must fight on to the end.

"The safety of our homes and the freedom of mankind depend alike upon the conduct of each one of us at this critical moment."

The British succeeded in stemming the Lys drive by the end of April, but at such cost that the German High Command was of the opinion that a third major thrust could destroy the British Army. This they delayed since they were already prepared for a great offensive against the French, which would use up French reserves otherwise available for service on the British front.

During these trying weeks, American units began increasingly to feel the war. The 1st Division, which had successfully stood off a large-scale German raid on Seicheprey in the St. Mihiel area, was shifted at the end of April to a relatively quiet area west of Montdidier in Picardy, at the tip of the salient the Germans had cut into Allied lines during their drives on Amiens in March. It was only relatively quiet; day after day the division suffered heavy casualties as the Germans kept up incessant shelling with shrapnel and gas and intermittent raiding. Division headquarters were in the deep but foul-smelling cellar of the chateau in Mesnil-St. Firmin. General Bullard's chief of operations, Colonel George C. Marshall, tried to sleep upstairs in fresh air, "But they drove me down when they began hitting this building with eight-inch shells which sounded like the end of the world."

Absorbed in their daily struggle against the foe, enlisted men, company commanders, and even the division staff had little notion of the larger movements of the war. General Bullard later wrote:

"The roar of great guns in battle was coming to us steadily from the north these days: the British were having a busy time on the other side of the Somme. But the sound at the time, and the communiqués the next day, were the only things that told us that we were near our British cousins. We saw nothing and thought little of them; we were quite fully occupied with our own affairs. It was a shock to me to find in after months that we had been literally alongside of them in battle and knew it not. The British headquarters were but a few miles from me. So it is in war. A soldier can see and know only that which is immediately before him and that none too well."

One of the officers in charge of ammunition did have a vivid overall view of the sector:

"We left the Lorraine front last month and are now on the French-British front taking part in the great battle. Our division is now a part of the 1st (French) Army. We have our own sector of the front of course but it is short. It is very active. The 75s fired an average of 1,250 rounds per gun yesterday.

"Last night I had an urgent order for 40 truck loads of 155 mm shells and I went on ahead to arrange for dumping it. We delivered it at a point 1½ miles from the trenches. Whether the Boche were trying to get the Corps dump or merely strafing the roads, I know not. Perhaps the shells that fell all around us were merely wild shots, primarily intended to reach our infantry. At any rate that is one reason why the service of ammunition is particularly hazardous; we are always exposed to shell fire, whereas if we were up at the front we would of necessity remain under bomb proof cover. Be that as it may, the brilliant flares, the signal rockets, the whining 75s, the roaring 155s, the clatter of horse batteries on the roads is enough to make any one sit up and take notice.

"A night ride up front affords a variety of experiences. It was after midnight (most of our work has to be done after dark); it was a wonderful sight. There was not a moment but masses of lurid gun flashed appeared all along the front and shells burst close around to rattle the glass in my automobile. The big fellows that passed high overhead made a noise like an express train. I saw but little actual damage last night. Most of the shells burst harmlessly in the fields on either side of us; but I did see a caisson blown up on the road and we had to dodge numerous craters in the road where shells had exploded.

"A couple miles back troops were engaged in organizing a new line of defense, erecting barb wire entanglements, emplacing guns, digging trenches, and so on; and back of that yet they may construct a third system of defenses. That is the method in trench warfare you know and what makes progress to the front so slow. Work goes along rapidly here. I noted a tendency on the part of the French to overload the ammunition wagons which caused some confusion and delay; but as a rule their road discipline is fine. I passed a column of 75s just as another column was coming from the opposite direction on a very narrow road. I did not see the second column in time to avoid it. I could not turn and a serious blockade seemed imminent; but nothing of the sort happened; the batteries did not even slow down; they just rolled off into the ditch and gave me the road, not a minute's delay and I did not have to stop.

"My train has been released to the artillery. Gen. Summerall is very strict. He has relieved about 30 officers and sent them to the rear echelons in training area. I stood by his side the other morning while the artillery was passing and he called an officer from the column for some violation of orders and sent him to the rear with his bedding roll. He sent him on foot, retaining the officer's mount. There was nothing for the poor fellow to do but catch a French truck and get back hundreds of miles to our training area.

"We are traveling light—50 pounds even for field officers. I had to leave most of my baggage back at an old chateau near Paris. May never see it again. Fortunately I brought my sheepskin coast for it has snowed three days this week and there was ice on the ponds two mornings.

"The roads are filled with refugees. I saw a most pitiful sight a day or two ago. Three women had hitched themselves to a wagon filled with their household things, another trundled a baby carriage behind with a six month old baby inside, while a dozen or more little children trudged along, all ill clad and looking very blue and miserable. How those women every managed to drag that wagon up these steep hills is a mystery to me.

"I am fortunate in having a Dodge limousine for my own personal use in handling the ammunition train of this division. I carry my raincoat, rubber boots, gas masks, helmet, pistol, and toilet articles in the car, and can sleep there in an emergency. Usually I have had no difficulty in finding a bed as our work is from villages considerably in the rear of our front. It's a queer life though—one night at some grand chateau the next perhaps in an open field."

The view of Ray A. Edwards, a private in the Supply Company of the 16th Infantry, was not as far-ranging, but his feelings were much the same:

"For a few days, now, I and one of the other clerks have been riding the wagons going for rations early in the morning, as the other men are all too busy, and we must have two men on each wagon. The mule 'skinners' will probably never be cited for great bravery, and may be ridiculed as too cowardly to go to the front, but it will be most unjust if such does happen, for, when others take to the dugouts, he must remain with his 'jar-heads,' exposed to view; and he does it with no great notions of his bravery. Good weather or bad, he must steer those crazy mules up to the very edge of what may be the great divide for him; but still, I believe, you would find less bucking and kicking in the supply outfit than in any other."

During the three months that the 1st Division was in the Montdidier sector, it suffered an average of 60 casualties a day; its worst ordeal came from a heavy gas barrage on the villages of Villers-Tournelle during the night of May 3 that incapacitated more than eight hundred soldiers. Sergeant Howard Cooper of the signal section of the 18th Infantry was stationed in Villers repairing telephone lines:

"On May 3rd, at 8 P.M., the Germans started to pepper us with mustard gas. Thousands and thousands of shells were fired

German infantry firing from a shell hole, Somme, 1918

Advance of the second wave of German shock troops through Bailleal, April 1918

Officer firing at a German airplane, Villers-Tournelle, May 20, 1918

on us and the gas attack lasted until noon the next day. For sixteen hours I worked with my mask on, never removing it from
my face. I kept on repairing line after line, and man after man
kept falling to the ground. We had an awful lot of casualties on
the occasion of this attack, but we stuck. There were only twenty-one of us out of one hundred and twenty-five men left to
repair lines from Regimental Headquarters. . . . [Five of us vol-
unteers] were all tired out and it was getting near daybreak. We
crawled our way through the fields down to the French lines.
We passed many men lying dead on the field of battle. Hungry,
worn and tired, we stuck to our jobs. At 12 o'clock off went our
masks. We could still smell gas, but it was very weak. I shared
my last drop of water with my comrades. Our bodies were burnt
by the gas, but we were only a handful of men left and we had
to stick it out until we could get relief. We were cited here for
our heroic work and ordered to leave for the hospital, which we
refused to do. For eleven days we stuck to the job, every day
getting weaker and weaker. On the 14th day of May, I collapsed
and was taken to the hospital. . . . On the 24th of May, after
being released from the hospital, I rejoined my outfit. . . . My
gas wounds, not being healed up, caused odors around my body
and again I was sent to the hospital. I was rushed to Field
Hospital, No. 13, then to No. 12, and thence to a French
Hospital where I received oil treatments. My body was soaked
with oil all the time. I was burned black. My speech was gone
and I could talk only in whispers."

"My new dugout is completed," Captain Arthur Sewall Hyde
wrote his sister on May 14, "for we had to evacuate the town after
the big has attack, and I lived for five days in a little funk-hole
under a sheltering bank on the hard ground. It was difficult to do
any paper-work under such conditions and the red tape goes on
merrily at the front in our army just as it does in garrison. I have
to make seven reports a day. Now I am comfortable again in a
cave dug in the chalk and an old mattress from one of the demol-
ished houses in the village is proving very comfortable.

"My work never lets up. The day is topsy-turvy. We have to
lay low all day to escape observation. The men sit on the edges

of their funk-holes like prairie-dogs and when the shells fly or aeroplanes sail overhead, they dive in under cover. At nine P.M. we emerge and do various work all night: digging trenches, wiring, carrying ammunition, buying the dead—and such tasks. Every officer is ordered to be with the company when at work.

"It is scary business to stand around in the dark while they work in the trenches and encourage them when the shelling begins, the rockets and flares all along the near horizon lighting up the weird scene, the Boche flash-lights simulating the aurora, the everlasting crack and roar of our own artillery all around us and the whine of the innumerable shells passing overhead, the sputtering of the machine-guns, and in the midst of it all the persistent singing of a nightingale down in the ravine. . . .

"Here I was interrupted by a gas alarm—I went out and sniffed and smelt something which resembled apple blossoms, and as the apple trees hereabouts are in full bloom, I was fooled for a minute. It was gas, much diffused by the breeze, and we only kept our mask on a few minutes."

The morale of the American troops remained remarkably high considering the serious fighting and continuing casualties, and the men grew rapidly in experience and confidence. By the end of May they were ready to undertake their first small offensive operation. They were ordered to capture the heights of Cantigny in order to obtain observation posts to survey the low-lying Aisne area to the east. After careful practice and planning, the 1st Division launched its attack on May 28. A liaison officer, Colonel Walter S. Grant of the General Staff, reported:

"The fight came off practically exactly as planned. I was able to observe it from an O[bservation] P[ost] north of Broyes on the high ground where I arrived at about 4:20 A.M. At this time some of our artillery was firing at intervals. At 4:45 A.M., our artillery, with the additional batteries put at the disposal of the division commander for the fight, started its neutralization fire on the hostile artillery. There was no sudden increase in the artillery fire at 4:45, but the volume of fire gradually increased. At 5:45 our artillery started its preparation and diversion fire. At this hour the increase in volume of fire was marked, and from my

O.P. I could observe the various areas and lines behind the enemy's front where this fire was being directed. It was a remarkable sight—great clouds of smoke rolling up from the shelled districts, against which the flashes of bursting shells stood out.

"At 6:40 the rolling barrage started. The infantry promptly moved out. Inequalities of the ground and the fact that visibility was only fair prevented my seeing the entire line, but I saw one company distinctly as it crossed a long stretch of open ground. It moved in two lines of two waves each and went forward as if it were at inspection—really splendid—lines straight, etc.

"The objectives were taken and our men proceeded to dig in. Up to this time there were no indications of any great losses on our side. Prisoners then commenced to come back and were all brought in to the cage at the division headquarters, where they were segregated, and given a preliminary examination.

"In the meanwhile our troops commenced to suffer from shell fire and from a machine gun at Fontaine-sous-Montdidier. . . . Major [Theodore] Roosevelt, [Jr.] in the morning had reported repulsing a counterattack (which personally I think doesn't amount to as much as it sounds). These small filtering parties led to the belief, however, that the Germans were going to counterattack later in the day—either that, or that their losses had been so severe as to demand the reestablishment of their front line in this way."

The Americans rushed to lay barbed wire and dig trenches as the Germans with extraordinary violence sought to dislodge them. They withstood a 72-hour artillery barrage and repeated counterattacks before the Germans finally accepted the loss of the village.

The capture of Cantigny was an enheartening demonstration to the Allies of the fighting qualities of the American troops. As it came at a time when the transports were landing 9000 men a day, it brought a glimmer of hope in black days. On May 27, the day before the testing at Cantigny, the Germans had launched their huge offensive against the French and were achieving frightening gains. Much depended upon quick American aid.

12

BLOCKING THE DRIVE ON PARIS

Suddenly in June 1918 American troops were rushed into bloody and sustained battle to help stem a great German drive on Paris. In one of their last desperate efforts, the German Army on May 27, 1918, opened an offensive against the French where they least expected it, along the Aisne sector, and achieved another spectacular breakthrough. In their initial rush on the first morning they captured the trenches along the ridge of the Chemin des Dames from which the 26th (Yankee) Division had recently been relieved. Traversing the Aisne River valley and brushing aside the weak resistance of retreating French troops, they dashed on to the Marne River. On June 1 they crossed it. In four days they advanced thirty miles, capturing 60,000 prisoners and vast quantities of arms and supplies. Paris, only fifty miles away, and indeed the entire French nation, seemed once more to be in acute peril.

To meet the emergency, General Foch hurried 25 French divisions into the Marne area, toward Chateau-Thierry—and fortunately by June there were several American divisions, each double the size of a European division, which he could call upon. Thus it was that thousands of soldiers, some of them already weary of service in the front lines and hoping for a rest, found themselves instead being rushed forward into furious battle. On foot, or in old buses or trucks, they were sent forth.

The 2nd Division, which had been scheduled to relieve the 1st Division around Cantigny, instead was loaded 28,000 strong into French camions driven by silent little Annamese from French Indochina. Stretched out in a procession fourteen miles long, the truck shirted Paris hurrying toward the front, wherever it might be. Joseph Feingold of the 4th Brigade, made up of two Marine regiments, remembered:

"The roads were blocked with a surging mass of humanity and trucks. One line was going away from the front, homeless, hungry and exhausted. French soldiers were also going back, broken in health and wounded. Not soldiers like our men, young and healthy, but old veterans of the war; old men, for all the young ones were at the front or dead. They were broken in everything but spirit. They would walk the roads with perspiration running down their faces and choked with dust; but they had a smile on their lips and motioned us by their hands what we should do to the Huns when we came into contact with them."

Late on the evening of May 31, the first American troops encountered the Germans. This was the 7th Machine Gun Battalion of General Joseph T. Dickman's 3rd Division, which reached the town of Chateau-Thierry astride the Marne River, and across the stream French detachments were falling back before the heavy attack of advancing Germans. Two gunners went to the assistance of the French, while each of the two machine-gun companies prepared to defend the bridgeheads. During the night the French blew up the main bridge just before the American machine gunners and their French comrades arrived to recross it; the marooned men fought their way to the railroad bridge, engaged in hand-to-hand conflict with German infantrymen, and recrossed to safety.

By daylight, the Machine Gun Battalion had emplaced all of its guns in protected locations commanding the two bridges. With nine guns they raked the railroad bridge with fire so heavy that the Germans could not cross, and with eight guns they fought off several German attempts to replace the ruined highway bridge. Together with French infantry, they prevented the Germans from occupying the southern half of the town. During the day, American infantry units arrived from Povins-Montmirail to reinforce the French along the Marne. Through June and the first half of July they held miles of the riverbank, digging defense positions and sending frequent patrols across the Marne to capture prisoners. These patrols and several sharp minor encounters cost the division 34 officers and 822 enlisted men killed or wounded.

Meanwhile the 2nd Division under General Omar Bundy was being rushed out the Paris-Metz highway and across the Marne, to stop the enemy advance northeast of Chateau-Thierry. There, on the afternoon of June 1, the troops were assigned to digging in along a defense line just beyond the village of Lucy-le-Borcage, while French infantry were delaying the Germans on the slope of hills about two miles away. The French officers urged no delay, since their exhausted troops had fought for six days without respite and could not hold for long. The Americans were only relatively fresh. General Harbord, commanding the Marines, reminisced, "My men had slept practically none the night of May 30th; were in buses all day the 31st and far into the night; slept practically none that night and had been marching since four-thirty that morning. They had little to eat, but they had been marching toward a fight, and both regiments were now at hand and ready. . . .

"The instructions from the French General were that we must 'hold the line at all hazards.' That was the order I transmitted to the Brigade. The companies were hardly more than in place when a message from the same General suggested that I have a line of trench dug several hundred yards back of them, 'just in case.' My reply was that, with the orders our men had, they were prepared to die if necessary to hold the line, but if started to digging trenches they would know it could have but one purpose and that my orders were not to be taken as given.

"So, I said: 'We will dig no trenches to fall back to. The Marines will hold where they stand.'"

The German vanguard reached the American line on June 2, and the next day the main body of troops heavily attacked the left side of the position. The first German prisoners could not believe that they were facing an American line, but so it was, since on June 3 and 4 the French troops in small groups retreated back through the front line, leaving it to the 2nd Division to defend. Against determined German assault on June 4, the line held.

Immediately the Americans, in keeping with their orders, planned counterattacks to try to regain some of the lost territory. These were to result in fighting bitter and heavy in losses far beyond the acreage involved, since the German High Command was determined to whip the American troops in order to lower their morale. The locale was to be a hilly spine of woodland, no more than a square mile in area, full of spindly second-growth trees and brush that helped hide huge boulders. From a distance, across a field of green wheat red with poppies bobbing in the wind, it seemed a delightful bit of forest. And so, if the French had been correct in their information, it would have remained, for they told the Americans the Germans were occupying only the northeast corner. The inexperienced Americans took the word of the French and did not send out patrols of their own—or they would have discovered that the Germans had transformed the thickets and boulders into an almost into an almost impregnable bastion. Instead of going around the woods and sealing them off, the Americans turned it into a place of testing, almost a miniature Verdun. All through June the 2nd Division sent wave after wave of attackers into the square-mile patch until, in the end, they cleared it completely of Germans and established their own fighting qualities—at a cost of some eight thousand casualties. This was Belleau Wood.

The attack began on June 6, and since it was to be a surprise no artillery barrage preceded it. When the Americans began to advance across the wheat field, it was they who suffered a frightful surprise as machine guns opened on them; the Germans had three lines of defense within the woods. Nevertheless, the Americans did advance a half mile and captured permanently the village of Bouresches. It was a day of frightfulness. Joyce Lewis, who was with his brother William serving in the 5th Marines, wrote a friend:

"Brother 'Billy' and I were of the first 1,250 to go 'over the top.' Eight hundred of these were either killed or wounded, almost before we got started. I saw Major Berry killed, and shortly thereafter 'Billy' went down. He was about two hundred feet from me. The boys were charging into machine-gun nests and Billy was running along the edge of a wheat-field toward a wood where Germans were concealed. The first bullet hit him in the top of the head and others lower down as he fell.

"In the charge, I got within fifty feet of the German machine-gun nests when a bullet plowed through the top of my skull. It was a bad wound, by no means healed to-day, five months later. As I lay there I could plainly see the German gunners and hear them talking. They could see I was not dead and I watched them as they prepared to finish me. They reloaded their gun and turned it on me. The first three bullets went through my legs and hip and the rest splashed up dust and dirt around my head and body. Evidently thinking they had done a good job the Boches turned their gun to other parts of the field. This was about 5:45 in the afternoon. That night, about two o'clock, one of my comrades, Robert Hess, of St. Paul, who later in the battle was himself killed, crawled out and started to carry me back to the lines. When he had gone some two hundred feet he stumbled, making a noise such as the Germans heard, and they turned their guns our way. Hess dropt me and, thinking it impossible for him to get me to the lines alone, he piled up a half-dozen bodies of my poor dead 'buddies' and barricaded my position. There I remained for several hours longer, and finally during a lull in the battle I was gotten back to the lines. The

German infantry advancing at Chemin des Dames, May 1918

Gun crew, Regimental Headquarters Company, 23rd Infantry, 2nd Division, firing 37 mm gun during an advance

Stretcher bearers removing a wounded soldier from Vaux, July 22, 1918

boys piled up around me were my own campmates whom I knew and recognized. Back of the lines the surgeons came out, finally, and seeing me, exclaimed, 'What, ain't you dead yet?' Then they took me into the hospital, fixt me up as best they could, and sent me to Paris in an automobile ambulance."

Happily Major Berry was only wounded in the arm and the losses were not as catastrophic as Lewis had thought, but as day after day went by, the fighting continued to have a nightmare quality. John C. Gieger, who participated in the attack of June 10, wrote:

"We crossed an open space of nearly a mile when we discovered that we had hit the Germans' second line trench.

"Still we kept going. Of the twenty-five who were with me, only four remained.

"Suddenly we spotted a machine gun. Without a thought the four of us started to charge it. Two of the men were killed immediately. I was shot in the right leg. The last man escaped. He told the other Marines of the machine gun and in a few minutes a second and bigger advance was made. They surrounded the gun and the crew wanted to surrender. But there's not much use taking as prisoners men who fire at you until they see they are overpowered. I don't remember any prisoners walking back from that crowd."

Added to these combat conditions, the troops had to contend with extreme fatigue. "The 2nd division has been moving, marching, entrenching, and fighting since May 30," General Bundy wired Pershing on June 10. "During that time, few men have had a night's rest. The gravity of the situation on its arrival here demanded the immediate placing of all regiments in the line. For the past five days, it has been engaged in close combat, offensive and defensive. The division holds a front of 10 kilometers. There are no troops to relieve them. As it is highly desirable that the ground gained and held by American troops be maintained by American troops, it is requested that a brigade of infantry be sent there at once for tour, relief purposes." Five more days went by before the 7th Infantry arrived to give the Marines a slight respite.

Even on relatively quiet days, the fighting in Belleau Wood was confused and unpleasant. Thus, an Operations Report on the 7th Infantry for June 21, 1918:

"Along about 4 o'clock this morning, or a little later, a terrible barrage was placed on the line, at the same time as an annihilating machine-gun fire from the enemy. These fires, so suddenly come upon, practically stunned Co. A. Their losses estimated at about 140 to 150 killed and wounded. . . . The officers and several enlisted men questioned by me all said that the enemy they actually saw were in groups of from 6 to 10 to 12, manipulating machine guns and rifles, and were dressed in American uniforms; that certain of them mixed with our troops and attempted to interfere with the plan of attack, saying that the line should not advance as our own people were up there and we should not kill our own people. At one point in the attack, when the line had engaged the enemy, a German in American uniform approached Lieut. Paysley of Co. A saying to him: 'My God, you are not going to fire on your own men out there in front of you; you are not going to kill your own men.' It being so apparent to Lt. Paysley that this officer was an enemy in our own uniform, that he immediately shot and killed him, in the excitement of the moment not obtaining insignia or identification from the body. It is quite apparent that the enemy so dressed tried to influence the movements in this attack. Shortly after the barrage and this terrible machine-gun fire was put on the line, and hand-to-hand fighting here and there, the engagement ceased."

Two days later Lieutenant Paysley was killed in the fighting.

From the German side, the fighting looked equally grim and deceptive. Major General Feldkeller, commanding the 87th Reserve Division, reported on June 25, 1918.

"At 5 P.M., strong hostile artillery fire set in on Belleau and the plateau between Belleau Wood and the village. At the same time, medium and heavy trench mortar fire was laid on that part of the woods held by us. At 6 P.M., the fire was extended also to the contact battalions and to the artillery. Since most of the mortar shells burst in the trees, the two left companies (3rd and

4th Cos., 347th Inf. Regt.), particularly, being nearer to edge of the woods, suffered very heavy losses.

"The hostile attack began at about 6:30 P.M. The battalion at first evaded the thrust. The battalion commander, Captain Kaulbars, having received timely report of the heavy losses of his companies, at 7 P.M., sent a telephone message, requesting that the 3d (Reserve) Battalion be alarmed. He then placed his assault company (1st Co.) in line by distributing it to the 3d and 4th Companies. At 7:12 battalion had resumed its advance against the wood. At 7:45 P.M., white rocket signals ('here we are') came from the depth of the wood. At 8:09 P.M., the report from an artillery observer stated that the north tip of the wood was again in our hands, and that the hostile artillery had quieted down.

"At 9:50 P.M., the infantry plane sent out by division confirmed that the infantry had again reached the old line.

"After a short pause, a violent barrage set in at 8:30 P.M., first on Belleau village then shifting to the north tip of the wood.

"The enemy followed with a new attack which penetrated between the 3d Co. and the remainder of the 4th Co., and rolled up the two companies (2d and 5th Cos.), 2nd Bn., adjoining on the north. A reorganization of the massed assault units for defense could not be effected in the short time available, particularly since, at the very beginning of the action, the [commander of the] 4th Co. had been killed and [the commander] of the 3d Co. fatally wounded. The prisoners captured by our counterthrust, according to the statements of the wounded, fell again into the hands of the enemy.

"At 10:15 P.M., there were left only the remnants of the 5 participating companies, which now reestablished themselves in the position held on the Torcy-Belleau road. . . .

"The total losses in the 5 participating companies of the 1st and 2d Bns., 347th Inf. Regt. were 7 officers, 433 N[on] C[ommissioned] officers and men. Of these, 2 officers and 64 N.C. officers and men returned wounded. Thus, the remaining 5 officers and 369 N.C. officers and men were killed or are missing.

"As later reported by a reliable officer who returned wounded, a part of the Americans had worn German uniforms with the insignia of the 109th Grenadier Regt. and, by calls in the German language, attempted to create confusion among our men.

"On the next day, artillery observers reported that at the edge of the woods, newly occupied by the enemy, men in German uniforms could be seen. Our close combat patrols sent out for reconnaissance in that direction encountered everywhere machine-gun fire, thus establishing the fact that it could not be a remaining nest of resistance held by Germans."

So ended the Battle of Belleau Wood. Several days later, after a heavy artillery bombardment, the 2nd Division easily captured the nearby village of Vaux. Clearly the Americans had proven their ability to fight; they proudly proclaimed a German intelligence report, of June 17, a copy of which they had captured:

"The American 2d Division may be rated as a very good division, if not even as an attack unit. The various attacks by both of the Marine regiments were carried out with vigor and regardless of losses. The moral effect of our firearms did not materially check the advance of the infantry. The nerves of the Americans are still unshaken. . . .

"The personnel may be considered excellent. They are healthy, strong and physically well-developed men from 18–20 years old who, at present, lack only the necessary training to make them into a very worthy opponent.

"The spirit of the troops is fresh and one of careless confidence. A characteristic expression of one of the prisoners is 'we kill or get killed.' "

This spirit carried over into the hospitals. Laurence W. Thomson, who had been hit in both legs with machine-gun bullets on the night of June 6, wrote home: "We marched right into the Huns and showed them what kind of stuff the marines are made of. They call us 'Devil Dogs'—some distinction."

Several weeks later, Assistant Secretary of the Navy Franklin D. Roosevelt visited the battlefield: "In order to enter the wood itself we had to thread our way past water-filled shell holes and thence up the step slope over outcropping rocks, overturned boulders, down trees, hastily improvised shelter pits, rusty bayonets, broken guns, emergency ration tins, hand grenades, discarded overcoats, rain-stained love letters, crawling lines of ants and many little mounds, some wholly unmarked, some with a rifle stuck bayonet down in the earth, some with a helmet, and some, too, with a whittled cross with a tag of wood or wrapping paper hung over it and in a pencil scrawl an American name."

This was in August, and not many kilometers away a number of American divisions were engaged in fighting along the Aisne-Marne sector. Belleau Wood had been only an opening engagement there. On July 15, a little farther south, in the area around Rheims, the Germans made a final vast effort to roll back the French toward Paris. Crossing the Marne south of Chateau-Thierry under protection of a smoke screen, they pitted 52 divisions against 34 Allied divisions—9 of which were American. The Allies were well prepared for defense in depth; the 3rd Division held the German attack on the right, but at points the Germans expanded their bridgehead to a depth of four miles. Three days later the Allies surprised the Germans with a major counteroffensive, smashing the bridgehead over the Marne. While the thrust was primarily with French troops, at several points Americans fighting recklessly spearheaded the attack.

Lieutenant M. P. Bledsoe of Battery A, 7th Field Artillery, serving in the 1st Division, wrote his sister:

"We had been in the line for several months then and we thought we were pretty well fagged, and so were greatly relieved when we started back to the 'rest camp'—but said rest camp proved to be the banks of the Marne! When we changed our route and began hitting it off with forced marches and headed toward Rheims, we all knew that something was going to happen and happen 'dam soon' and naturally we forgot that we were tired. The Captain had gone ahead a day or so and I was bringing in the battery. Of course, we had to come into positions at night. I'll never forget it! It took 2½ hours to travel the last half mile. The roads were literally blocked, jammed and packed with men and carriages of every description—caissons,

caissons, little guns and big guns, motorcycles, autos, hundreds of horses—men fighting and swearing at them; add to this two or three hundred tanks, a night as black as Hell itself, and over all a drizzling rain, and you can imagine what a tangled mess it must have seemed. However, we reached the battery position at 3 A.M., 'layed' the guns and had a bite of 'iron rations.' Of course, Fritz was not wise to what was coming off and was peacefully sleeping a few thousand yards away. Our rolling barrage was to start at 4:35. How many guns were in this sector, I don't know. I counted sixty-four that were in a few hundred yards of my battery. At 4:35, they all began at the same time. Mother of God! I have never heard such a hellish clamor! Fritz was literally blasted out of the ground, and the barrage started rolling forward. Following it came the tanks and then the doughboys. Said Fritz didn't have a dog's chance. Long before the barrage had reached the limits of our range, the prisoners were trailing past. When the range limit was reached, there was nothing to do but limber up and get forward in a hell of a hurry, and we kept gong until stopped by sheer exhaustion. Naturally all the dead men and wounded were not on Heine's side, but we have 'Kultur' one hell of a wallop."

And Gary Roberts of the 167th Infantry, 42nd (Rainbow) Division, wrote from a hospital:

"All of you cheer up and war a smile for I'm a little hero now I got two 920 of the rascals and finished killing a wounded one with my bayonet that might have gotten well had I not finished him. I'm only going to claim or give my self credit for two that I made hallow 'mercy comrade mercy.' But I want to tell you I couldn't be satisfied at killing them, how could I have mercy on such low lifed rascals as they are. Why I just couldn't kill them dead enough it didn't seem like. Believe me it was some fun as well as exciting. Now I'm sorry I didn't get to kill one for each of you. Perhaps I can get more next time. The first one I got was for momma and the other one was for myself for the trouble they have tgiven this old boy since I left Home."

In some of the fighting, American losses were frightful. The veteran soldiers in the 15th (Scottish) Division of the British

Army were dismayed when they relieved the 1st Division to march past American dead in regular rows. "It revealed the fallacy of some of Pershing's ideas," a British military historian, Cyril Falls, has written. "Able man and stalwart soldier though he was, his view that his troops were trained for open warfare, whereas those of their allies were not, was an exaggeration. So far the Americans had done what they had because in defense they were absolutely determined not to yield at any cost and in attack they meant to get through or die. Many died." Certainly Pershing had emphasized aggressiveness; on the other hand, he was angered when he felt a French commander wasted Americans troops on the Vesle River. The price for Americans was not as high as it had been for the British on the Somme, but of some 310,000 Americans who fought in the Aisne-Marne region, 67,000 were killed or wounded.

One of the soldiers picked up a letter, crumpled and dirty, lying in a field, and mailed it to its addressee. It was from Leo Cuthbertson, who writing on July 25, 1918, said:

"As we walked along the roads yesterday we could look on either side and see dead Huns—boys who had died with their boots on in defense of their country. Strange as it may seem, my heart is hardened to a point where such a sight, while pitiful, is a pleasure. For surely that is one way of defeating our enemy—put him in his grave. Some boys told me last night that the fields further up the line (about two miles) are covered with dead Huns. As I write this letter I feel somewhat nauseated from the odor of decayed bodies in the immediate vicinity.

"Last night I witnessed a truly pitiful sight—the burying of our boys. The sight of our comrades being laid away for their final rest, garbed in a U.S. uniform, makes one's blood run cold and increases a passionate desire to deal out misery to the enemy—and I believe before this war is over he will have had more misery than he bargained for."

13

FLATTENING THE
ST. MIHIEL SALIENT

Folks, we have them on the run,"
Charles Hershey, a wounded soldier, wrote his parents on July
28, 1918. "I hope we keep them to it, and I hope I can get a back
on the line soon and do my part in keeping them on
the fly."

The opening of the Allied counteroffensive on July 18
marked the decisive turning of the tide in the war. Not only had
Allies succeeded in parrying the German offensives for nearly
four months, but during that time as hundreds of thousands of
fresh, fit Americans arrived at the front, they regained numerical superiority. From this point on, the Allies pressed their
advantage against the Germans, and for month after month as
summer turned into fall, the Americans increasingly participated in routing the German armies.

Battle and hardships turned those Americans who had survived the spring and early summer into seasoned troops who

could transmit some of their skill and hardihood to the green replacements who were constantly coming into their midst. Their morale remained relatively high because they were winning, and because they felt their cause a righteous one. In training camps they had been told stories of German frightfulness, and their encounters with the Germans in battle had involved trickery and often came close to being no-quarter fighting. "The Germans opposite us were the ones who murdered the poor women and children on their advance though Belgium," Hershey told his parents. "They were soon cut to pieces and I hope we can still chop them some more."

Hardihood became commonplace. Hershey had "gone over the top" at 4:30 on the morning of July 18 when the counteroffensive began:

"I went over well prepared, as I saved my supper the night before and had it in my mess kit, and I had a little can of strawberries I had picked up, besides my hardtack. All this was on my back. Shortly after we crossed No Man's Land I developed the battle thirst and I was compelled to drink all the water I had, and still I was not satisfied. I saw a dead American soldier lying in the oats, so I took his pistol and exchanged canteens with him. Luckily the canteen was full, so that helped me out. Later many of us got German canteens that were full or nearly so of good cold coffee.

"The Germans turned their machine guns on us, and I with many others, was compelled to drop down in the high oats. I want to tell you that I was somewhat worried when the tossels of the oats fell down on my helmet and back. It sure worries a man and it was a great relief when some good comrade captured that machine gun nest.

"I was wounded while bandaging a good pal of mine, who was shot through the stomach by a machine gun. I was just wrapping the last time around when I felt a numbing sensation, and sure enough my shirt was torn by the fragments of a high explosive shell which struck about ten feet from us. My pal bandaged me and then he started crawling toward the rear, while I rested a bit from the shock. It certainly made me mad.

. . . I landed on my stomach and when I looked I found my pants torn around my knee and that I was wounded again. There was not much use of trying to go further, as I had only one hand to do anything with. I noticed that my can of strawberries and my hardtack had been blown from my back and that there was a tiny scratch on my back. When my 'eats' were gone I almost lost heart."

Collectively the soldiers met their vicissitudes in a similar jocular spirit. Lieutenant H. H. Heliwell described the experience of men in the 9th Infantry:

"After a trying and exasperating forty days in the lines at Chateau-Thierry, where we lived in the ground like gophers, only not so deep, and where shells were always getting in our way to make life a torment; where the nights were hell and the days dragged along like months, and where the grub was monkey-meat floating in grease; after all that, we were taken back to a small town for a rest. But, strange to say, we did not get that rest. Before the men had bathed or even changed their undergarments or recovered in any particular from their strenuous experiences in the lines, we received orders to entrain for a destination to be known when we arrived."

Without sleep or food, they traveled all night and all day to Villers-Cotterets, and after being given hot coffee—and nothing else—were marched eight miles to the front. At 4:00 in the morning they attacked the enemy:

"We went over on schedule time and reached our objectives on schedule time, and advanced seven miles inside of twenty-four hours, farther than we should have gone in fact. Don't forget that the men were doing this on empty stomachs and tired, very tired, bodies and legs. The men, some of them, drank from the puddles in the roads. . . .

"Some of them had not been in the lines before. They were replacements just assigned; yet they fought game to the very end. Will we lick the Kaiser? I'll say so, with men like those and twenty million more behind them just as good."

By the end of July there were not twenty million but a quite substantial 1,200,000 Americans in France, and General Pershing was determined to organize them into a separate army and launch them upon an offensive of their own. First he had to beat down his French and British allies, who wished to continue to use American divisions on their fronts. Pershing agreed that certain units could remain where most needed. Next he obtained permission to proceed with a plan he had long cherished, to employ the American Army in smashing the German St. Mihiel salient, which "stuck out like a sore thumb" south of the French fortress at Verdun. There it had remained, a threat and problem to the French, ever since open warfare had solidified into trench warfare in the fall of 1914. It crossed the Meuse River at the town of St. Mihiel, cut several important railroad lines, gave protection in depth against French bombardment of the industrial center at Metz, and could serve as a jaw in a German pincers movement against Verdun.

It had been worth the while of the Germans to develop heavy fortification in so useful a salient, even though its narrow extension into French lines gave it a basic vulnerability. The salient was not wide enough to serve as a jumping-off point in a new German offensive, and was in danger of being squeezed if the Allies attacked both sides. In 1915, the French had failed to reduce the salient; in 1916–1917 it had been quiet. To Pershing it seemed to offer a splendid opportunity for the Americans to drive forward on a front of their own, toward Metz, the Saar basin, and the industrial heart of Germany. Since the offensive would also threaten key railways running behind the German front, it would create vital danger for Germany.

The German High Command, well aware of the danger as its armies were worn down in the spring offensives of 1918, laid plans to withdraw from the exposed tip of the St. Mihiel salient to a less vulnerable and shorter line, the Michel Stellung (Michel position), which it carefully constructed. It would withdraw its forces systematically, according to a plan called Loki, but only when the High Command was absolutely certain that a major Allied offensive against the salient was about to begin. Therein lay the weakness of the German plan; its intelligence must be perfect if it were to order the withdrawal at the right moment.

At the end of August, Pershing, deep in preparations for the offensive, assumed command over the St. Mihiel sector, but at that very time Foch, recently promoted to Marshal, changed his plans. He asked General Pershing to limit the offensive, and then throw his units immediately into a larger battle farther north under French command. General Pershing agreed to Foch's proposals, but only if the troops in the area of the Argonne Forest would fight as an independent American army. Foch agreed that if Pershing after a limited St. Mihiel offensive mid-September would shift his divisions for an offensive west of the Meuse, to begin September 25, the Americans could themselves command ninety miles of the Western Front, from the Moselle River to the Argonne Forest.

Pershing rushed preparations both for the offensive and for the speedy transfer that must immediately follow. As he made his plans, he crossed part of the field of the first Battle of the Marne, marked by the crosses of soldiers' graves. "Whenever I passed through this district I could not help thinking of the dreadful toll in human life that modern war demanded," Pershing later remembered. "As we were now about to enter into an active campaign, the thought came to me, perhaps as never before, that many an American boy would likewise be buried on the battlefield before the contest in which we were engaged should come to an end."

Since early August, troops had been concentrating in the St. Mihiel area, and the Services of Supply had been rushing the construction of roads and railways, the erection of hospitals, and the building of water points and supply dumps. The greatest concentration of airplanes ever assembled up to that time was brought together. Almost fourteen hundred of them, many British and French, under the command of Colonel William Mitchell, guaranteed air superiority during the offensive. Over three thousand artillery guns (none American in manufacture), almost half of them manned by the French, were prepared to fire over three million shells. There were not nearly sufficient tanks available, only four hundred of French manufacture. Above all, the attack depended upon manpower: some 110,000 French soldiers and 550,000 Americans.

Most Americans quietly moved into the area did not know clearly what was in the offing. "We are out here in the woods awaiting orders," Hilton U. Brown, Jr., a lieutenant in the 7th Artillery, wrote on September 6. "We have been on the go for several days and have now reached a sort of destination where we have hung in suspense. . . . We moved from the quiet sector from which I wrote you last and have been doing a series of mysterious and puzzling maneuvers. If the Boche could observe them he could not be any more mystified than we are. We pull out of camp each night just at dark, and usually come to rest in a woods just as the sun rises."

Preparations went on so secretively that it was not until about September 6 that the German High Command became convinced that a major attack was likely, threatening German industry, mines, and lines of communication. They rushed work on the Michel Stellung and began removing some of their munitions and supplies out of the tip of the salient. Still, the American attack seemed so little imminent that it was not until September 11 that the High Command ordered a gradual withdrawal.

Many of the German soldiers had no yearning for additional fighting. P. Langner of the 6th Grenadier Regiment, writing on September 11, was worried only for fear that his commanders would order new attacks: "This would be a good place to wait for peace, but, of course, dear friend, you know that the 10th Infantry Division cannot bear anything quiet." Heinrich Kirschke of the 47th Infantry wrote from Pannes on September 11:

"When will that time come again that we can live together again so comfortably in Berlin? It looks very sad for our beautiful Germany. Who knows whether the Americans will not even yet break through? This morning at 3 o'clock we were again altered and thought the Americans were going to attack, but nothing as yet. However, we captured a couple of prisoners who said that they would be in Germany in eight days. This place is not far from Alsace Lorraine where Metz is soon reached. We few fellows cannot hold up this superior might and must all go helplessly into captivity and, of course, most of the prisoners are murdered. But then we have to be satisfied with our fate whatever happens. I shouldn't like at all to be taken prisoner for one is then entirely cut off from the dear home. Still worse than that is to be severely wounded. Better dead than that. Well, I have always had luck up to now and guess I'll get through somehow.

"According to all appearances we are approaching turbulent days. We are constantly alerted and it is feared that the Americans are going to attack in this sector. They are said to have assembled tremendous numbers of tanks and troops on the other side. In that case we are lost. But everything in our front line is balled up, so don't be surprised if you don't hear from me for several weeks. I am finally convinced that I couldn't be any worse off over there than I am here."

On that same day, Sergeant Elmer F. Straub of the 42nd (Rainbow) Division wrote from not far away (he was to be in Pannes the next night): "I have never seen so much artillery in such a small place in all my life before, one can see any kind of a gun used . . . and they sure are laid side by side: 75s, 155 how-itzers, 155 rifles, 120 howitzers, 120 long rifles and eight inch howitzers. These 120 long rifles are railroad guns and are sta-tioned directly in front of our battery. Behind us there are many railroad guns ranging from 12 to 21 inch type."

At eight o'clock on the evening of September 11, the men of Battery E, 1st Gas Regiment, made their way to the front lines to install Stokes mortars that would hurl intense-burning thermite bombs on the enemy. Somehow they made their way through the narrow, muddy trenches carrying loads of over one hundred pounds each. Sergeant William L. Langer wrote later: "There was not much activity in the trenches, certainly not enough to give reason to suppose that a large scale attack was about to start. The enemy, to be sure, kept up his Verey lights and fired at intervals. Still, most of us were quite startled and surprised when, about 1:00 in the morning, the sky lit up behind us and the American barrage began. . . .

"After depositing our loads at the position we started back for another. . . . And going back was quite a different proposition than going, for, as if by magic, the trenches had filled with men, most of them Marines . . . and troops of the 9th Infantry . . . who were to go over the top with the first wave. Those rows of cold, shivering men, equipped with grenades and with bayonets fixed, crouching in the mud of the trenches and waiting for the crucial moment, is another sight we shall never forget. . . .

"We were just about to start back for the trenches [with a second load of bombs] when the Boche suddenly opened up with a concentrated bombardment of the town. Everywhere the shells were bursting. For a moment we were undecided, but then we set out on a run. . . . We reached the trenches without mishap. The first wave was just about to go over, and our machine guns had just opened a rolling barrage to precede it. For green men it was a novel experience—this stuttering breathless chatter of the machine guns behind one. The trenches were in places so congested that to get through would have been impossible had we not struck on a rather clever idea. 'Heads up, men, high explosives, watch these sacks';—shouting words to that effect worked like magic and we secured an easy passage. . . . The infantry went over and we watched the lines follow each other through the field of barbed wire, over the German trenches and into the woods where the enemy had his artillery.

"We were so tired that it was quite agreeable to us to rest out there, with the aeroplanes swooping low over the advancing infantry and the hammering of the machine guns. Wounded men were already coming back, but so were the prisoners—not single or in small groups, but in droves or herds, as you like. Most of them were young and hale in appearance, though there were a few older, war-worn men among them too. I spoke to several of them and invariably they said they were glad to have been captured. One even stated that he was glad that the attack had been made, for he believed it would bring the end nearer. Such being the spirit, it was not hard to understand why large numbers of the captives were entrusted to two doughboys who,

A gas and flame attack seen from the air

Tank of Company C, 327th Tank Battalion, Corporal George Heeszh, driver, advancing September 12, 1918

with rifles slung, would march, one at the head, the other at the tail of the column, with an expression of endless self-satisfaction on their faces."

The Americans went "over the top" almost as relaxed and confident. One soldier wrote home to Newburyport, Massachusetts, "When I went over I don't know how I felt. I imagined that all the Infantry would go forward all crouched over with their bayonets all set to jab a Dutchman and was surprised to see the doughboys smoking cigarettes and their rifles slung over their shoulders. I expected to see them falling all around me, but they didn't." Later, when the German artillery began shelling, casualties began. "It was some hot for awhile. They got a lot of men, but only a few of our company."

At ten in the morning, Sergeant Straub's battery started forward: "We went through Baupaume, Seicheprey St. Baussant, Essey and finally into Pannes. The road was certainly a sight, there were three columns of troops going forward on this one narrow little road, The road itself was in an awful condition, full of shell holes, bridges out and all torn up. The Engineers were working on the bridges and filling up the shell holes, wounded were being bought back this way, some few of the whippet tanks that had taken part in the drive were stuck in the marshes by the sides of the road, others were lying there silent, probably silenced by a German shell or so, still others were puffing noisily along the road going toward the front. We were on our slope of the hill and we could overlook the whole valley that not twelve hours before was 'No Man's Land' and now it is crowded with human bodies, both dead and alive. The drive had been a surprise to the Germans and they had left everything behind in their hurry to get out. . . . In the small villages that we passed through we saw many, many French civilians who had lived in their old homes under German military rule ever since the beginning of the war. When our officers would pass them they would all come to attention showing that the Germans had made them love and regard them as 'THE RULERS' of the land. . . . Far in front of us we could see fires and smoke where the Germans were set-

ting things on fire as they retreated and group after group of
from 20 to 200 German prisoners passed us as we went along.
. . . There we ran into a German canteetn and in it was anything a fellow could want, officer's quarters, maps, books, field
glasses, pistols, automatics, food horses and any kind of
equipment one could wish for. Right in front of the canteen
stood a wagon all loaded with things from some German officer's quarters. We went through it and found ivory toilet sets,
the best of turkish towels and a thousand other things worth
real money. We went into the canteen and there we got cigarettes, cigars, candies, soap, towels, matches, cakes and much
other food and then we went down into the cellar of the canteen and there to our surprise sat two American 'doughboys,'
dirty, just full of mud, packs on their backs and rifles at their
sides, but Oh, Boy they were sure drunk because the cellar was
filled with champagne and beer and they certainly had gotten
their share of it."

Private R. R. (Mick) Wallace described his experiences that
day more succinctly: "We shot Germans, captured Germans and
a lot of freight cars loaded with supplies and beer, so I have
drank Dutch beer, eat straw bread and spent German money. I
lost some mighty good pals . . . tho."

One of the cooks in the 89th Division, W. E. Thomas, wrote
his friends: "Our objective . . . was a little beyond Thiaucourt
towards Metz, and the doughboys liked to never have stopped,
ran clean away from the artillery support and finally come to a
halt by orders, but not by any resistance. . . . I followed up with
my kitchen as soon as I could; the roads were all blowed up, so
I was at Flirey until I could move, and on Sept. 14th moved to
Bouillonville, but that was too close and a little too hot, and
they moved us back to Euvezine at which place we stayed only
a few days, arriving back on a hillside close to Bouillonville,
where we stayed until a few days, arriving back on a hillside
close to Bouillonville, where we stayed until Oct. 7th. . . . I was
with our officers back always, but in range of gas and beaucoup
shelling, which we received night and day. It was a thrilling life,
a thrill every hour of the day or night."

The St. Mihiel offensive caught the Germans by surprise at a most awkward moment when they were moving some of their divisions; their none-too-reliable 77th Division of Reserves was especially shattered. At noon, Berlin time, on the first day of the battle, the German command ordered the Loki movement to start immediately, and taking losses in men and material, pulled its troops back toward the Michel Stellung. On the next day, with most of its troops rescued, but having paid the price of 15,000 men taken prisoner and quantities of supplies, the German command braced itself for an attack on the new line. So thin were their defenses that General Douglas MacArthur, commanding the 84th Infantry Brigade of the 42nd (Rainbow) Division, scouting on the night of September 13, walked undetected into the environs of Metz. A victory so disruptive to the Germans that it could end the war seemed within grasp, but General Pershing could not order a thrust toward Metz. Instead, he had to obey Marshal Foch's instructions, and having achieved the limited objectives allowed, at a cost of less than 9000 casualties, rushed his men northward for the new and still larger offensive in the Meuse-Argonne area. The Americans left with their spirits high and those of the Germans depressed. "They sure knew they were up against a real foe, the Americans," wrote Private Thomas. "That St. Mihiel drive was the deciding blow. Since then the Huns have had no spirit."

14

ACES AND AIR ARMADAS

During the critical battles on the Western Front, air supremacy was of vital aid to whichever side possessed it. Through the great German offensives from March into July, the Germans frequently controlled the air and inflicted punishing damage. Later, even as American infantry divisions were redressing the balance on the ground, American airmen flying French planes were gaining control of the skies—and returning the punishment to the German forces. Thus even in the First World War, massed strength came to count most in air warfare—the sum total of the exploits of hundreds and even thousands of airmen.

Americans gloried in these exploits: bombing and strafing behind the German lines, disrupting enemy supply lines and troop morale; shooting down German observation balloons and protecting those of the Allies; checking on German and especially engaging in "dogfights" with German patrols. Many were the American triumphs, but they were not always as one-sided as either the troops below or newspaper readers back home liked to think.

In July 1918 as the Germans broke through at the Chemin des Dames and swept to the Marne River, the Allies were as hard-pressed to stem the onslaught in the air as on land. The Germans not only massed far more airplanes against the French, but the planes themselves, a new model Fokker, were distinctly better than those of the Allies. Thus the German communiqué of July 19 read:

"Aviation. Hostile columns advancing to the battlefield were the objectives of our battle aviators. Our pursuit aviators shot down 32 hostile machines. Lt. Loewenhardt achieved his 38th and 39th, Lt. Bolle his 23rd and Lt. Goering his 22nd air victory."

The 3rd Division headquarters reported:

"Throughout the battle south of the Marne, and the advance toward the north, hostile aircraft flew over our troops with impunity, observing for the enemy artillery, bombing and firing upon all concentrations with machine guns. Many of our casualties were due to the work of these planes. In spit of . . . repeated requests of the Division Commander, our planes put in their appearance only very tardily and never for any extensive period of time. It is absolutely necessary that from a tactical standpoint and from that of morale that our air force attain and maintain supremacy over those of the enemy."

Colonel Mitchell found it no easy task to attain this level of excellence and numerical superiority. Like the ground forces, the air corps seasoned its men in the quiet sector stretching south of Toul. Beginning in April, several squadrons serving under the French took responsibility for a sector between St. Mihiel and Pont-a-Mousson, and at the very outset, on April 14, downed two German airplanes. Lieutenant Alan F. Winslow, who together with Lieutenant Douglas Campbell shot them down, wrote:

"On Sunday morning April 14th, I was 'on alert' from 6:00 A.M. 'till 10:00 A.M. with Lieut. Douglas Campbell. We were sitting in the little alert tent, playing cards, waiting for a call. Our machines were outside, ready at a moment's notice. At 8:45 I was called to the 'phone, told by the information officer . . . that two German aeroplanes were about two thousand metres above the city. . . . We were rushed down to our machines in side cars, and in another minute were off in the air.

" 'Doug' started ahead of men, as I was to meet him above a certain point at five hundred meters, and then take the lead. I gave him about forty-five seconds' start, and then left myself, climbing steeply in a left-hand spiral in order to save time. I had not made a complete half turn, and was at about two hundred and fifty metres, when straight above of me in the mist of the early morning, and not more than a hundred yards away, I saw a plane coming toward me with huge black crosses on its wings and tail. I was so furious to see a Hun directly over our Aviation field that I swore out loud and violently opened fire. At the same time, to avoid my bullets, he slipped into a left-hand reversement, and came down, firing on me. I climbed, however, in a right-hand spiral, and slipped off, coming down directly behind him and 'on his tail.' Again I violently opened fire. I had him at a rare advantage which was due to the greater speed and maneuverability of our wonderful machines. I fired twenty to thirty rounds at him and could see my tracers entering his machine. Then, in another moment, his plane went straight down in an uncontrolled nose-dive, his engine out of commission. I followed in a straight dive, firing all the way. At about six feet above the ground he tried to regain control of his machine, but could not, and he crashed to earth. I darted down near him, made a sharp turn by the wreck, to make sure he was out of commission, then made a victorious swoop down over him, and climbed up again to see if 'Doug' needed any help with the other Hun."

Campbell needed no help; he had destroyed the other plane nearby. He and Winslow dashed to the site of the wrecks:

"On the way there—it was only half a mile, I ran into a huge crowd of soldiers—blue and khaki—pressing about one man. I pushed my way through the crowd, and heard somebody triumphantly say to the surrounded man in French: 'There he is;

now you will believe he is an American.' . . . Needless to say, I felt rather haughty to come face to face with my victim, now a prisoner, but did not know what to say. It seems he would not believe that an American officer had brought him down. He looked me all over, and then asked me in good French if I was an American. When I answered, 'Yes' he had no more to say."

In the weeks that followed, as the Americans inflicted losses upon the Germans in a ratio of three to one their spirits soared, and (as with the infantry) perhaps they became a bit overconfident. One evidence of their buoyant feelings came when they were forbidden to date American nurses in a nearby hospital because they brought the nurses back so late. In response to the ban, several airplanes in formation flew over the hospital, festooning it and its environs with long ribbons of unrolling toilet paper.

Deaths were more sobering, especially on May 19, the loss of the leading American ace, Major Raoul Lufbery, who had transferred from the Lafayette Escadrille. Lufbery, who had downed eighteen German planes, was killed in combat only six miles from Toul. He was buried the next day while the airplanes of the 1st Pursuit Group, led by Lieutenant Edward Rickenbacker, came diving low to drop flowers as a tribute.

And death seemed always imminent. "The duration of life at the front in the French aviation service is about sixty actual flying hours, and English statistics figure as low as forty hours," Henry Brewster Palmer of the Lafayette Escadrille wrote his brother. "It is great sport, and all that I ask is that I be given a chance to take a few Boches with me when I go." But Palmer died in a hospital, of pneumonia.

A few weeks before he himself was killed in an airplane accident at the front, Lieutenant Chales Hastings Upton of the 50th Aero Squadron wrote:

"There is something more awe inspiring about an airplane crash than any other accident that may cause death. . . . I thought I had become hardened to death—I am not—my desire to fly is still with me. I do not fear my own death; there is too much beyond; but I fear to see my brothers go. . . .

"Who can stand beside the open grave of a comrade, hear the volleys fired, and the sweet notes of 'Taps,' see the airplanes swoop down to drop garlands over the spot, without feeling that there is something Greater? As the last note of 'Taps' sounds out over the spot, one has a vision, if you like, of a soul gone to a well-earned rest and to happiness."

Few aviators were so lyrical when their friends were killed. Most typical was the painful personal note R. Blessley wrote Louis Bennet, an American lieutenant in the Royal Air Force, August 13, 1918:

"Yes you're right. 'War *is* hell.' Jarve went West this morning. Even though I've been over at his squadron, #56, all afternoon, I absolutely can't realize it. It doesn't seem to come home to me at all. Poor old Jarve—how we shall miss him. And such a boy. And one of the very few who have kept straight through it all, thank God. He was diving on the target and evidently had his eyes so fixed on his sights, that he didn't notice the ground until it was too late, and then tried to pull out too fast. We only got out yesterday—he to #56 and myself to #60. Am enclosing a picture I found in his things which he evidently intended for you."

Eleven days later, Bennet himself was missing. He had shot down nine balloons and two enemy aircraft.

While thus living on such close terms with sudden death, the aviators became fatalistic, and determinedly left talk of flying behind them when they were in their quarters. "Barracks flying," remarked Lieutenant William M. Russel, "is absolutely tabooed." When he sat with his fellow aviators around a poor coal fire during bad weather: "If anyone should make the grave mistake of talking flying, a stick or poker is placed in his hands and the chorus sings, 'Show us how you would do it, Mr. Bones.'"

"It is good for the men to forget their work when they are not on duty," Lieutenant Jerry C. Vasconcelles wrote home. "Some go from the dance never to return, but one never thinks of that."

In their barracks, the aviators, though believing in the righteousness of the Allied cause, seemed less hateful toward the

Germans than some of those they had left behind in the United States. Sergeant James Norman Hall of the Lafayette Escadrille (who soon became Captain Hall in the Air Corps) in the winter of 1917–1918 wrote to the *New Republic* in protest against the persecution of the violinist Fritz Kreisler, who had served briefly in the Austrian Army at the start of the war:

"At our mess, here on the western front, we have among our phonograph records, Tschaikowsky's Chanson Sans Paroles, interpreted by Mr. Kreisler. We play it again and again. We are fifteen pilots in the Escadrille Lafayette, and Mr. Kreisler aids and comforts us, not only daily but many times daily. Technically we are his enemies—but only technically. Should he not then be proceeded against by the Austrian authorities as a traitor to his own government? I offer this as the only kind of argument which will be likely to appeal to that type of Junker American which is carrying on hate-campaigns in the United States."

The daily routine, even in the relatively quiet spring of 1918, drew heavily upon the airmen's time and energy. From a hospital where he was recovering from shellshock and frostbite, Vasconcelles explained:

"Our work over here consists of three strenuous performances:

"First, patrolling the line of our sector. This means regular hours of flying—from one to three a day.

"Second, 'alert,' which means that we are on duty by flights from dawn until dark and we must be at the hangars for a third of that time, as there are three flights to be made. After we receive messages we must be in the air within three minutes— then we know that the Huns are coming.

"The third duty is escort duty. When a bombing machine from a photo or bombing squadron wants to go across into Germany, we send up fast scout places to protect it.

"I have been in six of these scraps, attacked by the enemy planes six times, but have been on escort duty each time and so it was impossible to go after them, for the first duty of a scout is to protect the convoy.

"On the day when I had my hands frozen and lost my hearing, I was hit by 'Archie' or an anti-aircraft fire. The plane was knocked 100 feet straight up and was thrown into a spin. The altitude and its effect I didn't realize until after we had made the landing, when I discovered that my hands were numb, my cheeks black and burning and I could not hear out of my left ear."

Soon Vasconcelles was again flying, and by the end of the war was an ace with six victories to his credit.

No matter how skilled a pilot had become in aerial acrobatics and mock dogfights during his many months of training, his first patrol out over the enemy lines was a thrilling experience. Even though these flights would soon be routine, the first one, for a man of no combat experience, was nerve-racking. Lieutenant Russel, a brave man, who had gone through training and testing crashes with aplomb, wrote candidly:

"We flew at an altitude of between four and five thousand metres, well back of the German lines, looking for whatever trouble might be found. If any had come, I believe that I would have been of little assistance. Although at a high altitude, and bitterly cold, beads of perspiration broke out all over me. I was safe enough, however, huddled up in the middle of the squadron with experienced men on all sides. My instructions were to witness everything, learn directions, and keep out of a fracas unless it should be absolutely necessary to help others or defend myself—observation, and not fighting. I saw many Boche machines but no fighting. Below me all the time was Hell's fire, actually."

Within three weeks, Lieutenant Russel was writing with zest of his four hours per day in the air: "The strong wind blows on your face all day, and you are ever on the alert, continually watching like a hawk the move of every machine above, below, and around you, with one eye fixed steadily on the sun, if that is possible." Within four weeks he was killed in combat near the Vesle River.

It was in July 1918 along the Marne that the outnumbered Americans, flying Nieuport 28s against the German Fokker D-VIIs, fared poorly. It took weeks of arguing for Colonel Mitchell to obtain new, fast Spads to replace the worn-out Nieuports. Meanwhile, his squadrons sustained punishing losses.

The most publicized was that of Theodore Roosevelt's son Quentin. On July 11, Lieutenant Roosevelt was victorious. He chased three planes in formation, thinking they were Allied; when he caught up with them, discovering they were German, he shot down the last of the three and dashed back across the Allied lines just ahead of the other two. July 14, Bastille Day, was different. A German newspaper, the *Kolnische Zeitung*, reported:

"A formation of seven German aeroplanes, while crossing the Marne, saw in the neighborhood of Dormans a group of twelve American fighting aeroplanes and attacked them. A lively air battle began, in which one American in particular persisted in attacking. The principal feature of the battle consisted in an air duel between the American and German fighting pilot, named Sergeant Greper. After a short struggle Greper succeeded in bringing the brave American before his gunsights. After a few shots the plane apparently got out of his control; the American began to fall and struck the ground near the village of Chamery, about ten kilometres north of the Marne. The American flyer was killed by two shots through the head. Papers in his pocket showed him to be Quentin Roosevelt, of the United States army. His effects are being taken care of in order to be sent to his relatives. He was buried by German aviators with military honors."

Far too often, the American aviators were seriously outnumbered. Lieutenant Hamilton Coolidge wrote at the end of July:

"Nine of us on patrol saw a formation of six Boches planes below and our leader signaled to attack. Just as we started down, however, eighteen more Boches appeared over the edge of the clouds. We saw at once that we were in a bad fix. We swung round as quickly as possible, but they were by this time close 'on our tails' and the 'tracers' began to fly past us. I don't mind saying I was thoroughly scared—twenty-four against nine is poor odds especially when one is over enemy territory. Looking back I could plainly distinguish every feature of the enemy planes nearest to me. They were single seat Fokker biplanes. We became somewhat scattered in our hasty retreat, so I can speak only for myself. I kept my motor wide open and kicked my rudder to and fro which gave my machine a zig-zag motion and made it a difficult target. As luck would have it my plane didn't suffer any bullet holes. Fortunately our Spads are very fast: surely that was all that saved us."

From early in the summer, Colonel Mitchell tried to end the attrition resulting from inexperienced aviators, slow planes, and small patrols. In June he had achieved notable success by concentrating his 250 planes, augmented by British bombers, against German ammunition dumps supplying the Marne drive. Gradually the fliers became more experienced; Spads outflew the Fokkers; the numbers of planes increased. On September 12, when the Americans began the St. Mihiel offensive, Mitchell had over fourteen hundred airplanes under his command. Lieutenant Coolidge wrote his mother:

"We went out in groups of three or four, flying at a height of perhaps two hundred feet. Our objective was to see everything possible on the ground and to try to establish the location of the lines. I headed for a group of four. . . . Well, you never saw such a sight or heard such sounds. We started down our lines just at the edge and every second came flashes and white puffs from our batteries. We were so close that every explosion rocked us about frantically and often threatened to dash us into the tree tops. In fact sometimes our little ships were almost unmanageable. . . . The air was filled with Allied aircraft of all types and strange to say not a Boche appeared. Since then, however, they have come out in large numbers."

The Germans arrived too late; the Allied air concentration at St. Mihiel was overwhelmingly successful.

Along the Western Front during the summer and fall, the greatest objective of the opposing pursuit pilots was each other's observation balloons. This provided one of the great spectacles for the soldiers on the ground. "I saw a balloon shot down," wrote Hunry T. Kenealy. "My heart seemed to sink within me as the balloon went up in flames. The next day I saw two more go up in flames, but mother, that is the game of war." And Sergeant Merrill E. Henry wrote his sister, "About an hour ago I saw a Dutch airplane dive for an American observation balloon and shoot at it. The men in the balloon jumped and came down in parachutes." American observers were so skilled in parachuting that although they jumped 116 times, only one man was killed.

German observation balloons directing artillery fire, protected by anti-aircraft batteries and air squadrons, were dangerous targets. Nevertheless, American pilots shot down 73 of them. Lieutenant David E. Putnam, fresh from service in the Lafayette Escadrille, on June 15 shot down a German biplane, then headed back:

"I had flown perhaps three minutes towards our lines when a German balloon loomed up directly ahead of me. 'Well,' I said, 'I've got no incendiary bullets, but there's no harm in shooting at it.' No sooner said than done. I pulled both triggers. Pfoof!!! The balloon burst into flames, and it did look queer. I supposed that there would be just one burst of flame and that would be the end. No; the thing remained in the air, a flaming mass, for perhaps twenty seconds, and then dropped slowly to the ground where it continued to burn. But how the anti-aircraft guns did shoot at me. Bang! Bang! Bang! Just a continuous roar. 'Flaming onions' also were coming up from the ground. Into a cloud I went. The shooting was even more terrible there, so out I dove. Twisting, turning, circling, I finally reached our lines and made tracks for home."

The most audacious, talented balloon-buster was Lieutenant Frank Luke of Phoenix, Arizona, who in a few days in September became the second-ranking American ace of the war. Luke was a "loner" who fought most of his battles with only the aid of his friend, Lieutenant Joseph Wehner. His war on balloons began on September 12, when he heard Captain Vasconcelles remark that destroying a balloon was the most difficult assignment a pilot could undertake. He went out and set one on fire. On September 14, he downed two more; on September 15, another three. Then he devised a new technique, to attack the balloons at dusk, and on September 16 he and Wehner bagged three. September 18, he and Wehner made the most remarkable record of all—two balloons and three planes—but Wehner was killed. Luke was sent to Paris on

Operating a Graflex camera from an observation plane

Lieutenant Edward Rickenbacker in the cockpit of his Spad, 94th Aero Squadron, near Rembercourt, October 18, 1918

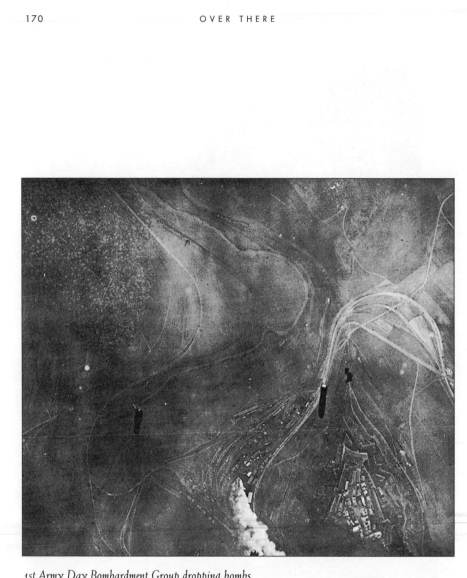

1st Army Day Bombardment Group dropping bombs

leave, but returned early, and on September 29 he simultaneously was placed under arrest and recommended for the Distinguished Service Cross. But before he could be grounded, he took off one last flight. He dropped a note to American observers: "Watch three Hun balloons on the Meuse." He downed each of the three, but was hit by anti-aircraft shrapnel, and could not gain altitude. He swooped over the town of Murvaux, strafing German troops, and careened down into a meadow below. The Germans shouted to him to surrender, but he stood defiantly in the meadow, shooting at them with his pistol until he himself was killed.

"Luke was the greatest fighter who ever went into the air," declared Captain Rickenbacker. But it was Rickenbacker, who had gone from auto racing to chauffeuring General Pershing to flying, who amassed the greatest total of victories of any American ace—26 compared with Luke's 18—and somehow survived the war. Captain Hall later described him, standing alone, "not quite smiling nor quite austere." To the newer men he seemed a sort of god: "A kind of quizzical, friendly smile touched his eyes. His lean body, slack in an easy posture, spelled capability, a lazy grace that might instantly become decisive action."

Such was the aura surrounding the aces.

There were numbers of aviators, flying hazardous scouting patrols or bombing missions, who took serious risks without as great opportunities to be singled out as heroes. There were, for example, the naval aviators flying patrols along the French and British coasts, hunting for submarines, helping protect convoys, and participating in attacks on the German dirigibles raiding London. Much of their work was dull as well as dangerous, over rough water where frequent engine trouble was more likely to be disastrous than over French meadows. Ensign J. W. Homer, who by June 22 had already flown 301 hours of patrol duty out of the R.A.F. Station at Polegate, described one of his blimp flights:

"Yesterday, I went on patrol at 6 A.M. and got into the fog (we are almost always out of sight of land) and flew around for about four hours. I was just going to lay a course for home when I sighted land to the south where it ought *not be*. On investigation it was Cape Barfleur. So I flew inland until I reached a French Airship Station and landed for a few minutes. . . . Then I went home (about eighty miles, arriving at 7 P.M. thirteen hours over the water). . . . Have been for five hours without seeing anything except gray sea below and gray fog all around—and have come home when it was so thick that I couldn't see the station a quarter of a mile off—just had to find the beach, then find the town I knew, then follow roads and railways about a hundred feet off the ground until I got to the station."

Sometimes attacks upon submarines or Zeppelins and fights with German airplanes punctuated these otherwise routine patrols. Most often airplane trouble caused mishaps. On the day before the Armistice, Ensign Francis Hartley, Jr., was forced to land his flying boat in the English Channel when its strut broke. His radio was out of order, but he sent carrier pigeons telling his location, and after seven hours of being tossed by the waves was rescued by a submarine.

Bomber pilots and bombardiers lived even more perilously. The 1st Day Bomber Group was thrown into the Battle of St. Mihiel where, flying in much-too-small formations against some of the best German squadrons, it was badly mauled. The 20th and 12th Squadrons were the first to be equipped with Americans airplanes, De Havilland 4s with Liberty motors. These bombers were so disappointing that they could carry only two bombs apiece rather than the anticipated ten; they were so vulnerable that the aviators called them "flaming coffins." On its first mission on September 14, the 11th Squadron lost two planes but, Lieutenant Paul S. Greene later wrote, the next day was even more calamitous. "Out of a formation of six planes which crossed the lines, only one succeeded in staggering back in a riddled condition." Reorganized and equipped with Breguets, the 11th Squadron flew with notable success, belying its earlier nickname, the "Bewilderment Group."

Through the Meuse-Argonne campaign from the end of September into November, the numbers and efficiency of both pursuit and bomber groups rapidly increased. Pursuit planes not only fought off enemy patrols, but dropped packages of cigarettes wrapped with encouraging messages to the dough-boys, and strafed the Germans. Lieutenant Hamilton Coolidge thus harassed the enemy on the first morning of the Argonne offensive:

"How my old heart just hammered with excitement as I dove beside that road, not fifty feet high, and recognized those Boche helmets! In a twinkling I was past them, gained a little height to turn in safety, and came diving down upon them from the rear. I just held both triggers down hard while the fiery bullets flew streaming out of the two guns. Little glimpses was all I could catch before I was by. Another turn and down the line again. I had a vague confused picture of streaming fire, of rearing horses, falling men, running men, general mess. Turn again and back upon them. This time I clearly saw two men heel off the seat of a wagon, then more awful mess. A fourth time I turned and came back. One gun stuck but the incendiaries still blazed on. Horses rearing, on fallen men; wagons crosswise in the road; men again dashing for the gutter. I craned my neck to see more and to be sure not to run into trees or houses beyond. Suddenly a ra-ta-ta-ta and a series of whacks like the crack of a whip broke loose. I knew only too well that the bullets were coming very close to crack that way! I *rocked* and swung and turned and the rattle died away behind. I found myself trembling with excitement and overawed at being a cold-blooded murderer, but a sense of keen satisfaction came too. It was only the sort of thing our poor dough-boys have suffered so often."

On October 27, Coolidge, by this time a Captain leading his flight, was killed near Grandpre by a German anti-aircraft shell.

Bombing raids became formidable. On the late afternoon of October 8, an armada of 200 bombers, 110 pursuit planes, and 53 triplace planes flew over the German lines in two great echelons, dropping a total of 32 tons of bombs. Twelve German planes were destroyed and only one American plane lost.

On November 6, 1918, thirty bombers dropped two tons of bombs on Mouzon and Raucourt. For an hour the planes circled over the field, slowly rising to an altitude of 14,000 feet, then flew, amid bursting anti-aircraft shells, to Mouzon. Lieutenant Gardiner Fiske of the 20th Squadron wrote:

"As we reached Mouzon luck caused a sudden rift to appear in the clouds and the town was plainly visible. I steered the pilot, by the reins attached to his arms, for the town, swinging the formation to the right. Getting the edge of the town in sight I gave the 'all set' signal by firing off a Verys light with seven green balls. At this point always comes a tense moment. The town passed back along the bar of the sight, reached the cross-bar and passed it. I pulled back the lever and let go our bombs. Waiting a few seconds to be sure all the Squadron had dropped theirs, I signalled to the pilot that all was well and to go home. Leaning over the side of the plane as far as possible, I tried to see the effects of the bursts, noticing one on a barracks and some flames near the railroad."

The Squadron had to fight its way home past opposing German planes:

'We arrived back at the field to await the hardest part of the whole raid. After making our report we watched the sky for the missing planes to come in. One hour passed; then two; finally we heard a month later that one plane had gone down in flames and two others had been forced to land in German territory. This was our last raid, as the rain god answered our daily supplications from Nov. 6 to Nov. 11."

One of the two bombers forced to land was that which Lieutenant Samuel P. Mandell was piloting. German bullets cut an aileron and knocked out the engine; from 12,000 feet it came spiraling downward to crash near the canal in Martincourt. The Germans took away the observer, Lieutenant R. W. Fulton, who was scarcely injured, but left Mandell, whose leg was broken, propped against his airplane, guarded by soldiers. Some hours afterward a German infantry captain came by, took a rifle from one of the guards, and shot Mandell to death.

Five days later the Armistice came. General William Mitchell viewed with satisfaction the overall achievements of the Air Service; the Americans had shot down 927 German airplanes and balloons while the Germans destroyed only 316 a ratio of three to one. He exulted, "We Americans had developed the best system of air fighting that the world had ever seen." But he and his men were tired, and were happy that an end had come to hostilities. "I was glad to see the terrific loss of life being stopped."

15

INTO THE ARGONNE

Across the rugged terrain of the Meuse-Argonne region, a million two hundred thousand American soldier hurled themselves against the fiercely defending Germans. From the end of September into early November 1918 they engaged in what became the death struggle of Imperial Germany. For 47 days they attacked through what General Pershing once described as a "vast network of uncut barbwire, ... deep ravines, dense woods, myriads of shell craters, ... [obscured by] heavy fog."

The objective was to cut the rail lines near Sedan upon which the Germans depended for the supply of all their troops to the northward into Flanders. To protect this vulnerable line, the Germans during the previous four years had built formidable defense systems to a depth of about thirteen miles, to augment the discouraging defenses that nature had devised. For hundreds of years the Argonne had stood as an almost inviolable barrier between the realms of the French kings and the German princes. When a French general early in the Revolution awaited the Prussian Army in the passes through these forested hills he proclaimed: "Behold the Thermopylae of France." But the Argonne could be outflanked—and indeed one of the problems of the Americans in the fall of 1918 was the speedier advance of Allied armies traversing easier terrain to the north. Because the Germans who were so powerfully entrenched there could not be allowed to outflank the oncoming Allies, the Americans had no choice but to plunge straight into that difficult region.

The immediate problem for the American command at the conclusion of the St. Mihiel offensive was to move most of their divisions northward to the new battlefield within the space of about ten days. The difficult logistic task of transferring 600,000 Americans was the responsibility of Colonel George C. Marshall, Jr., of the General Staff. He later reported:

"The two great difficulties in connection with these movements, aside from the uncertainty of knowing when any particular unit could be safely withdrawn from the St. Mihiel battle were:

"1st—The movement of the troops across the rear zone of the corps engaged in the St. Mihiel battle during the period when all the roads were congested with the movement forward of ammunition, rations and engineer materiel. Units had to be moved from east of the Moselle across the corps zones.

"2d—The limited number of roads available for the movement of the large mass of troops to be transferred to the Argonne front, coupled with the fact that all movements had to be executed entirely under the cover of darkness. The Toul—Void—Bar-le-Duc Road was the motor highway, and the other two roads were employed for the movement of the foot troops and the animal drawn vehicles, except in a few instances where tractor artillery had to be sent over them."

Complications were legion; nevertheless, Marshall was able afterward to state: "Despite the haste with which all the movements had to be carried out, the inexperience of most of the commanders in movements of such density, the condition of the animals and the limitations as to roads, the entire movement was carried out without a single element failing to reach its place on the date scheduled, which was, I understand, one day earlier, than Marshal Foch considered possible."

The plans for attack provided an even greater challenge:

"1. Mission: The mission assigned the army . . . was to penetrate the Hindenburg position on the line Dun-sur-Meuse–Grandpre. This was to be followed by a development toward the line Stenay–Le Chesne which would turn the line of the Aisne River. The Meuse was the eastern limit to the attack. The attack was to be made in conjunction with an attack of the French Fourth Army between the Aisne and the Suippe.

"2. Terrain: The terrain presented unusual difficulties. The attack had to be made along the high ridge or water shed between the Meuse and the Aisne Rivers, and it was flanked on the east by the commanding heights of the Cotes de Meuse and on the west by the wooded hills of the Argonne Forest. Along this high ridge, and forming obstacles to the advance, were: The commanding hill of Montfaucon, the wooded heights of Romagne and Cunel, and the heights of Andevanne and the Bois de Barricourt. The terrain over which the attack was made may be likened to a deep defile, blocked by three successive barriers.

"3: This position, strong by nature, was heavily fortified and well protected with wire. The enemy's first position ran generally through Malancourt–Vaquois and a second position through Montfaucon. Through Cunel-Romagne heights and Grandpre, there was a third position, the Kriemhild Stellung, a part of the famous Hindenburg Line. At the time of the attack, the enemy held the front with about six divisions."

The first part of this operation required penetrating the German lines to a depth of about sixteen kilometers to reach the line running from Dun-sur-Meuse to Grandpre. It took about a month to accomplish.

The initial attack was fought from September 26 to September 30.

Traffic jams at Esnes. Supplies for the Argonne drive moved forward at a two-mile-an-hour pace.

All that was left of the church on the crest at Montfaucon

Many of the troops who had not been engaged at St. Mihiel assembled near the lines in the days before the battle under deceptively peaceable conditions. Lieutenant Francis Reed Austin of the 28th Division wrote on September 21:

"Am back with the company again, and we are in the heart of the largest and most wild and beautiful forest in France. It reminds me somehow of Maine, but everywhere there are tall oaks instead of pines. It is a lovely September afternoon with the clouds floating by through the opening in the trees and trees bending to the gentle breeze. Another Lieutenant and I are sitting at a little table censoring mail and making a few notes on the organization of our platoons."

But four days later, on September 25, Austin wrote a friend:

"It is half-past nine and I am in the loveliest little dugout writing by candlelight. At 10:30 we move up on to the line, and after a four-hour bombardment we go ahead. It is my first, and all I pray is that I am worthy of the trust of my boys and the trust of you all at home. My boys are the finest of our whole splendid country, and I realize many are not to return, but they have a spirit of love that can never die. Just before supper we assembled under an oak tree and I told them everything and that the only thing that counted was to do their best for those they loved at home.

"They are singing and playing cards up there now with their rifles all cleaned and pistols ready. Just simple farmers ready to give whatever sacrifice is asked of them. I shall never be more happy than as the leader of these boys if I am worthy.

"I am not writing this to my mother or to any one but just you, for I know you understand. In this game as a platoon leader the chances are pretty good of being killed, but it is the dandiest of them all, and please tell my mother, if anything does happen, how much I loved them.

"My memories of my friends at home and little picture of my mother in my inside pocket make me just happy."

Not many of the soldiers about to go into combat were as eager as Lieutenant Austin. A Mississippian, Private Horace L. Baker of the 128th Infantry, 32nd Division, as a new replacement, joined a battle-seasoned company less than three months after he had been sworn into the Army. After several days in billets in a village on the banks of the Marne in September 1918, he noticed trucks arriving and parking along the main streets. The experienced men said, "Boys, that means another trip to the Front." In the next few days they moved forward, and on the night of September 25 marched in twos into the village of La Voye, where they rested:

"The rest period was prolonged. It began to rain softly as though the heavens were weeping over the sacrifice of so many lives that was so soon to be made. Yanks always want to go someplace else, so becoming impatient, the cry, 'Let's go,' resounded. . . . A truck bound to the rear was piled high with something. After it passed two or three of the fellows declared that it was loaded with the bodies of dead soldiers, averring that they could distinguish their feet. I know now that it wasn't so, but was prepared to believe anything." Baker did not go into the front lines that night; his regiment was held in reserve. "I had feared that we would go in, relieve some division and make the attack ourselves."

Sergeant William L. Langer and men of the 1st Gas Regiment visited the front lines that night as they had for several preceding nights: "At night . . . ammunition, as well as the guns, [was] carried over the hill to the position, which was a gap at the foot of the famous Hill 263, our target. The attack was to be a surprise and the line was to be held by the French until the zero hour, so it was essential that our operations should be quietly carried on. I remember that it was no easy matter . . . there in the moonlight, to follow a French guide through the trenches, when every twig brushing against a helmet and the noise of every misplaced step sounded so loud that one would think it was heard in Berlin."

For three hours before dawn on September 26, 1918, 2700 guns bombarded the enemy lines. At 5:30, nine divisions of infantry attacked along a thirty-kilometer front from the Meuse River to Vienne-le-Chateau. Some of them attacked in an early-morning fog that gave way to one of the few sunny days of the entire offensive. Edwin Newell Lewis wrote:

"At 5:45 the Major said, 'Let's go!' He boosted the lieutenant to the parapet and was in turn pulled up by hand to take his perch on the edge of the weirdest panorama of mist and mystery that mortal imagination could conjure up. No Man's Land, which should have beckoned straight into the heart of the Argonne, was shrouded in a thick, white fog. It seemed to close in from all sides on that little infantry company, isolating it entirely from the colossal Allied advance. . . .

"Beyond and through the fog the flashes of bursting shells flickered. The ear was confused by the muffled echoes of friendly artillery. The eye was confused by the haze, which kept from vision all objects more than 100 feet away and curiously distorted the few stumps and posts that clung to the side of the slop at their feet. It was almost as though the infantry was asked to go over the top blindfolded."

Captain Frank Tiebout of the 305th Infantry wrote not long afterward:

"Could anyone who was there ever forget . . . the anxious consultation of watched; the thrill of the take-off; the labored advance over a No Man's Land so barren, churned, pitted and snarled as to defy description; the towering billows of rusty, clinging wire; the flaming signal rockets that sprayed the heavens; the choking, blinding smoke and fog and gas that drenched the valleys, and then—one's utter amazement at finding himself at last within the German stronghold which during four years had been thought impregnable! This was certainly a long way from New York!

"A few corpses lay strewn about in the wreckage of emplacement, camp or dugout; a few dazed willing prisoners were picked up here and there; but for the most part the Boches had fled, their only resistance being a feeble shell fire, machine gunning and sniping. They had pulled out as rapidly as possible . . . to their second line of defense.

"Despite the intensity of the shelling, the maze of wire revealed no open avenues and there was difficulty in keeping up with our own rolling barrage as it swept over the ground before us at the rate of a hundred meters in five minutes. Pieces of cloth and flesh stayed with the rusty, clinging barbs; a number of men were impaled on spikes cleverly set for that very purpose. With difficulty the leading and supporting waves were reformed in line of 'gangs' or small combat groups before plunging on into ravines, there to become lost or separated from their fellows until after climbing to some high point above the sea of fog they might determine again the direction of advance by a consultation of map and compass and a consideration of whatever landmarks rose above the clouds.

"No concerted resistance was met with until about noon, after three kilometers of wooded terrain had been covered. There a stubborn machine gun resistance and a heavy shell fire persuaded the Second Battalion, reinforced by companies of the First, to dig in while they spread their panels on the ground to indicate to the Liberty planes overhead the point of farthest advance. At last we were to get some assistance from the air! Casualties there had been in great numbers from enemy shelling and from lurking snipers; but like North American Indians, we continued to stalk our prey from tree to tree."

The men of Company H, 364th Infantry, crawling along an open slope, held back by German machine-gun fire, spotted a rabbit that darted out of a shell hole toward the German lines. "Instantly, many Enfields cracked, the rabbit fell, 'killed in action,'" wrote Chaplain Bryant Wilson. "That important mission accomplished, the men proceeded to outflank and capture the Boche machine guns." Wilson and Lieutenant Lamar Tooze chronicled the advance through the forest:

"Cheppy Woods bristled with machine guns, placed to command the roads and light tramways along which most of the skirmishers had to advance because of the density of the underbrush. ... And those machine gunners of the First and Second Prussian Guard divisions obeyed their orders to hold at all costs. They would continue to fire their guns until hopelessly surrounded and only then would they come out of their concealed positions, both hands high above their heads, shouting 'Kamerad.' The machine guns were cleverly placed and camouflaged. The only thing which disclosed their locations was the puppety-pup sound of the Maxim guns they used, a sound distinguishable from our own Vickers. The gunners' helmets were streaked with multi-colored paints so as to blend with the earth and brush of the emplacement. Many wore the Red Cross brassard. Hedges, straw stacks, and buildings were the favorite positions for these guns and we soon learned to recognize likely locations of gun emplacements.

"Cheppy Woods looked like a summer resort. With the true German desire for comfort, walks had been built in all directions, picturesque rustic bridges spanned a small stream, the dugouts were complete with furniture, lighted by electricity, heated by small iron stoves, and the exterior painted. Arbors had been made where the soldiers quaffed their beer. . . . When men from the First Battalion were mopping up the woods, they entered a building which had formerly been used as a German canteen. It contained a good stock of beer, cigars, and cigarettes. Some of the articles bore the stamp of the Y.M.C.A. Evidently, they had been captured from the British and French during the spring offensive. The men did a good mopping-up job and it was a 'dry' canteen when they left."

Along the entire front, from the Argonne Forest to the Meuse, the initial attack went exceedingly well; at some points the troops advanced five miles and cracked the German second line of defense. The crucial objective that first day was the commanding German position, Montfaucon, the "Mount of the Falcon," from which the Crown Prince had commanded his assaulting forces against the French fortress of Verdun. The 79th Division was held up as it advanced toward Montfaucon through a valley and a large wood and was not able to assault the heights until 6:00 in the evening. Heavy German artillery and machine-gun fire drove back the American forces. At dawn on the rainy morning of September 27, the 79th and 37th Divisions renewed the battle and by noon carried the heights. This achievement was as much as General Petain had thought the Americans could accomplish in the entire fall campaign. One Frenchman wrote expansively:

"They captured Montfaucon, the eagle's nest, and its butte, considered impregnable since we, in 1914 and 1915, expended against it so much effort and so much blood. It was a magnificent conquest. Montfaucon (342 meters high) dominates the whole region from the Meuse to beyond the chain of the Argonne. This peak constituted ever since 1914, I can testify, a painful obstacle in the eyes of those defending the northern part of the camp of Verdun."

But the two days required to win Montfaucon gave the Germans time to bring up their reserves and to slow the Americans along most of the battle line. Also, the old No Man's Land, churned by shell and shot since 1914, was a most difficult obstacle to cross with heavy artillery. Consequently, the artillery could not support the advancing infantry on September 27. Sergeant Langer had visited this obstacle the pervious afternoon:

"For a wide belt through the forest the land was desolate. Trees, as well as the underbrush, had been shot away or left in a charred condition. The entire area was covered with fields of barbed wire and cut in all directions with great trench systems or dugouts. But most striking was the effect of the shell-fire and mine explosions, which left the whole landscape torn and scarred. Some of the mine craters were at least one hundred feet in diameter and forty feet deep, enormous wounds where the very bowels of the earth had been torn out. At a loss adequately to describe the scene, a German writer . . . asks his readers to imagine the ocean at its roughest and then imagine it instantly changed into clay. Such is the 'Fille Morte' [Dead Girl] line."

The construction of serviceable roads across this lunar morass became a compelling urgency. Lieutenant Worthington Blackman wrote home:

"We were switched from the reserve to the work of road-building, laying boards over mud, tearing shacks and dugouts to pieces in order to get the boards, even sawing down trees of over 18 inches in diameter and splitting them in two, for roads. The engineers, pioneers and others actually tore up the ruins of two towns, and carried the rock on their backs for a mile or more, to fill up mud holes and shell holes. . . .

"When it became evident that the roads could not be repaired in time to beat the Boche reinforcements to [the front], our division went into the front lines, relieving the division which had made the attack. My battalion was selected to occupy the front line. There was no question of trenches on our side—when the men had stopped going forward, each man had selected a shell-hold, and with his little shovel or pick had dug himself in, excavating a hole about two feet wide, five feet long and three feet deep, making a bank from the dirt dug out. . . . And we lived in those holes, without fire day or night, and with nothing over our heads, for three days and two nights, and it rained nearly half the time while the thermometer ranged from forty to sixty degrees all the time."

Such was life in the funkholes or foxholes. Some troops were more fortunate in obtaining quarters in former German dugouts. Wrote Sergeant Langer of the night of September 27:

"It was very dark and quite late when we reached Varennes, the famous town in which, some century and a quarter ago, Louis XVI and his family were stopped and turned back as they were attempting to flee the country during the great revolution. There were very few troops in the place when we arrived and consequently we had our choice of the dugouts. We chose those around the German Headquarters and officers' apartments. The walk had been a long one and we were tired, so tired that we hardly minded carrying the bloody forms of four dead Boche out and then sleeping in the damp bunks where we had found them."

Not only transportation but also inexperience was causing difficulties. Only five of the nine divisions used in the first assaults had participated in earlier offenses, and four of the divisions were dependent upon artillery units with which they had not trained. "Young officers did not know how to regroup their men after the initial advance," Colonel Marshall later wrote, "and when the time came to push on, they were unable to carry out their mission. . . . With better trained divisions in line much greater progress would have been made at this period."

On September 28, when the artillery had caught up with the infantry, the forces pushed ahead a mile and a half, but on the next day the Germans, reinforced by six rested divisions, held their ground. By October 1, the first phase of the battle was at an end. The American divisions in the front lines, bloodied and wearied from four days of heavy fighting and rapid advance, were relieved by new divisions. Vast quantities of artillery, ammunition, and supplies were moved to the forward positions. The American forces along much of the front east of the Argonne Forest had reached the outposts of the Hindenburg Line. As the A.E.F. prepared for a fresh assault, and as, to the north, the French and British pushed back the Germans, it became obvious to the German High Command that the future held nothing for them but further disaster. On September 29, Ludendorff and Hindenburg asked their government to negotiate an armistice. "The High Command insists on its demand . . . for the immediate forwarding of an offer peace to our enemies," Marshal von Hindenburg wrote the Imperial Chancellor on October 3. "There is now no longer any possible hope for forcing peace on the enemy. . . . The situation grows more desperate every day and may force the High Command to grave decisions." Three days later, the Chancellor, Prince Max of Baden, through the Swiss government opened negotiations with President Wilson.

16

BINDING THE WOUNDS

From the first frightful days of August 1914, many an American dedicated his or her life to giving succor to the Allied wounded. Idealistic stretcher bearers, ambulance drivers, doctors, and nurses, working long hours and sometimes themselves wounded or killed, aided the suffering soldiers. College men, joining the American Field Service, drove ambulances along the fronts in Belgium, France, and Italy. Red Cross workers were active even in the Balkans. As early as the spring of 1915, Dr. Harvey Cushing was serving with the Harvard Unit of a military hospital, the Ambulance Americaine, at Neuilly. In the fall of 1917, the ambulance and truck drivers of the American Field Service were enlisted in the United States Army, but continued to serve the French Army.

The admiration with which American ambulance drivers regarded the wounded French soldiers was unbounded. Franklin B. Skeele of the Stanford University section of the American Field Service wrote in September 1917:

"I do wish there was some way of telling you just how stoical to suffering the French *poilu* is. This is an impression that grows on me, with every wounded man that I carry. One has to become accustomed to so many heart-tearing scenes. . . . Boys of eighteen, men of forty, all give their lives and suffer for ideals that mean more to them than life. And then comes our part—to get the wounded *poilu* quickly to the hospital and to the skilful surgeon, for time means life. And yet one must drive carefully, for every jar means agony."

The wounded *poilus* were warm in their appreciation. A young American woman serving with the rank of lieutenant in a French military hospital developed a relationship with her charges almost like that between mother and sons. After they recuperated and returned to the trenches they remembered her. She wrote:

"In all the months I don't believe I've ever mentioned the exquisite compensation that comes almost daily in the shape of cards and letters from my children—'*bonne petite maman*,' '*Notre gentille Mademoiselle Miss*,' etc."

As Americans began to sustain wounds at the front and found themselves in French hospitals, they reciprocated in their warm appreciation for French orderlies and nurses. "A sister of M. Clemenceau is a nurse in my ward (or at least she is around a great deal) and she certainly is a noble character," wrote Hilton U. Brown after he was wounded near Cantigny in May 1918. "She has been decorated three times and has such a motherly nature that one can feel her presence in the room, even if one is sleeping."

Meanwhile the Medical Department was preparing for the large-scale casualties that would follow the throwing of two million men into battle. They planned base hospitals containing 200,000 beds and advance hospitals with 25,000—some 250 miles of standard wards. At the time of the Armistice there were 145,000 members of the A.E.F. hospitalized. During the big offensives, the handling of the wounded was organized on a huge scale, and in a routine fashion. From his bed in a Paris hospital on October 23, 1918, Colonel William J. Donovan described the process to his wife:

"I will tell you in detail what is done with human baggage from the first aid station on.

"At the battalion first aid station they tied a tag to me—

LT. COL. W. J. DONOVAN,
G.S.W. right knee,
Corbet, M.O.

meaning I had received a gun shot wound in the right knee. From there I was carried on a stretcher about 1½ kilometers to the Regimental dressing station where my wound was dressed and I was placed in an ambulance. A tough 3 kilometer ride over shell-torn roads to the Field Hospital. I was hauled out and placed on the ground. It then being determined that there was no immediate need of an operation I was sent on to the Mobile Unit. This was about 4 kilometers further back, and all these rides were damned uncomfortable.

"At this hospital I was taken in during a pounding rain. They took a complete record of my name, regiment, rank, nature and date of wound. Then they stropped me and rubbed me over with a warm sponge. It being the first in many days it was very welcome. Then then anti-tetanus injection. Then on a stretcher and put in a row in the waiting room off the operating room awaiting my turn. I waited there with eyes closed tried to get a little repose. I heard someone say 'Hello Colonel' and beside me was an enlisted man from my old battalion who was a runner and who had been hurt after me.

"Placed on the operating table they saw no need for an operation and putting my leg in a splint turned me into a ward. I was put between sheets.—Think of it! Beside me was an officer shot through the stomach and dying, across two officers coming out of ether and asking the nurse to hold their hands or smooth their brows. In the next ward a bedlam of delerium. . . .

"Pancakes for breakfast and then prepared for evacuation. Our cards containing our history were attached, and we were loaded into ambulances and sent to Evacuation No. 10. It was in a pouring rain and the road was terrific. I had with me several

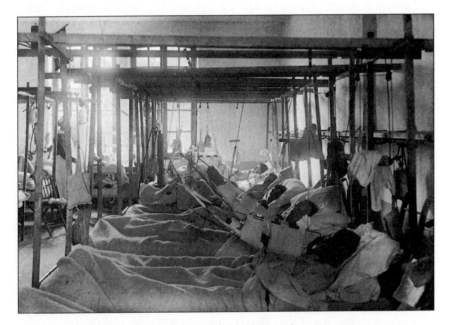

Fracture ward, Evacuation Hospital No. 1, Sebastapol, November 30, 1918

badly wounded officers who groaned the whole time, and I was not very comfortable, myself, so that on the road things were not happy.

"At the Evacuation Hospital we were handled like pieces of freight. Put on a rack, and when your turn came put in front of a checker who carefully noted your record. Then to bed. I was given a room. I was in an old French barracks hospital. The nurse was a sister of Rose, the hammer thrower, and looked to me husky enough to handle any of us.

"Two days here, the hospital overflowing, and then we were put on a French train, sixteen of us, officers and men in a car. The stretchers and slings were most uncomfortable. We had coffee without milk, canned corn, beef heated, and nothing else. I passed it all and dug up some Y.M.C.A. crackers I had been saving. We had a French orderly on the train. An old Breton, most obliging. He knew no French yet always knew what the men wanted. All night long this patient fellow worked, always awake and always smiling.

"Early in the morning we arrived here. I have a room with another officer. This was once the American something club. A club for American girls studying art. It is in the Latin Quarter. The food is good and wholesome, the nurses are not beautiful but nice and competent. My floor is full of generals and colonels, the two other floors captains, majors, and lieutenants."

It had taken much hard work to organize the handling of casualties so efficiently. The early arrivals in the Medical Corps spent weeks either building barracks or preparing building for use as hospitals. Dr. William H. Baker of the 168th Field Hospital, a private at the time, wrote December 6, 1917:

"We had a job cleaning up an old building that was built, or said to have been built, in the early 1700's. . . . I thought by the looks of the dirt we hauled out of it that it must have been built about 1492 and never swept since the day it was finished.

"We cleaned the place up and opened a hospital. In about four days we were relieved and moved to a village about seven miles away. More cleaning. Maybe move again. . . . The hospital we are opening now will in all probability accommodate about 1,500 men. We are so close to the firing line that we can hear the reports of the big guns."

Others were preparing to operate hospital trains. Private Paul C. Bibbee of Hospital Train 58 wrote with enthusiasm: "It is just as promised and much better. Sixteen large Pullman cars designed by American engineers and built in England. All are finished in khaki on the outside and two large red crosses in white setting on each side of each car. . . . The ward or patient cars are all finished in white enamel. Each contains 36 beds. The beds which are fastened to the wall three tiers high are so arranged that they can be folded against the wall out of the way when not in use."

The period of preparation did not last long, and indeed many of the doctors and nurses were quickly assigned to the British and French where, like the ambulance drivers, they found the work long, exhausting, and hazardous. Dr. C. H. Arnold of Lincoln, Nebraska, a Captain in the Medical Corps, went "over the top" with a British battalion near Albert on June 1:

"My aid post was in the front line so my work started as soon as our boys 'went over.' I shall never forget the place and although I was working like a madman to get the wounded dressed and back to places of safety I have a vivid recollection of most things that went on around us. Wounded were straggling in from all directions, stretcher-bearers were working at the double and soon my corporal and I were swamped, but we kept steadily at it going from one to another, the routine being occasionally broken by the arrival of a dangerously wounded officer or man whom we turned to and got started down the line as soon as possible. . . .

"We continued to dress the wounded and to splint their broken limbs until 9 A.M. when just as I was finishing the dressing of an officer who had a bullet through his head back of his eyes, I felt something like a brick hit my steel helmet. At first I thought it was a piece of shell which burst near by, but as I put my hand up and felt the hat where it had been torn and then the blood running down my face and neck I realized at last that the boche had 'got me.'

"It proved to be the work of a sniper who was hiding in a shell hole 200 yards away. The bullet tore a hole in one side of my helmet and a hole out the other side, split my scalp open as it passed through and just grazed my skull. . . . A few minutes later the same sniper caught a lad directly through the head a few yards away.

"I stayed till all the wounded had been cared for, both ours and the wounded Huns. A medical officer from an air post close by relieved me as my post was the more centrally located and I went down the line. . . .

"I was pleased to be able to come down on the same hospital train as the young officer I was dressing when the sniper spotted me. He is in the hospital now and doing well . . . although he will be permanently blind in both eyes. . . .

"Oh, yes, I forget to mention that we gained our objective and at last report were holding it O.K."

Stretcher-bearers and ambulance drivers also found themselves frequently under fire and the targets of Germans. What it was to be an ambulance driver with the 42nd (Rainbow) Division, Private O. Mensing of the 117th Sanitary Train explained to his sister on November 9, 1918:

"Ten days ago I was on detached service with the Tennessee Ambulance Co. with my mules. I had to haul patients from the front to the dressing station where the Motor ambulances relay them to a hospital. It was raining constantly while I was there, and it was impossible for motors to get through, so the mule ambulances were kept very busy. I sure had tough pickins while I was there, but Thank God, I lived through it alright. The first night that I was there I had good luck. There were no shells and everything was quiet, but the next days and nights after that were rather rough sea. The road that I had to drive four mules over was simply a trail through war devastated country, and many shell holes which I had to dodge. But that wasn't half of it, I did not mind that so much, but I was frightened at times when the Germans were sending over a barrage and the shells bursting around me. That made the cold chills go up my spine every once in a while. . . . It isn't so bad when you are walking and can duck to the ground or crawl into a shell hole, but when you are helpless in an ambulance with wounded patients moaning and asking you to help them it is a horrid sensation. I had mud thrown all over me and could hear that shrapnel from the high explosives sing through the air. We had four mules killed and two drivers were blown up out of the Company on this front."

Life was no easier for nurses near the front. Because she spoke French, Florence Bullard was rushed to a French Army hospital near the front during the German drive in March 1918:

"I arrived here in this deserted village in due time. Everything in the place was evacuated except the hospital where I am, and we are installed in the cellar. It is a sort of coal-cellar, completely underground. The Army is only twelve miles away from us and only the wounded that are too severely to live to be carried a little farther are brought here.

"I found on my arrival that my duties were to be interpreter for the English-speaking ones and the care of them. I have not seen daylight for eight days now and the stench in this cave is pretty bad; no air, artificial light, and the cots are so close together you can just get between them.

"Side by side I have Americans, English, Scotch, Irish, and French, and a part in the corners are *Boche*. They have to watch each other die side by side. I am sent for everywhere—in the little room they have curtained off with blankets for an operating-room, the dressing-room, and back again to the rows of men. Another part of the cellar is curtained off for the officers.

"Of course, some only stay twenty-four fours, because they send them away just as fast as it is possible, for even this cellar is too dangerous a place to be in. The cannon goes day and night and the shells are breaking over and around us. As yet I have never had a moment's fear, but one is so busy and with hand and heart too full to think of your own self. . . .

"I have had to write many sad letters to American mothers. I wonder if it will ever end and we will live a life other than one of confusions and tragedy. . . . I almost feel guilty to have stolen even this moment from my wounded."

From Coulommiers, not far behind the lines, during the Second Battle of the Marne, June 20, 1918, Emily Vuagniaux of Mobile Hospital T wrote her parents:

"We are in our tent and it is raining. Have been on duty 12 hours, but the excitement keeps us from knowing we are tired. We arrived here last Friday and have worked hard and long as we could stand it, sometimes 18 hours straight. I have the operating room and they run four tables days and night and have between 200 and 300 patients right off the field, so you may known we are quite close in. . . . Our tents have no floors, so it makes walking quite rough."

Sometimes conditions in these hospitals became chaotic. On July 22, 1918, Dr. Harvey Cushing described in his diary his efforts to restore order at a severely bombed hospital near Crepy-en-Calois:

"The hastily manned hospital near the station at Crepy had been hard hit and was evidently untenable—obviously necessary to evacuate. For this purpose an ambulance train, No. 54 U.S.A., was drawn up alongside the badly smashed-up station—equipped to transport 360 lying cases; it was about to leave with 622 wounded of all kinds, mostly severe.

"Altogether 2000 casualties had been routed through Crepy with the aid of a few surgeons and dentists from Mobile No. 1. With them were [Dr. Harry] Kerr and [Dr. Hugh H.] Trout, who had just reached France and been pitchforked into this mess to do strange operations under stranger circumstances. . . . They began to take in Thursday afternoon—had 604 last night alone, and they're rather done in. . . .

"At the station, wounded had been lying out all night in the storm untouched—waiting for the train. Bert Lee in desperation finally wangled some empty lorries and sent a large number of them, thoroughly drenched, to this place. . . . operations all night in a Bessonneau tent we finally managed to get set up— amputations of the thigh-sucking chest wounds—mutilations— German wounded. I recall a young Seaforth Highlander subaltern and a Jock of the Gordon. . . . wounded by the air raiders who passed over near midnight—the only two wounds which I saw that were not stinking.

"All told it was a bad night. Sometime about dawn, while waiting for the next head to be shaved, I lay down on an empty operating table, went promptly to sleep, and fell off. Morning has now come and it all seems very far away. I've had coffee, a shave, and will take a nap—the flies permitting—before we go on again."

So it went to the end of the war. Private Andrew C. Raber of Field Hospital 16, 2nd Division, wrote friends:

"From Charpentry, on the 7th of November we moved to Bayonville, where we were swamped with patients, mostly marines from the 5th and 6th regiments; total exhaustion and sick, gassed and wounded; mud knee deep. The artillery was hub-deep in mud, four to twelve mules to the gun, moving them forward; ration wagon stuck, trucks stuck, turned over, dead animals, strewn ammunition, damaged guns, in fact everything in desolation, destruction of property and human life.

"The 9th we moved up again to Sommathe and set up in church and hotel; swamped again; 1500 patients came in; all worked day and night for two days and nights. Our company was increased 75 men which afforded us a relief. Church was full, tents and hotel wherever there was any room for a man to lay. Then the 11th we moved to Beaumont, where we were swamped again—when the armistice was signed—well, honestly, we were all so fagged out, men and officers, that we didn't believe or realize what the armistice really meant at the moment it was signed. But later we certainly rejoiced after we got a minute to think."

17

"The Period . . . of Heaviest Strain"

As negotiations for an armistice began to unfold, the gigantic battle of the Meuse-Argonne, along with comparable British and French assaults, roared on in full fury. The negotiations were of little comfort to the American troops, since the slowly retreating Germans desperately contested almost every foot of territory. General von der Marwitz warned his 5th Army on October 1, 1918, that the Americans were thrusting toward the vital rail lines and essential iron mines of the Reich. "The fate of a large portion of the Western Front, perhaps of our nation, depends on the firm holding of the Verdun front," Marwitz asserted. "The Fatherland believes that every commander and every soldier realizes the greatness of his task, and that everyone will fulfill his duties to the utmost. If this is done the enemy's attack will be shattered."

General Pershing later reminisced, "The period of the battle from October 1st to the 11th involved the heaviest strain on the army and on me." The urgency of pressing the Germans gave little time for the improvement of transportation, the regrouping of troops, and even the training of new arrivals from the United States. It was not easy to keep the men almost constantly on the attack in the incessant cold rain. And some officers felt Pershing's displeasure:

"A few commanders lacking in those stern qualities essential to battle leadership or in physical stamina so necessary under these conditions were inclined to pessimism or inertia. An exhibition of either of these tendencies was quickly reflected in the troops. The real leaders, those indomitable characters whose spirits rose to master every difficulty, stood forth, a tower of strength to me during this period of the fighting. For the thing to do was to drive forward with all possible force."

Even during the comparative lull in the fighting before Pershing launched a second major drive, many of the regiments were engaged in intense local fighting. Much of the 305th Infantry was pinned down in the thickets of the Bois de la Naza and in a nearby precipitous ravine. Captain Tiebout wrote:

"Both sides maintained an almost constant rifle and machine gun fire. . . . To provide drinking water, one man would painstakingly crawl from one hole to another collecting on a stick a dozen or so canteens which he would bear to some point in rear. Movement or noise of any kind seemed to draw forth a raking fire of greater intensity. . . .

"For the better part of four days, we stove against these positions. Artillery could not be used to advantage because of the proximity of our lines to those of the enemy and the likelihood of short bursts in the tree-tops. 'The American Army never retreats,' and those higher up would not consider for a moment withdrawing troops while a sudden barrage might be laid down. We prayed for that artillery, but got precious little assistance. Rifle grenades fouled in the trees. . . .

"The 2d of October brought forth a succession of bloody attacks on various parts of the line. Those in higher command could not or would not appreciate the unspeakable difficulties of the situation and demanded that the opposition be shattered at once."

An unfortunate Captain who had, under orders, taken over positions from another regiment in the Ravine de la Fontaine aux Charmes, before he could redeploy his men was visited by a Corps Inspector. The Inspector, investigating the delay, removed the Captain, reporting that his men were "soldiering"—lying down on the job. "This was rank injustice to a very able leader," commented Tiebout, "and to the poor devils who had been crawling around on their empty bellies for a week, seeing their comrades dropping like flies."

That afternoon, the 305th Infantry attacked "Machine Gun Hill" or "Suicide Hill" in the Bois de la Naza, and suffered over three hundred casualties. One of the men in Company F wrote:

"At 3:30 we lined up our gangs and started over that most terrible hill. We were at once under direct machine gun fire, the worst yet, and it seemed as if the air was so full of bullets that a man could not move without being hit. A man standing upright would have been riddled from head to foot. That's what happened to Lieutenant Gardner, leading E Company. We were approaching the crest of Suicide Hill, advancing very slowly on our bellies. The only order that could be heard was 'Forward,' and Company F was game. It was awful. The poor boys were getting slaughtered as fast as sheep could go up a plank. No one could ever describe the horror of it. The screams of the wounded were terrible, but we stuck to it. We could not see a Boche; once in a while one would stick his head out of his machine gun emplacement only to his sorrow. . . . The Boches made our company look like a squad; all that was left was a handful of men."

On that same relatively quiet day, Ocotober 2, the so-called Lost Battalion of the 77th Division, moving in advance of the rest of the division through the secondary German lines in the Argonne Forest, became completely surrounded and had to fight for days without supplies or aid until the division broke through to it. The battalion, consisting of six companies of the 308th Infantry and some men from the 306th Machine Gun Battalion, were ordered to advance in the Argonne Forest "without regard to the exposed condition of the flanks." The battalion, under the command of Mjor Charles W. Whittlesey, succeeded in making its way up a small valley, and by dark were established on a slope about a half mile beyond the front line of the division. They dug funkholes, and spent a quiet night.

At 6:00 the next morning, Major Whittlesey sent back Company E under Lieutenant Karl Wilhelm to attack on one side of the ravine and connect with two companies fighting their way forward from the main lines:

"I started out soon after daylight but after getting a half mile away from the Lost Battalion, was startled by a voice on the hill tip above saying:

" 'What Company is that?'

"Three or four men immediately answered: 'It is E Company.'

"Something in the tones of the voice made me suspicious and I sent a scout up the hill to see if he could get any definite information. At the end of ten minutes he did not return, so I crawled up the hill a short distance myself and again heard talking, the men peaking in German although I could not distinguish what they said. Returning to the Company I gave the order to move ahead but about this time a terrific rifle and machine gun fire commenced, the Germans firing at us from above and also both flanks—while from across the little valley snipers started working.

"I took ten men and worked for a hundred and fifty yards to see if there was a possible chance for the Company advancing between the machine gun firing from the foot of the hill and the Infantry Company above us on the hill. After five of these men had been shot I determined that this was not feasible and started back toward the remainder of the Company, only to find that the Germans had swung down in between myself and the rest of the Company. We were cut off from the Company. The only thing left for us was to head straight up the hill and back into German territory. When we had advanced five or six yards we found that there were Germans all around us. They were shouting to one another and evidently had some idea we were in that vicinity, so we crawled into thick underbrush and lay there all during that day.

"A little path some fifteen yards away from us evidently led to a German gun position of some sort, for all during the day the Germans were passing and repassing by two and threes—so close that we could hear what they said. In my party was a sergeant, a corporal and two privates, and after dark we decided that it would be much sager to work back in smaller groups as two or three men would make less noise than would five, so Sergeant Callahan and myself started working along this little path which led in the general direction of the American lines. It took us from 8 P.M. to 12 P.M. that night to go an eighth of a mile, and we had to be exceedingly careful about noise. Every few minutes we would crouch at the side of the path while Germans would go by talking, unconscious of the fact that we were hidden there. Finally, near midnight we came upon an open plain a half mile across, which was more or less illuminated by flares which the Germans were throwing up every few minutes. Directly in front of us were three stretches of barbed wire each about 30 yards wide and protected by machine guns located every few hundred yards.

"After a short rest we started working through this barbed wire—our progress being necessarily slow at every time a flare went up we would have to stand perfectly rigid until it had died out. They fired frequently with machine guns—searching the wire for any enemy that might be there, but as luck would have it, we got through safely and crawled across the open plain to our own posts."

When Major Whittlesey became certain, by noon on October 3, that his battalion was surrounded by Germans, he delivered an order to all Company commanders:

"OUR MISSION IS TO HOLD THIS POSITION AT ALL COSTS. NO FALLING BACK. HAVE THIS UNDERSTOOD BY EVERY MAN IN YOUR COMMAND."

For the next four days, the battalion was out of communication with headquarters, except for messages that Whittlesey sent by seven carrier pigeons on October 3 and 4. By noon of October 3, the last of the food had been eaten, and the only spring in the area had a German machine gun trained on it. A

Taking a message from a pigeon sent from the front

quarter of the men had already been killed or wounded; bandages were used up; and there was no medical officer with the battalion. Major Whittlesey and Captain George McMurty later wrote:

"In their excitement to storm the position and capture the entire American force, the Germans neglected to maintain the silence usually associated with surprise attacks. One of our officers on the left flank who understood the Teuton tongue, heard enemy officers discussing preparations for the next attack which was launched shortly before 5 P.M. They seemed to be calling the roll.

" 'Rudolph,' a guttural voice would call.

" '*Hier.*' The answer came from the bushes above the outposts on the extreme left.

" 'Heinrich,' the same voice called.

" 'Ich bin hier,' was the answer.

"More commands in German followed and then, after a shout of 'Nun, alle zusamen' the attack was started. It combined rushes against the left and right flanks with a second grenade attack from the ridge. The ravine rang with the echoes of machine guns, chauchats and rifles. Our machine guns worked splendidly and the enemy must have suffered heavy losses from this source alone.

"This attack, the most severe attempted by the enemy while the Americans were surrounded, was repulsed on all sides. Quiet stole over the closely huddled funk holes as darkness settled down."

At 10:55 the next morning, Whittlesey released the next to the last pigeon:

"Germans are still around us, though in smaller numbers. We have been heavily shelled by mortar this morning. . . .

"Men are suffering from hunger and exposure; the wounded are in very bad condition.

"Cannot support be sent at once?"

The only reply in the afternoon was an American artillery barrage which, beginning on the ridge, gradually moved directly into the battalion's positions, sending shrapnel flying among the men, and tearing away the underbrush that hid them from enemy snipers. Whittlesey, dispatched his last pigeon:

"We are along the road parallel 276.4.

"Our own artillery is dropping a barrage directly on us.

"For heaven's sake, stop it."

For over an hour and a half the barrage continued, killing and wounding 30 of the battalion. Happily the pigeon reached the American lines, and the barrage the next day avoided the pocket in which the battalion waited. American airplanes went overhead from time to time dropping messages and packages of food, but all went wide of their mark. Lieutenant Maurice V. Griffin later wrote his wife:

"The picture I have of you has a hole in it from a piece of shell. I have four bullet holes in my overcoat, and my trousers were torn to pieces by a grenade, but I only had my knees cut besides the bullet in my shoulder. The strap to my field glasses was cut by a bullet, my gas mask was cut in half by shrapnel, and my helmet has a dent from a bullet. But they did not get me. The last . . . days we had nothing to eat but tree leaves and roots. Most of our drinking water was rain water from shell holes."

On the afternoon of the fifth day, a private came limping along the slope from the German lines, carrying a cane to which a white handkerchief was tied. He had been caught by the Germans and sent back with a message urging Whittlesey to surrender:

"The suffering of your wounded man can be heared over here in the German lines and we are appealing to your human sentiments.

"A withe Flag shown by one of your man will tell us that you agree with these conditions.

"Please treat the Lowell R. Hollingshead as an honourable man. He is quite a soldier we envy you.

"The German commanding officer."

Whittlesey smiled grimly at the thought of the Germans appealing to their humane instincts, and ordered the white panels used for signaling airplanes to be removed at once so that nothing white would show within the American lines. When the indignant enlisted men heard of the surrender demand they told each other what they thought Whittlesey must have said: "Go to hell!" Thus a legend was born.

With ammunition almost gone and the troops weak from hunger and exposure, the battalion was settling into a night of hopelessness when, at little after 7:00 P.M., three companies of the 307th Infantry finally arrived. The next afternoon, October 8, the survivors slowly made their way out of the valley to Regimental Headquarters; of the 554 who had fought their way in on October 2, only 194 were able to walk out.

How did the "top brass" regard their achievement? General Robert Lee Bullard, commanding the III Corps, granted "they had the right stuff in them," but could not resist labeling them "the largest collection of 'babes in the wood' that I ever saw." Bullard said of Pershing that "underneath his easy manner was inexorable ruin to the commander who did not have things right"—and some of this spirit rubbed off on Bullard. But Pershing, later listing Whittlesey and his Lost Battalion among the exemplars of heroic American fighting qualities, was deeply troubled over their predicament. It was a factor in his decision to order the 28th and 82nd Divisions to attack the left and rear of the enemy around Chatel-Chehery and Cornay in order to force them out of the Argonne Forest. The attack was successful; not only was the Lost Battalion rescued but the Germans withdrew from the entire Argonne area.

During the fighting on October 8, Private Alvin C. York of the 82nd Division performed some of the most renowned feats of the war. He was one of a patrol of seventeen men sent to destroy several German machine-gun nests that were holding a wooded slope. The patrol slipped quietly behind the enemy lines and into a clearing where it surprised a German battalion commander and a number of soldiers. The patrol attacked, and most of the Germans had thrown up their hands to surrender when a number of Germans on a nearby hillside began firing, killing or wounding nine of the patrol. York took command of the patrol, leaving them to guard the German prisoners. Shielding himself in part behind the prisoners, York returned the fire of the attacking Germans, killing more than fifteen of them and forcing the remainder to surrender. York then ordered the prisoners to form a column, and with the seven remaining members of his patrol as guards, marched them back to the American lines. The line of prisoners increased along the way as they encountered additional Germans and forced them also to surrender. He delivered a total of 132 prisoners, including five officers. York received the Congressional Medal of Honor.

York was not alone in his courage and resourcefulness. For example, another winner of the Congressional Medal, Private Michael B. Ellis of the 1st Division, fighting on the hillsides north of Exermont on October 5, managed to silence no less than ten machine guns, killing or capturing their crews.

On the other hand, General Bullard some years later pointed out that not all the American soldiers were heroes:

"Far back of our lines and camps my provost marshal . . . began to gather large numbers of American soldiers that had straggled from . . . various divisions. The French villages were full of them. Relative to the number of American soldiers that had been here, the stragglers were few, but actually their numbers were great. Popular public impressions to the contrary notwithstanding, we had in our army dead-beats and deserters, evaders of battle and danger. When to-day after the war, I read in their histories the bragging of some of our divisions of the fierce warrior bravery and high sense of duty of all their men, all, without any exception mentioned, I cannot help remembering the great numbers of their dead-beats that we herded up."

Deadbeats were proportionally few; men sick of the war were legion. One private, who had been wounded at Soissons and after convalescence returned to the line, wrote frankly:

"I arrived at the Argonne October 7th. The place smelled badly from dead. . . . It was on the 17th day of October that I was hit by a high explosive across the back, which put me out of the game and kept me out of the war permanently. I was happy to be hit again, because life in the trenches, plugging through the mud and water up to the waist, sleeping in wet, damp dugouts is unspeakable. When you have to live on a cracker and a glass of water for two and three days that is what is called real hardship."

Far from being a "dead-beat," this man had received the Croix de Guerre for participating in a raiding party on October 10 that captured 41 German machine guns and took 57 prisoners.

Regardless of their feelings, the Americans swept on. The First Army had resumed the offensive on October 4, gaining permanent possession of Exermont, several days later forcing the Germans to relinquish the Argonne Forest, and by the 10th had captured one after another of the wooded ridges on Romagne Heights, up to the main German defense line—the so-called Hindenburg Line. Three divisions, the 3rd, 32nd, and 80th, had already penetrated the line. Two other American divisions, fighting with the French were clearing heights east of the Meuse River.

Farther north in the Somme, the 27th and 30th Divisions, serving with the British, at the end of September had helped break the Hindenburg Line near St. Wuentin, and through October were pressing onward. The terrain was flat, but the mud, if anything, deeper, and the fighting no more pleasant than elsewhere. Civilians were suffering almost as much as the soldiers. When troops of the 30th Divisions entered Montbrehain, they came upon Madame Josephine Vassaux, whose 80-year-old bedridden husband had been killed by an Allied shell during the bombardment that preceded capture of the town. For five days Madame Vassaux sat beside her dead husband until he could be buried.

Corporal William M. Taylor of the 362nd Infantry saw his two closest friends killed near Ghent, and was himself wounded, but wrote from the hospital:

"The most vivid thing which I can remember of all that I saw during my last march before I was wounded. We were marching toward Ghent through smoke from the German guns, firing at a nearby village. We met three women carrying tiny babies, and an old man who was carrying his son, a legless Belgian soldier. They all looked half starved and like hunted animals."

Through October, as the tide of war was ebbing toward Germany, it was leaving behind little but devastation and heart-break.

18

BEHIND THE LINES

At the front, exhausted troops lived for the moment when orders came to march behind the lines for a rest. A lieutenant in the 305th Infantry wrote of watching his men as they came out of the line in mid-October 1918:

"I stood a tthe foot of the trail leading into Camp de Bouzon watching the stream of faces that passed—white, weary faces which told more eloquently than words of the utter fatigue, the nerve-shattering strain, the loss of good comrades, the rains and the cold and the hunger of twenty-one days advance in the fighting—of twenty-four days in the line—of twenty-two kilos advance. Ragged, mudcaked, unshaven outcasts they seemed, scarcely able to plant one foot in front of the other, stumbling down the trail, eyes staring vacantly—hungry for sleep; bodies as hungry for shelter, warmth, baths and clean clothes as for hot food."

First to succor them behind the immediate front lines were the volunteer workers for the Salvation Army, Red Cross, Y.M.C.A., and other organizations. Sometimes there was sour criticism of the men working for the "Y" but seldom of the women. One soldier praised especially the Salvation Army:

"Right up under the guns you see these women with their baskets serving hot drinks to the doughboys. In every advance zone you will always find this organization. It is always in the places where the boys need help and the closest hut to the lines you'll find is the Salvation Army."

Others similarly praised the Red Cross and the "Y" and with good reason. Eloise Robinson described her life just behind the lines in a shattered French village:

"It was a gay life in that little town. No water, unless we walked three-quarters of a mile for it along a shelled road, and then we had to boil every bit we drank. Mud, mud, mud till I shall always dream of it, and dirt until I felt as if I had never seen anything else. But always those blessed boys to do something for, so we didn't really mind. One afternoon I made fifty-five gallons of fudge, and gave it away. Another time it was candy out of corn sirup, with canned butter from the quartermaster, who was always our ally and would give us anything he possessed. Almost every day it was cookies, and every day hot chocolate and cigarets. The boys were so happy over everything we could do. I made enough for every boy in the battalion and all the runners coming through and the supply company and the M.P.'s along the line to have about a quarter of a pound apiece. And a general. . . who came by and stopped to ask directions and the cause for the crowd—the whole battalion was lined up in a perfect tangle before my field stove—went away in his limousine beating a tin cup full of the hot candy that had just come off the stove and had not had time to harden, with an army spoon.

"And then every afternoon I took about six hundred newspapers in a little cart which the Huns had left behind them and made the tour of the boys in the dugouts on the hillsides where no car could go. How those boys did scurry out of their poor little holes like rabbits out of their burrows! . . . I had on the cart a German gas *alerte* that one of the boys had given me, and I used to blow that. They knew it meant papers, and how they did come running! I couldn't let them gather too many at a time, though, because if a shell came over it would 'get' too many. But they didn't seem to mind, and we had our stock jokes.

"We weren't in one town all the time, but moved with the division. . . . The colonel of the regiment . . . every night . . . had a big army milk-can of water brought to us, hot from one of the field kitchens, so that we could each have a bath in our rubber tub! Talk about thoughtfulness! I don't know when I have ever appreciated any delicate attention from any man more. We ate in the field kitchens, going down and standing in line with our mess kits under our arms and waiting for our turn. Sometimes we had to go to the officers mess, or they would have been cross at us. And once for five days I cooked for nineteen officers on an improvised brick stove, because the kitchen was lost."

The soldiers were ecstatic in their gratitude toward these women. "They treated the Red Cross workers as though they were goddesses and nothing was too good for us," said Mrs. Sidney Walker.

Nevertheless, soldiers did spread some wild stories about the American women. Foster Rhea Dulles, historian of the Red Cross, had written: "The scurrilous charges of immorality (rumors circulating that several boatloads of pregnant women had been sent home) had no real basis in fact, but . . . there were some grounds for the popular belief that a number of the Red Cross girls were more interested in their own good times than in concentrating on the needs of the doughboys." Opportunities for romance among the Red Cross, Y.M.C.A., and Salvation Army women, and with the nurses, were relatively lacking, Nevertheless there were a few marriages. On May 25, 1918, Lieutenant Harry Bausher of the Medical Corps married Nurse Mary Butler in the A.E.F. chapel at Chaumont.

Toward Y.M.C.A workers, especially men, the soldiers were not always appreciative, and many of them damned the "Y" for selling tobacco they thought they should receive free:

"A while back I bought a package of cigarettes at the 'Y' and inside of it there was a card telling that it was donated by a girl in Philadelphia and to please write the donor a card. That's the kind of stuff we are compelled to put up with and I guess you heard Christmas all about us going to receive a Christmas bag from the Red Cross. Well, it's now one month [after] Christmas and no box yet. The Red Cross is all right, I guess, for some people, but not for me, as they've cooked their goose with soldiers as well as the Honorable Y.M.C.A., as it's all a big graft and I hardly know whether Mr. Censor will let this pass but I hope so as it is all the truth and it's what the people [who] are donating in the states should know . . . you are being jipped out of your kale."

The selling of gift tobacco, General Johnson Hagood of the S.O.S. explained later, occurred because it was impossible to keep shipments separate. " 'Gift tobacco' got mixed with the rest and was sold, not only by the Y.M.C.A., but by the Army," he wrote. "In order to adjust this I myself gave orders that if a soldier bought any tobacco anywhere which upon being opened was disclosed to be a gift, he could go to any army commissary and have his purchase duplicated free, without returning the original."

Significantly few of the complaints about the "Y" and other organizations came from men fresh from the front. Harold G. Merriam, an English professor from Reed College, who was encountering difficulties in running a canteen in the Toul sector, noted the difference. In mid-October a hundred trucks and ambulances carrying a thousand men stopped by his Foyer des Soldats (which was supposed to serve only French soldiers, and was empty of supplies):

"The boys were a fine lot, though having just come out of the Argonne, where it is said the bloodiest fighting of the war for Americans took place, they were in need of many physical comforts and luxuries. Unlike other bunches, when they discovered my canteen empty of all but excellent hot coffee, they expressed appreciation of the coffee. You could have seen a startled H G M when the boys actually thanked him for such a fine Y, when I hadn't a cake or cigaret or bit of chocolate for them! Other lots have damned both me and the place. . . . I said to myself that I would supply them with everything they could desire or bust. And I did—not bust, but supply them."

It took Merriam two days and much traveling and arguing to obtain the supplies. He loaded two ambulances to capacity, and brought to the Foyer "eleven thousand francs worth of cigars, cigarets, cakes, chocolate, and chewing and smoking tobacco." The "Y" charged the men 7 cents for a package of Camel cigarettes that sold for 15 cents at home. But the price in French money (with which some of the men still remained unfamiliar) was 35 centimes, leading some soldiers to wrote home that they had to pay 35 cents for the cigarettes.

Merriam was not pleased that the "Y" devoted so much of its energies to canteen work of this sort. To his friends at home he wrote:

"To the Y.M.C.A. has falled the hunger and coarser task doing the delivery work to soldier wherever they may be. . . . The Red Cross has organized itself as it has had funds and persons, regardless of how many units might be howling for service. It is therefore well organised, and when found, at stations and elsewhere, it seems to the soldier a very haven of refuge. But it is not always found. It is like a fine house with fine hospitality, found here and there but when found a haven of delight. . . . The Salvation Army, with small funds at its command, could not attempt what the Y with its large funds could. It seems to me to have satisfied itself with organizing a few houses of welcome that it could make very much like home. It has lassies who make doughnuts, as does the Red Cross, and pies and fix up its rooms in a homelike manner, with an air of femininity. At the same time it has succeeded in keeping its principles better than other Christian organizations. It observes Sunday, deprecates swearing and foul speech, deals gently with men, is lovable—as I have seen it. The Y.M.C.A., on the other hand deals roughly and in the large, thinks it necessary to be a 'man among men,' tolerates swearing and foul speech, observes Sunday hardly at all under the plea that the physical needs of

the men must be attended to. The Y undertook the job of catering to the luxurious appetites of men and that catering has
almost absorbed its efforts. . . . A certain depth and breadth of
experience, and I think a few grey hairs, are needed by the Y
man. The boys as it now is, do not hesitate to swear around the
Y men most abominably (you well know that I am no prude on
this subject of swearing) and talk about their escapades with
women and wine with utter lack of shamefacedness—in other
words they seem to expect little spiritually of the Y man. . . .
The American boy is a spoiled boy, and the Y is a largely
responsible. Take all this with a grain or two of salt. Yet in
essence it is all true. Some day I will set myself the pleasanter
task of relating to you what I think the Y has done well."

Others who had been in "Y" work longer than Merriam
argued that unless the "Y" concentrated upon filling the physical needs of the troops, especially on Sundays, the soldiers
would quickly drift elsewhere their needs might be filled in
ways the "Y" and Army regarded as less acceptable. Even in the
little village where Merriam ran his canteen, the problem existed. He had a frank conversation with his landlady: "Then we
spoke of neighbor whose grown-up girls have been set to the
occupation of serving men sexually instead of digging potatoes
. . . and Mlle. Marie said, 'Ah, it is unfortunate, what harm the
war has wrought; the girls can get . . . plenty of men now and
make a good living, but after the war what will they do—the
officers will be gone and they will stay here and they won't
know how to work."

And there was the almost irresistible temptation to get
drunk. "Do you know, Ma," wrote one infantry lieutenant, "I'm
just beginning to realize why officers . . . on leave want to raise
so much Cain . . . it's being cut off for so long from civilization
and from amusements, from news from the outside world. . . . I
know that if I drank at all, and that if I didn't have a wife and
family at home to keep me on the level, there would be nothing on earth that would keep me from raising h—if I ever got
into a big town." Another wrote: "There is a whole lot to the
case as presented thus by one of my men: 'Lieutenant, what the

hell is a man goin' to do if he don't get vin-rouged-up once in a while? They keep us either on the line or confined to training areas where we can't get to even a good village, let alone a city. And a soldier's a human bein'. If he don't get a chance to let off steam once in a while, he'll go crazy!' "

For most of them, liquor could wait in their priorities. What they most wanted after being relieved during an offensive was hot coffee and food, next sleep, and then a bath and clean clothing. Only after that were they eager to turn to recreation, either of the sort approved or disapproved. Claude I. Jenkins made clear the reasons for this sort of priority:

"I didn't change clothes from Aug. 12th till Oct. 20th. When I got to the base hospital at Angers, and no bath in that time either. No hair cut for longer than that. Over a month without taking my clothes off. A month without a shave. Three weeks no washee face. You may be sure not because it wasn't needed but because it couldn't be helped.

"I did wash my hands on average of once a week whether they needed it or not. Could take a chance and wash our hands in the water of shell holes but didn't dare use that on our face for fear of getting gas in our eyes.

"We were lucky to get a little water to drink that wasn't poisoned or gassed, and while in the front lines we were very lucky to get one canteen of water a day."

Jenkins could have added that his clothes were vermin-ridden. It was not much fun at the time, but most soldiers joked about the "cooties." Corporal Andrew Crosby wrote:

"Burned all my clothes the other night and put on new. Like grapenuts, 'there's a reason.' Jimmie, my side kick, claims that he found cooties with three service stripes and that they were carrying helmets, gas masks, and wearing cross de guerres. Now I think I am uninhabited. Neighboring tent burned down. They say casualties were 6,192,383 coots."

These were the concerns of the 168th Infantry when, on October 21, it was pulled a short distance back:

"It is a remarkable how much brighter the world looks to a man in a new pair of breeches and a whole shirt, especially when the sun is shining for the first time in two weeks. . . . For several weeks there had been no opportunity for washing clothes, and the men had been wearing that underclothes they had, or none, or clothes salvaged from equipment abandoned by the Germans. Now vermin-infested clothing was discarded or boiled out in the syrup cans that appeared over individual fires all along the hillside, and one by one the companies journeyed four kilometers down the valley to an old German bathhouse for a hot shower." Captain Morris Esmiol of the 340th Artillery wrote on October 1:

"I am ashamed to say I had a bath tonight for the first time two weeks. The cooks gave me a canvas wash basin of hot water, and I know I had the same sense of luxury that the old Roman aristocrat must have felt as he descended his marble steps to take his morning ablution."

Having eaten, slept and bathed, wearing clean clothes once more, the troops bounced back in morale and were ready for recreation. Five hours' maneuvers per day could not entirely quench their enthusiasm while they were in a rest area, wrote Captain Frank Tiebout of the 305th Infantry: "Even the daily drill in attack formation, the reception of replacements and the reorganization of combat 'gangs,' the incessant practice with grenades, with German 'potato-mashers,' with pistol, rifle and automatic and with captured German machine guns could not make all the clouds look a dark gray."

There was time left for shooting craps, playing cards, playing baseball or volleyball, and, if one were far enough behind the lines, to go sight-seeing (if one were also lucky enough to obtain a pass). Some nights there were movies; there were amateur shows, and occasionally there was a visiting star like Elsie Janis, who sang popular songs and told funny stories. Miss Janis, serving in the Y.M.C.A. Theatrical Corps, wrote in her diary, May 2, 1918:

"Gave my afternoon show up back of the lines in what is called a rest camp. I imagine it is so called because the mud is deep that if you once step in it you rest there. The fellows had just come out of the line. The show was out of doors—the stage

Baseball game between the 1st and 2nd Battalions, 1st Engineers, Varmaise, June 16, 1916

German machine gunner, killed at his post, Villers devant Dun, November 4, 1918

American of the 2nd Battalion, 339th Infantry, guarding warehouse where oatmeal is being unloaded, Archangel, October 27, 1918

two tables 'wished' together. The boys seemed rather shocked to see me at first. I don't wear a uniform, and I'm the only girl I've met who does not. They were fine, though. They gave me souvenirs they had picked up, pins, medals, German coins, etc.

"When I had finished I asked if they had any home talent, so a nice-looking boy got up and sang a parody which he had written on 'The Sunshine of Your Smile.' . . .

"Bless their hearts! They are all cheery, and ready to do all they can. They like France, but they love America, and the slogan up here is 'Heaven, Hell or Hoboken by Christmas!' "

Some entertainment was a little less genteel and very popular. Merriam wrote home:

"Then the evening rush descended on us . . . and right in the middle of it unexpectedly blew in five American girls (all of them had been on the stage in America) to give a concert. I got the stage ready, dispatched messengers to spread the news, though the hall was already full. . . . One of the girls was of the cheap actress type, painted and with hair fluffed, and eager to distribute signed photographs. She took the boys by storm. They played about forty kinds of instruments, dressed in several costumes, did the conventional stage wiggles, and had some racy vaudeville stories."

Men also enjoyed the baseball games, some liking them even better than sight-seeing. Harry Gwyn, who earlier had boasted of capturing two Germans, informed his mother, "I had a chance a few days ago to go to the birth place of Joan of Arc, but I preferred to play ball and of course we lost. The score was 8 to 6. It was the first game we had ever lost."

Large quantities of the soldiers were inveterate sight-seers; privates and generals alike visited cathedrals and chateaus, and wrote endless appreciative accounts of what they had seen. The memoirs of more than one high-ranking officer read almost as much like a tourist guide as a military history. General Harbord, one of the most enthusiastic of these sight-seers, wrote after a trip with Newton D. Baker, "I would soon get the cathedral habit if I traveled much with Secretary Baker. It is only when I travel with him that I seem to have time to visit them."

An ambulance driver, LaPoole Strehlke, was one of the fortunate few in the A.E.F. allowed to enjoy a leave in Paris during the war. He wrote his mother:

"Tonight I went to the opera and saw Faust. It was very good, of course. The orchestra was better than the Boston orchestra I think. Heard them play the music two winters ago in Thais. The opera house is a most wonderful building, situated in a square on the Grand Boulevard. . . .

"In time spent in walking I formed the idea that Paris could not be seen in ten days, so I shall not attempt it. Rather shall enjoy things as they come and do those things and feel the comforts of civil life."

Paris was so overcrowded, and offered so many opportunities for vice, that leave there was seldom permitted until after the war. Those troops that were allowed in were taken on rapid, carefully escorted sight-seeing tours. Nevertheless there were sufficient Americans in Paris in 1918 to require the service of a good-sized organization of military police.

In order to provide weary soldiers with a complete change from military routine, the Y.M.C.A. arranged with the A.E.F for the establishment of Leave Areas in French resort towns. There several hundred thousand men for seven days lived in luxury, almost as free as though they were civilians. The first, and most visited, was Aix-les-Bains (immediately nicknamed "Aches and Pains"), which opened in February 1918. In October, "Pete" Swinney of Sterling, Colorado, wrote his brother:

"Here we are away down in Savoy . . . and you may wonder what we are doing so far from the firing line. Well, it was like this. The C.O. called up Top Sergeant George Caudel one day by phone and asked him how he and a bunch of the fellows would like a few days out of hell. . . .

"All right, a bunch was picked, five from our battery and twenty-six from the regiment, given a week away. . . .

"There are some swell places here as it is one of the highest-up watering places in Europe. We are quartered in one of the finest hotels you ever saw, and good old Uncle Sam is taking the best of care of us. He pays $2.50 per for each one of us, we don't

have to get up in the morning, don't have to go to bed at
night till we want to, eat, sleep and see, and when we want
anything special push goes the button and the Frenchy porter
does the rest.

"There are lots of fine hotels, swell boarding houses,
'Ponshons' they call them here, and beautiful residences, fine
baths, pretty parks, and the mountain scenery is fine. The
mountains are all covered with trees and bushes and at this time
of the year their leaves are all colors, red, brown, green, yellow
and every other tint, making it a pretty sight from the hotel. . . .

"It was one of those swell places where the big bugs of
Europe used to come to indulge a little game of draw poker or
swap off a small country or two among each other. This war has
stopped all that, for the time, anyhow, and now we are enjoying the luxuries the rich folks built for themselves. It is great,
Bob, and I wish you could be in on it. You bet the Logan County
bunch will have something to tell when they get back to their
homesteads."

Swinney failed to mention the greatest attraction at the
Leave Areas. "Have you ever longed and sighed, for a dance
with, or even the sight of, an American girl?" inquired
Lieutenant Carlos M. Fetterolf. At Aix-les-Bains and the other
areas there were indeed American girls, Y.M.C.A. workers
whose assignment it was to talk with the soldiers, lead them on
hikes and picnic with them, and dance with them. True enough,
twenty or thirty soldiers accompanied one girl on a hike and
picnic, and at the dances the ratio was sometimes fifty to one.
The Y.M.C.A. later reported:

"The system of 'tag' dancing, by which, when a whistle was
blown, every man might cut in, made sure that every man got a
partner. . . . The dancing was a strenuous addition to the duties
of the girls. They worked all day in the canteen, or hiked with
the picnic parties; there was no possibility of resting while the
orchestra played, for girls were too scarce, and they were
caught from one partner to another often without missing a
step. Dancing slippers had little chance against hobnail army
shoes; the rule was proposed by the donkey turned out in the

poultry yard: 'Let every one look out for his own toes.' But somehow the girls endured it and kept smiling."

The men enjoyed themselves with a sense of urgency, the leaves were so brief, the aftermath so grim in promise. Swinney wrote cheerfully:

"I expect the week will go mighty fast, but we are going to see all we can before we go back to that infernal hell again. I am feeling fine, in splendid health, and feel just like 'stepping out.' And this will do all of us so much good that we will step into those Huns harder than ever next week."

19

"We Must Strike Harder than Ever"

By the middle of October, German negotiations for an armistice were well advanced. Major Whittlesey (freshly promoted to Lieutenant Colonel), resting with the reserve of the 77th Division in quiet, pleasant forest, on October 15 received a message he was asked to read the men. It reported that the Germans had accepted President Wilson's "Fourteen Points" as conditions for the peace: "When the men heard it, the following morning—a Sunday, as I recall it—you can imagine how rosy life looked under the Greenwood tree!"

Another battalion commander at Grandpre, about to be ordered to attack, reveived the same message with the warning that he must not tell his men. There was to be no slacking of effort while the two sides negotiated. General Pershing on October 17 sent a strong message to the corps and division commanders:

"Not that Germany and the Central Powers are losing, they are begging for an armistice. Their request is an acknowledgement of weakness and clearly means that the Allies are winning the war. That is the best of reasons for our pushing the war more vigorously at this moment. Germany's desire is only to gain time to restore order among her forces, but she must be given no opportunity to recuperate and we must strike harder than ever. Our strong blows are telling and continuous pressure by us has compelled the enemy to meet us, enabling our Allies to gain on other parts of the line. There can be no conclusion to this war until Germany is brought to her knees."

The great offensive blow of October 14–16 had almost achieved this goal. On the first day of the renewed drive, the 32nd Division took the town of Romagne, and captured Cote Dame Marie, which Pershing regarded as "perhaps the most important strong point on the Hindenburg Line." While the 42nd (Rainbow) Division fought through part of the Bois de Romagne, its 84th Brigade under General Douglas MacArthur operated like a vast pincers squeezing the formidable heights of the Cote de Chatillon, which MacArthur looked upon as "the keystone of the whole German position." The 77th Division took St. Juvin and part of Grandpre. The heights had been captured, and the Americans were within heavy artillery range of the German rail system. The price was heavy.

Lieutenant Colonel William J. Donovan of the 165th Infantry, 77th Division, wrote his wife a few days later:

"I wrote you last, did I not, from the Bois de Montfaucon? We were suddenly ordered forward to relieve another Division, the 1st. The same old jumble of troops and camions and trains on the road, only now the roads more slippery and more in need of repair. Our way led past freshly killed and yet unburied Germans, through unmistakable smell of dead horses to a farm in a valley where we parked our wagons and disposed of our men. The farm house had been used as a dressing station for one of the regiments of the other division. Outside was a huge collection of torn and bloody litters, broken salvaged equipment, reddened underclothing and discarded uniforms, all of our own men—the cast off of the dead and wounded. Within, however, was a nice fat Y.M.C.A. man in a suit of blue overalls and a sombrero. He was in attendance at a big cauldron of cocoa while on a stand beside him was bread and, best of all, beef. There could have been no better meal. They then arranged a bed in one of the ambulances into which the Colonel and I crawled. I slept until 6. . . .

"The division preceding us had a terrific fight just three days before and the ground was a stew of dead—Boche and American. One attack had evidently been made in the morning mist and as it cleared an entire company was caught on a little rise. The bodies were laid out in rows. It was easy to determine the formation and the plans of the different leaders. In one hole we found a wounded German who had lain there three days afraid to come out—in another, a wounded German and wounded American who had crawled to the same hole, shared their water and cigarettes, and then, rolling into the German's blanket, had gone to sleep. . . . I then went over the position.

"The support line was in rear of a long ridge running some 3 kilometers. This was the ridge the Germans had held commanding the valley. I went to their machine gun positions. Gun after gun was there with the gunners lying beside them, dead. From these positions I could look back across the valley and then it was easy to see how heavy a toll could be demanded for entrance there. . . . On the other side of the valley were two knolls which were the westerly continuation of the ridge you have read about as the Cote de Chatillon. This was our advanced position. . . .

"Two nights of this and then early on the morning of the 14th we received orders that the attack would be made in the morning. There was a multitude of things to do and the orders coming so late they could not be done properly. The brigade on our right was to advance first, all the guns being concentrated to assist it. Then two hours later all the guns were to concentrate to help us. The party started. I moved to the forward position which they were shelling heavily. I could see no advance on our right. Our hour struck and promptly the leading battalion moved out. The Germans at once put down a heavy barrage and swept the hill we had to climb with indirect machine gun fire. The advance did not go well. There were green company commanders with the companies; liaison was not maintained; the barrage was not followed closely; there was not enough punch. There were times when I had to march at the head of the companies to get them forward. They would follow me. New men need some visible symbol of authority. I could see nothing coming up on our right or left. They were crowding in, the resistance was becoming stronger. The preparation had been hurried, proper instructions had not been sent; officers had been killed or wounded, N.C.O.s the same; vast quantities of new untrained elements. We found our way to within 500 meters of the line. You know the Germans were entrenched with three parallels of wire and a position they proposed holding. The attack as is always the case, finally languished. I sent for another battalion. It was late in arriving and in coming into position. Not until 8 P.M. did I get it across, but it too was beaten back. Orders then came to stabilize for the night. I was in a little shell hole with my telephone operation. For mess I had an onion, which was delicious and raw, and two pieces of hardtack. At 1 A.M. the telephone went out and it was impossible to get in touch with the rear. Patrols were sent out to tie with elements on our right and left. I knew an attack would come in the morning, but I had no orders. I did not know how or where it would be launched, what artillery preparation, nothing. The night passed only too quickly. I sent back for food but the lieutenant with his party never returned. Ammunition came up and then at 6:20 the orders for an attack at 7:30. With such short notice it was impossible to get proper word to all units and to make the best disposition. A heavy mist was hanging. I went around to the men and talked to them. All of this was close to the German line. We had gained two kilometers the first day, the 14th. I should not have been there but remained so because it would have had a bad effect on the men if I had taken position further in rear.

"Tanks were to be near to help us. Zero hour came but no tanks, so we started anyway. I had walked to the different units and was coming back to the telephone when—smash, I felt as if somebody had hit me on the back of the leg with a spiked club. I fell like a log, but after a few minutes managed to crawl into my little telephone hole. A machine gun lieutenant ripped open my breeches and put on the first aid. The leg hurt, but there were many things to be done. The tanks then came along the road but almost immediately turned back either on account of smashed mechanism or wounded drivers. The situation was bad. There was more defense than we thought and the battalion was held up. Messengers I sent through were killed or wounded and messages remained undelivered. We were shelled heavily. Beside me three men were blown up and I was showered with the remains of their bodies. No communication with the rear as the telephone was still out. Gas was then thrown at us, thick and nasty. Five hours passed. I was getting very groggy but managed to get a message through, withdrawing the unit on the line and putting another in place. Then they carried me back in a blanket. I told them to put me down but they said they were willing to take a chance. It was a tough hike. At last the shelter of a hill. I turned things over to the major, turned in a report, and then was taken on my way to the hospital."

On the German side, little was left except hope of survival. Georg Bucher, one of the dwindling few who had been fighting since 1914, a so-called "front-hog," was full of sadness. Most of his comrades were gone, men like Max Gaaten, whom Bucher had saved from a court martial at Sisonne: "With pailfuls of red wine he had fuddled the Saxons guarding a big barn in which *francs-tireurs* [resisting French civilians], sentenced to be shot the next morning, were confined. This he had done so that a pregnant women might escape unobserved, with her two children, into the fire-reddened night." Gaaten and Bucher's other comrades were almost all dead, and boys were filling out the regiments that faced the Americans:

"There were rumors of peace, which were not true, and propaganda which revealed all too truly the terrible condition of the homeland. Ruin stared the army in the face—that army which stood helplessly before a mighty enemy bristling with weapons. . . .

"Silently too we received orders one day, against all our secret hopes, to go up the line; it was all the harder for us since we knew that the end could not be far off. How cautiously we made our way through the communicators! We ducked at the sound of every explosion—which we had never bothered to do before. The old hands sought for the deepest, safest dug-outs and did not scruple to leave to the young recruits the hundred and one things which were risky—digging, repairing, the wire fetching up the rations. Their desire to live cried out against the discipline which, though it had forced them to be the efficient and unquestioning tools of the war-makers, was at last giving way. The thought of an attack was more terrifying to them than to the young soldiers who were still so inexperienced, so touchingly helpless and yet, in spite of everything, so willing. . . .

"Dull, hollow explosions sounded outside. With startled faces we pulled out our gas-masks, fitted them to our faces and replaced our helmets. Then we leapt out into the trench, carrying handgrenades. Tanks had broken through our line on the right of us, although our own sector was still under fire and a mist of gas filled the trench. . . .

"There were no waves of infantry, only those tanks moving rapidly amid a hail of hand-grenades and trench-mortar shells. They were coming straight for our part of the trench. One of them was nearly blown to bits—smoke and flames belched from it. Our trench-mortars had got right on to it—a stout fellow that sergeant-major! If only we had had armor-piercing machine-gun ammunition and tank-defenses!. . .

"It seemed that nothing remained for us but to defend ourselves till we were killed or captured. The first waves of the attacking infantry were already moving through the rotting corn. We did not stop to fire at them, for suddenly there was a wild stampede leftwards along the trench—there, where we were still not entirely cut off, was our only hope of escape. We jumped up out of the trench—it was no longer of use to us—

and began to fire from the ground behind it. Enemy aeroplanes were flying over the anti-tank guns and artillery positions, their machine-guns mowing down the crews and the troops who were hurrying forward to counter-attack. The guns mounted in the tanks were still blazing away furiously and, to add to our terrors, we saw that the infantry had almost reached our abandoned trench.

"That however saved us. Gasping for breath, we tore off our masks, for the gas was no longer hanging about above ground. Some machine-guns in concrete emplacements were behind us and their fire kept the enemy from emerging from the trench while we worked our way leftwards, running from shell-hole to shell-hole. There was just a chance that we should get away.

"About forty of us were left. The little artillery officer and the trench-mortar sergeant-major, who were still some distance to our right, surrendered with some twenty men to one of the tanks. The officer, sergeant-major and five or six others were shot down—the poor devils were in the cross-fire between friend and foe. The other flung themselves on the found and bellowed for mercy. I saw that they were allowed to go back into the trench—and into captivity. They were lucky!

"We rushed from shell-hole to shell-hole. The wildness of the enemy fire must have been our salvation."

Field Marshal von Hindenburg gradually committed more and more of his troops to the American sectors, from an original 16 divisions to some 34 by the end of October. But the American armies grew even more rapidly. Hindenburg later confessed, "The pressure which the fresh American masses were putting upon our most sensitive point in the region of the Meuse was too strong."

To keep up the pressure, the American commanders continued to rush inexperienced troops into the front lines wherever they were needed, and rested the seasoned regiments for further combat. Supply lines were taxed to the utmost, and transportation continued to be a nightmare. Once when ammunition was running short, trucks, and wagons were lacking, and the transportation jam was too acute in any event, a regiment moving toward the front was sent back twelve miles to a dump. Every man was then marched forward lugging a shell on his shoulder.

As for traffic jams, Corporal Andrew Crosby of the 148th Field Artillery wrote his aunt:

"At such times it is wonderful what a shell in the immediate vicinity will do to stimulate traffic. There are times, tho, when a truck breaks down completely. If this is on a narrow, one-way road, it is no time at all until the road will be crowded with trucks for miles back. Nice situation when there is a Fritz balloon observing proceedings. Then the M.P. gets busy. M.P. is a cross between a speed cop (here they howl if you are not going fast enuf), a traffic cop, justice of the peace, interpreter and sheep herder. Usually he has the vocabulary of an army mule skinner. He proceeds to call for volunteers from the road workers. These are always willing to quit the job of making little [rocks] out of big ones to give him a hand. They push the offending truck to the roadside. If there is not room they lift one side up and tip it up off the road. You ought to hear the Frogs howl when their pet truck . . . is tipped over with four wheels spinning idly in the breeze. But it is the war, and things must go onward."

As men and supplies arrived at the front, the American command laid plans to participate in one last great offensive against the Germans to begin on November 1. Marshal Foch wanted the Allied armies to attack the reeling Germans relentlessly all along the front. The American objective remained, as it had been, to cut the railway line running through Sedan. Further, they hoped to capture that famous fortress city itself, which had been the key to the German victory in the Franco-Prussian War.

At the outset the fighting was again ferocious. Private Shanahan of the 311th Infantry wrote home describing the start of the offensive from near Grandpre:

"We were in a valley at the foot of the last wooden hill of the famous Argonne Woods. Here on the last hill the Germans placed their all. Dotted here and there, every few yards, were machine guns; also many machine-gun snipers located in the trees along the ridge of this hill. We had remained here for eight days, and during that time I was obliged to work both day and night. During first four days or ninety-six hours I had but five hours' sleep. This is almost unbelievable. During the day we helped carry the wounded to the first aid, also ammunition and what food we could procure, and during the night stood guard or sentry duty, holding the lines with the Germans within hearing distance. We held these lines until it was our turn to go over the top again.

"Well, to make it short, we were tired out the morning of our last trip, which I believe was the worst in the present war. We were called together at the foot of the hill at 1:00 A.M. and were told by our officers we would hear within two hours of the greatest barrage in history, which was in progress along the entire front. The barrage started at 3:00 A.M. and lasted for many hours. During the barrage we made preparations for our last trip over the top. We filled our canteens with muddy water and were glad to find this water; shell-holes which collect the rain are the means of our drinking water at times. We also greased our bodies for protection, or rather relief, from mustard gas, as we expected much gas, having a tough section of the front. . . . For a stretch of many miles in back of this last hill was nothing but smooth plains or farm land of beautiful Alsace-Lorraine. We had, as we expected, our toughest battle, the Germans had their machine guns lined up everywhere; we began at 5:00 A.M. and fought until 6:00 P.M. We shot many shells at them and my rifle was hot from the heat of the continual fire. . . . After driving the greater part of the Germans a few hundred yards away and killing the most of them it was about 6 o'clock, or dark. We established ourselves on the spot and jumped into the dug-outs the Germans occupied but an hour ago, and there, with our own dead lads and very many Germans lying about, was our temporary line. We threw hand grenade at the Germans and blew up many of their machine guns. We started after them again the next morning and found—they had 'flown the coop.'"

At some points the Americans had shattered the German lines; the V Corps, in the center, advanced five miles. The

Germans had no choice but to retreat along the entire American battle line, even though this in turn required rapid withdrawal along the lines to the north in Belgium. And although the Germans fought skillful rear-guard actions, the race toward Sedan continued day after day. By November 4, the German Army was badly disorganized, and General Pershing was hopeful both of destroying parts of it and driving into the German mining and industrial area of Briey and Longwy. He began to covet the prize of Sedan even though it lay in the prescribed path of the French. The French command seemed agreeable to Pershing's suggestion that the boundary line between the American and French Armies should be ignored and that the Americans might cross northwest beyond their agreed limits if they outran the French. On November 5 an order was issued:

"1. General Pershing desires that the honor of entering Sedan should fall to the American First Army. He has every confidence that the troops of the I Corps, assisted on their right by the V Corps, will enable him to realize this desire.

"2. In transmitting the foregoing message, your attention is invited to the favorable opportunity now existing for pressing our advance throughout the night. Boundaries will not be considered binding."

The result was not what Pershing has envisaged; he had expected boundaries not to be binding only between the French and American Armies. The 1st Division of the V Corps, in the center, cut sharply left in front of the 42nd (Rainbow) Division of the I Corps. General Douglas MacArthur of the Rainbow Division went forward, fearing Americans might fire on Americans, and was halted by a suspicious 1st Division patrol. Its leader, encountering this commanding figure in his soft garrison cap and muffler, feared he was a German officer and put him under arrest. No casualties ensued, but a great snarl, as the two American divisions raced left across the path of the advancing French 40th Division, and by November 7 reached the heights commanding Sedan. Thereupon, the French warned that they might have to bombard Sedan even if the Americans were in their path. The Americans halted their advance and the

French could not catch up in time for either ally to harvest the glory of capturing Sedan—the stronghold where France had been humiliated in the Franco-Prussian War. But the Americans on the heights achieved the essential goal; they effectively cut the German rail lines by bringing them within range even of their machine guns. Germany had no alternative but to accept Allied armistice terms, stringent though they were.

20

ON FAR-OFF FRONTS

More than a few soldiers, enlisting to fight the Germans on the Western Front, found themselves shipped to far-off places where their activities seemed to have little to do with the great offensives and counteroffensives of 1918. There was the token force in Italy, expeditionary forces to Russia and Siberia, which stayed—and fought—long after the Armistice, and even a few men who found themselves in Cuba or Haiti.

Some of these men were philosophical about the strange turn the war took for them. U. W. Showalter wrote from Cap Haitien, April 1, 1919, "We are having a taste of real warfare down here until the Cacos are cleaned out." But Private Lionel P. Atwood, writing from Santo Domingo in the summer of 1919, spoke for many a soldier stranded from the Caribbean to Siberia:

"For the most part we are 'duration-of-the-war' men who left good homes and good jobs to fight for a great cause. We left willingly because the cause was worth the sacrifice many times over. But against our will and choice we were literally shang-haied down here to partake in a work which not only was dis-agreeable to us, but not, in our opinion, worth the price which we have had to pay, i.e., dependent parents and families at home and promising careers. This job may be necessary, that is not for us to say, but it should be handled by men who enlist in the Marine Corps for a living and not an emergency. . . .

"We still believe in the American people, the old American democracy founded on justice to all, and we are writing this with the hope that our democracy may know of our plight. With this knowledge assured, we feel confident that something will be done to effect our return to the States."

In time these men did come home, filled with a sense of grievance.

Quite different was the experience of the handful of soldiers sent to Italy. Because of the extreme need for troops on the Western Front in the spring and summer of 1918, only one reg-iment, the 322nd Infantry, arrived at the Italian front. Its mis-sion was to build the morale of the Italians and dismay the Austrians, by giving the appearance of being several regiments. Stationed in October 1918 at Treviso near the front on the Piave River, its battalions would set out conspicuously morning after morning on different roads, wearing different uniforms and equipment. After nightfall, each battalion would slip back into Treviso as quietly as possible.

The kind of ruse was scarcely necessary, since the Austrians were weak. On October 24, the Italian opened the Vittorio-Veneto drive, and the Austrians retreated so speedily that the most difficult task the 332nd Infantry faced was to try to catch up with them. After hard marching, on November 3, the regiment attacked the Austrian rear guard defending a bridgehead on the Tagliamento River near Ponte della Delizia. Crossing on a foot-bridge, they took the Austrian position, and pushed on to Codroipo, where they captured large quantities of supplies. There the Austrian Armistice of November 4 at 3:00 P.M. ended their fighting. They had lost only one man killed and seven wounded.

In addition to the Infantry, 54 bomber pilots participated in attacking the Austrians. Perhaps most useful to the Italian Army were 135 Americans rushed to Italy in December 1917 to man American Red Cross ambulances serving with the Italian Army. One of these drivers, severely wounded by shrapnel, was Ernest Hemingway, who later described the Italian rout at Caporetto in *A Farewell to Arms.*

Numerous visiting Americans turned up along the quiet lines in Italy during the summer of 1918, among them Samuel Gompers, President of the American Federation of Labor, and Representative Alben Barkley of Kentucky. Barkley was one of a delegation of six congressmen who on September 6, 1918, visited the front lines and later dined with the King. He wrote in his diary:

"We then returned to Pavia, washed up and were taken several miles out to the villa occupied by the King, Victor Emmanuel III, who had invited our party to dinner. . . . He was dressed in the uniform of an Italian General, was quite democratic in his bearing. He shook hands all around and then we were seated and engaged in conversation chiefly concerning the war. The King showed himself well informed, as well as frank. . . . Soon dinner was announced, we all went to the dining room, where I was seated to the King's left, Jas. Aswell to his right. The meal was well served, but simple such as might be found on the table of any well to do family. . . . He is a man of small stature, being but little over 5 ft. high. He talked freely of the war, and said his country needed 30 to 35 divisions of allied troops in order to be justified in making an offensive against the Austrians."

The next month proved King Victor Emmanuel to have been too pessimistic. For Navy and Army men landing in northern Russia in the summer and early fall of 1918, there was neither optimism nor pessimism—only confusion. Yet the reasons for being there had been presented to President Wilson by the British in compelling fashion. There was the need for a second front against the Germans to take the pressure off the Western Front. Secondarily, the large Allied stores of supplies at Murmansk and Archangel must be guarded from the Germans, who were threatening to thrust through Finland to seize them. Finally, the Allies wished to block German plans to establish a submarine base in the area.

At the beginning of August, the Allies seized both ports and chased the Bolsheviks south. Participating under British command were sailors from the U.S.S. *Olympia* (Admiral Dewey's flagship during the Spanish-American War) who found themselves stranded and fighting far inland in Russia. J. Sam Perry, who participated in these initial exploits, wrote home:

"I had been doing everything from convoy duty on destroyers to and from England and France to land duty in Russia around Archangel and Kola with British marines before arrival of American soldiers in that sector. There were 100 sailors from the Olympia and a handful of B[ritish] R[oyal] M[arines] but we took our objective with comparatively small losses; only two killed and three wounded, though the other 95 got surrounded and nearly starved awaiting ammunition and then it didn't come so we marched about 80 miles through the swamps of Dvina River where we secured it and turned on the Bolsheviks. Had it not been for a seaman by the name of Hardaway from Montgomery [Alabama] who rode barebacked a horse for 40 miles, attempted to hire another, failed, took it by force and rode another 40 miles along the enemy flank and gave notice of our close pressure we might all have swung from tree tops there in cold Russia as some of our comrades did. Hardaway was decorated by the British government with the D.S.O."

Through the almost interminable Arctic winter of 1918–1919, the Americans manned outposts along a 450-mile front, at times engaging in sharp fighting. They suffered some four hundred casualties. Yet for most of the men, Russian duty was simply dull and meaningless. On April 11, 1919, Corporal Herman Waldhart wrote his mother:

"I thought I would answer your most welcome letter, which I received yesterday, and which I was certainly glad to get. I am feeling fine and hope this will find you the same. This is the first mail I have received since last November, so you can imagine how happy it made me feel to get a letter.

"I have pulled through all the battles that I have been in without injury, and am not feeling any the worse. The weather here has been pretty cold, but it is warming up some now. I am out in the wilderness on a post station and don't have very much to do. . . .

"I don't know for certain when we are going to get out of here, but I surely hope it will be soon."

The Armistice in November 1918 had brought an end to the military reasons for the occupation of northern Russia, and the United States did not want to be dragged into a war against the Communists. Nevertheless, 40 Americans were killed before, at the beginning of August 1919, the American force operating out of Archangel officially ended its operations.

To the soldiers involved, the Siberian adventure was no less confused, but was larger, and was far more significant in its purport. Ten thousand Americans participated, beginning in August 1918. The announced reasons were to guard military stores, to aid former Czech prisoners of the Russians who wanted to fight the Central Powers, and to stabilize the area around Vladivostok. The factor about which no one talked was the presence of 73,000 Japanese troops in eastern Siberia. If they continued to occupy the area indefinitely, they would by their presence close off Manchuria from American business interests and upset the power balance in East Asia.

Even Secretary of War Newton D. Baker did not seem to recognize this large purport to the Siberian expedition. He later confessed, "Siberia was like Sergeant Grischa, who had no conception of what it was all about but knew that the once orderly world was in a state of complete and baffling disorder."

Confusing though the intervention was to the Army, it followed orders from Washington. Although other commanders in Vladivostok, especially the British, were openly hostile toward the Bolsheviks, the American officer in charge, General William S. Graves, kept his forces strictly neutral among the contending factions in the great Russian civil war. General Graves was appalled by the atrocities and cruelties committed by the contenders. United States soldiers did not attack Bolsheviks in

Siberia, but did fight vigorously when the Bolsheviks tired to capture section of the Trans-Siberian Railroad they were guarding.

Americans in Vladivostok, like the Secretary of War, were
baffled, but not especially troubled. T. P. Ferguson of the U.S.S.
Brooklyn wrote in September 1918:

"Vladivostok is said to be in better condition than any other
Russian city, and conditions are bad enough there. There is
enough food and enough of everything in Russia but no adequate transportation or government to get it where it is needed.
You would be surprised at some of the methods they have for
transportation and it is so large and rich a country. They are
finding themselves and our army is welcome among them and is
doing some good work from all reports. The army railway service is going to help perhaps as much as anything in bringing
about the desired results."

Earl Thompson, in the Army medical corps, took a sight-
seer's interest in Siberia in October 1918:

"I was on guard yesterday, guarding an old Russian church.
They have several churches around here and some of them are
wonderful buildings. . . .

"As we go along the country roads the little Russian children
run out to see us. Some of them have learned to say hello, and
others to salute us. It doesn't take them long for them to pick up
little things like that. If we have anything to eat we divide with
them, so they are always watching for us. Things are high here,
that is everything except peanuts and street car rides."

For those in the Red Cross, there was serious and meaning-
ful work to be undertaken, sending supplies and medical aid
along the five-thousand-mile track of the Trans-Siberian
Railroad. The Allied troops and White Russian forces under
Admiral Kolchak kept the lines more or less open. An anti-
typhus train operating between Vladivostok and Perm in the
Ural Mountains bathed over a hundred thousand people, disin-
fected their clothing, and gave them new clothing.

What the Americans saw of the Russians, engaged in bitter
civil war, was not encouraging. Earl Thompson wrote at the end
of the first winter in Siberia:

"I wish some of the rank socialists at home could be here and live under conditions which now exist where socialism and Bolshevism have been in power. I believe they would soon get some of their wild ideas out of their heads. The socialists here believe that all factories should be turned over and divided up among the laborers, and all the hotels should be turned over to the servants to do as they see fit. Can you imagine what kind of mixup would follow in a country where most laboring classes cannot read or write?

"I do not think people in the states realize what a serious thing it would be for the whole world if the Bolshevists gain power here in Russia."

Gradually the Bolshevists did establish their power, and on April 1, 1920, the American expedition in Siberia came to an end.

21

THE ARMISTICE

At eleven o'clock, everything got so quiet that the silence was nearly unbearable," A. R. Sunde of the 89th Division wrote his friends. "We were wet and cold, hungry and tired and after the company had assembled to give thanks to our Creator for the wonderful quiet that reigned, we were allowed to build fires and could remove our shoes and stockings and dry them out and get warm. . . . It sure did seem strange. That night it was actually so quiet that I could not sleep until late in the morning, tired as I was, and I laid around the fire we had built until I finally dozed off for a few hours."

One soldier thus celebrated the Armistice on November 11, 1918, and among the infinite reactions and modes of celebration, his was as close as any to being typical.

General Pershing, viewing an Armistice as considerably less satisfactory than total victory, on October 30 presented his recommendations to the Allied Supreme War Council:

"Judging by their excellent conduct during the past three months, the British, French, Belgian and American Armies appear capable of continuing the offensive indefinitely. Their morale is high and the prospects of certain victory should keep it so. . . .

"German manpower is constantly diminishing and her armies have lost over 300,000 prisoners and over one-third of their artillery during the past three months in their effort to extricate themselves from a difficult situation and avoid disaster.
. . .

"Germany's morale is undoubtedly low, her Allies have deserted her one by one and she can no longer hope to win. Therefore we should take full advantage of the situation and continue the offensive until we compel her unconditional surrender."

If the Allies did nevertheless decide to grant an armistice, a temporary cessation of hostilities, Pershing proposed that "the terms should be so rigid that under no circumstances could Germany again take up arms." This in the end is what was done. The Allies drew up stringent military and naval terms that would make it impossible for Germany to resume the war, but labeled them "Armistice" rather than "Unconditional Surrender." Pershing thought then and later that the German Army was so badly beaten that it would have no choice except to surrender. He deplored the fact that the Armistice permitted Hindenburg and the High Command to march their men home with flags flying and to blame the defeat upon the betrayal of politicians rather than the collapse at the front. Pershing's views had weight in determining American policy during the Second World War.

On the afternoon of November 7, civilian German delegates crossed the Allied lines and opened negotiations with Marshal Foch, meeting in two railway coaches on a siding in the forest between Compiegne and Soissons. The radio message from the German government authorizing signature did not come until 11:00 on the night of November 10; it was 5:00 on the morning of November 11 before rough terms could be drafted. In order to end the carnage as soon as possible, the last page of the Armistice document was written first and signed a few minutes after 5:00. The end of hostilities was set for 11:00—as quickly as word could be sent to all the forces.

Before the word could arrive, many an American attacking party along the Meuse and St. Mihiel fronts was about its grim business, sustaining serious casualties in some instances. Lieutenant Francis Reed Austin of the 28th Division earlier had been notable for his chivalric actions during the fighting. On the morning of November 11, at Haumont beyond St. Mihiel, Lieutenant Austin won a Distinguished Service Cross, and lost his life. The citation read:

"Lieut. Francis Reed Austin led a platoon of machine guns and two one-pounders with their crews under cover of a fog within the enemy's lines and attacked at close range a strong point held by 25 men and 10 machine guns.

"After this position had been reduced, concentrated machine-gun fire from the flanks forced Lieut. Austin and his party to withdraw. Exposing himself in order to place his men under cover, Lieut. Austin was mortally wounded but he directed the dressing of the wounds of his men and their evacuation before he would accept aid for himself."

Too, there were commanders who out of fighting zeal, rigidity, or perhaps their love of glory, ordered their troops to proceed with planned attacks, even though clearly the preliminary warning that the Armistice was to take place at 11:00 had been intended to save lives, not signal a final bloodbath. Frank P. Sibley, correspondent at the Headquarters of the 26th (Yankee) Division, to which General Pershing had recently sent a new "driving" commanding officer, reported:

"At Division Headquarters men met, shook hands, smiled in infinite satisfaction, and hurried on about the business which the new state of affairs bought in its train. . . .

"Things began to happen swiftly. First came the order for the artillery preparation, already thundering away in the north, to continue to the moment of the cessation of hostilities, but for the infantry not to advance. Then on the heels of that order came another,—that the infantry would advance until 11 o'clock.

"The Yankees' line was concave and it was the desire of the commanding officer and the Corps to straighten out that concavity, therefore the worn-out doughboys must make one final effort."

At least one battalion commander exercised realism in carrying out these orders. Major Sherman Shumway's first orders, reaching him at three in the morning, had been to advance; he marched the companies, hungry and cold, three miles to the jumping-off point in Wavrille Wood. Before they could attack, the order came not to advance, so the men waited, and happily the revised order to advance until 11 o'clock did not arrive until 10:40. "By the time this too had been relayed to the company commanders," reported Sibley, "there was not much time left. The battalion advanced across a sloping field and into the lee of the embankment of the road. There, just at eleven, it stopped."

Another officer with the 26th (Yankee) Division was less fortunate. Lieutenant Harry G. Rennagel of the 101st Infantry wrote his family:

"I left the hospital November 10th, reaching my outfit about ten o'clock the next morning, the fatal one; we were all talking, laughing and waiting for the gong to ring when orders came to go over the top. We thought it a joke—it was a grim one of Fate's, for we jumped off at 25 minutes to 11 and advanced but very slowly for we knew that there were many machine gun nests ahead of us. At 10:55 a minenwerfer fell among my men and I was told one wanted to see me. I hurried over and there lay five of my best men. One fatally injured, hole near heart, two seriously injured and the other two badly hurt. We took care of the injured men and then I knelt beside the lad whose eyes had such a look of sorrow that my eyes filled with tears.

" 'What is it old man,' I asked.

" 'Lieutenant, I'm going fast. Don't say I'll get better, you know different and this is a pretty unhappy time for me. You know we all expected things to cease to-day, so I wrote my girl, we were to be married when I returned, and my folks that I was

safe and well and about my plans, and now—by some order I
am not going home.'

"A glance at my watch, 11:05. I looked away and when I
looked back—he had gone . . . I can honestly tell you I cried
and so did the rest."

For most men at the front it was a morning of incredulity—
there had been so many false rumors of peace. The 168th
Infantry was marching to Briquenay, and at 10:50 had fallen out
for a ten-minute rest, wrote John H. Taber:

"A staff captain riding past in a limousine leaned out and
called excitedly, 'The Boches have signed an armistice. The war
ends at eleven.' Did he think we were a lot of greenhorns? An
armistice, with the guns briskly booming up front, while above
the two airplanes were maneuvering for position and rattling
away at each other! That was a good one. Ha ha!

"At eleven o'clock the regiment was put on its feet . . . and
started on the way again. 'I reckon as how Big Bertha kinda
called that captain a liar,' sang out a lad near the head of the column as a distant boom came back on the breeze. A bit later
someone else remarked that it was getting mighty quiet up
front. There wasn't a sound. Nothing but the steady tramp,
tramp of heavily shod feet."

And it was a morning of intermittently intense bombardment as every artilleryman on each side seemed to be trying to
shoot every remaining shell in his possession. "But there
seemed to be little hate in that morning's barrage," wrote
Sibley. "The guns weren't pointed anywhere in particular; they
were just headed in the general direction of Germany and
turned loose as fast as they could be fired." Everyone wanted to
fire the last shot:

"In one battery each man took a shell and waited in line for
his turn to fire the gun. In another battery, five officers took
hold of the lanyard, and all fired the last shot together. In still
another a long rope was made fast to the lanyard of each of
the four guns. Some two hundred men got hands on each
rope, and one man, with a watch, went out forward. At the
hour he dropped a handkerchief." Eight hundred men tugged

on the ropes; eight hundred could claim they had fired the momentous shot.

Lieutenant Walter A Davenport described the spectacle on the St. Mihiel sector:

"About 9:30 A.M. on November 11th, the Germans must have gotten word that the Armistice had been signed. We were dug in the mud of the Bois de Domartin. . . . Every Boche gun between Dommartin and Metz inclusive opened up on us. My God, how they strafed us. Everything from minenwerfers to 210's descended upon those woods. The soft ground billowed like the ocean. But we were dug in and the forest is very heavy, and our casualties were very, very small.

"And our artillery came back at them.

"From 10 o'clock to 11—the hour for the cessation of hostilities—the opposing batteries simply raised hell. Not even the artillery prelude to our advance into the Argonne had anything on it. To attempt an advance was out of the question. It was not a barrage. It was a deluge.

"All along our front the earth was flying skyward geyser-like. And above us roared about 50 Allied planes watching the effect of our shots. . . .

"We had synchronized our watches. On my right flank I had eight machine guns. They had kept up a constant stream of fire during the artillery riot. About 10:45 A.M. the boys with the Chauchats, and the ordinary Springfields, and Enfields had joined in just that they might be in the party. I do not know how many thousand tons of steel, copper, cupro-nickel, and lead were poured into, over and upon Jerry, but it was fearful to see.

"Nothing quite so electrical in effect as the sudden stop that came at 11 A.M. has ever occurred to me. It was 10:60 precisely and—the roar stopped like a motor car hitting a wall. The resulting quiet was uncanny in comparison. From somewhere far below the ground, Germans began to appear. They clambered to the parapets and began to shout wildly. They threw their rifles, hats, bandoleers, bayonets and trench knives toward us. They began to sing. Came one bewhiskered Hun with a concertina and he began goose stepping along the parados followed in close file by fifty others—all goose stepping.

"Our lads stood up watching the show. We had quite a time watching them lest they take pot shots at the concertina player. One of my snipers begged the chance to 'slip a cold one' into a Boche who stood 'at ease' all alone leaning on his rifle.

"We kept the boys under restraint as long as we could. Finally the strain was too great. A big Yank named Carter ran out into No Man's Land and planted the Stars and Stripes on a signal pole in the lip of a shell hole. Keasby, a bugler, got out in front and began playing 'The Star Spangled Banner' on a German trumpet he'd found in Thiaucourt. And they sang— Gee how they sang!"

That night, the lights went back on everywhere, Lieutenant Frederick F. Sullivan of the 28th Division wrote his wife:

"Both sides were getting rid of their night illumination paraphernalia, flares and verey lights, rocket signals, etc., and the whole front was blazing like a grand Fourth of July celebration.

"Lights could be seen in all the towns, fires were blazing in every place, in fact, the whole of France which had been darkened at night in fear of air attacks was blazing forth into light. I imagine Paris, after four years of darkness, blazing forth with arc lights, electric signs, etc. It must have been wonderful."

For the fortunate Americans who were in Paris on Armistice Day it was indeed wonderful. A corporal in the Air Force, Willis Burdick, wrote his parents:

"I have vivid recollections of wild pandemonium, seething crowds, of deafening din, shouting men and women, of a waving sea of multicolored flags, of songs, of national hymns sung with tremendous volume and fervor; of Americans embracing French, of French English . . . ; of loaded automobile-trucks pushing through the densely populated boulevards, the occupants acclaimed with cheers by those on foot, of continual processions from one end of an avenue to another; of flag bedecked government buildings and private homes; of salvoes from salute cannon all over the city; of military bands filling the air with martial music; of brilliantly illuminated streets at night."

Company M, 6th Regiment, celebrating at Remoiville

On guard in the funk holes, Gibercy, November 12, 1918

Colonel Stephen Bonsal, who was soon to be President Wilson's interpreter at the peace conference, came upon one sober face in the celebrating throng, that of an Italian journalist he respected. "Yes," said the journalist, "we have armistice; the formidable hour has struck."

That did not become apparent until later. Most of the fighting men were too dazed that day either to celebrate especially or to worry much abou the future. "Of course the fellows had a smile on their faces but there was not any rejoicing to amount to anything," wrote Sergeant Elmer F. Straub. Soon after the arrival of the 168th Infantry in Briquenay, wrote Taber:

"From the steps of the shell-torn church Chaplain [Winfred E.] Robb announced that the war was over. It really was beyond comprehension, this glorious news—too much to grasp all at once. No more whizz-bangs, no more bombs, no more mangled, bleeding bodies, no more exposure to terrifying shell fire in the rain and cold and mud! It would be difficult to adjust the mind to the new state of things.

"Now the band, silent for weeks, and out of practice—for at the front where silence was something more than golden, there wasn't much opportunity for practice—got out its instruments and blared forth 'Over There.' 'We won't come back till it's over, over there' didn't seem like an empty boast any longer. The long fight had been won, and now we would see our homes once more."

22

THE WEARY ROAD HOME

By the morning of November 12, 1918, the American soldiers had grasped the reality of the Armistice and began to wonder how soon they could go home. Few had any illusions but that the road home would be long and weary, and so it was for most of them. Although the return movement of troops began quickly and accelerated at a phenomenal speed, time dragged and irritations multiplied. The months after the Armistice were sour ones from the Rhine to Brest; vicissitudes cheerfully accepted in the trenches continued, and because they were unnecessary galled. Bitterness and disillusion grew and swelled over into the postwar years. And yet for these basically healthy, optimistic young men there was some fun and adventure in the war's aftermath.

One of the engineers, Lieutenant Watson Avery, wrote his father on November 14:

"We are building a road across what was No Man's Land last Monday morning. It is a very wonderful feeling to walk about in perfect security and work in daylight without precaution on land that so recently was disputed territory. We will have a road open to the German outpost line by tomorrow night.

"I have no idea what we will do, where we will go, or most important of all how long we will be on this side of the pond. We know of course that there is to be an army of occupation in Germany but whether or not we will be part of it we do not know; are simply assuming that that is a good guess in view of the fact that we are on the line at present. In any event now that the thing is over I am exceedingly anxious to get home and the sooner the better it will suit me. I joined the army to fight, not to be a policeman."

Some of the front-line troops remained at the Armistice line for some days, some returned at once to the training areas, and others after a specified period moved into the American occupation zone in the Rhineland. For their commanders it was a nervous, difficult time, since for some days they tried, on the one hand, to rush demobilization, and on the other, to maintain the wherewithal to resume combat if Germany did not renew the Armistice at stated intervals. After the first month it was clear that Germany could not possibly resist further, and tension decreased.

For most of the men at the front, the two weeks immediately after the Armistice brought long, punishing marches of one hundred to even two hundred miles in shoes so worn out that most of the soldiers suffered from raw, bleeding feet. Private William H. Straney of the 353rd Infantry cheerfully commented: "We could have enjoyed this trip much more if we had been traveling by some other means, although hiking beat dodging bullets, G.I. cans and whiz bangs, and laying out in a hole in the ground in the mud and water."

That was about all that could be said for these forced marches. John H. Taber later described the vicissitudes of the 168th Infantry:

"Although accustomed to outdoor life and its discomforts, even those hardened veterans were beginning to succumb to the rigors of the winter. . . . Those who remained were clad in old and tattered uniforms, their shoes were virtually a thing of memory, and the ration at this stage was nothing to boast of. In fact, they lacked everything but a heavy load of useless ammunition. . . .

"Early on the morning of the 16th of November the regiment formed up for its move beyond the Meuse. . . . Just as the column passed over the pontoon bridge erected by American engineers to replace the German-mined stone structure spanning the Meuse at Dun, it was met by four men of the 166th Infantry who had been captured six weeks before. These were the first repatriated prisoners to pass through our lines, but a short distance farther on we were greeted by a contingent of French, Russian, and Italian prisoners, unkempt, half-starved, haggard, but happy. Some of them had been walking for three days without a bite to eat."

During the next few weeks, the American Red Cross brought back a number of American prisoners. One of them, Corporal Paul Thompson of the 5th Marines, who had been wounded and captured October 2, wrote home on December 12 describing his experiences as a prisoner:

"I rode in a German Red Cross ambulance for about six hours to another field hospital where I stayed three weeks in dwelling houses with old wooden cots which had paper-cloth mattress covers filled with wood shavings. We had old blankets that never had been fumigated I don't believe, consequently they were very lively with little animals. . . . We got the same food as the Germans, three slices of dark bread with a cheap butter or jam, and a coffee made from parched barley or wheat and always barley soup at noon."

As for the troops marching toward the Rhineland, on November 17 at 5:30 A.M. they crossed the Armistice line on their way. As they passed through previously German-occupied towns of France and Belgium, and crossed Luxemburg, they enjoyed for the first time some of the delights of victory. Irving Curtis wrote:

"In Belgium we were warmly welcomed in a way such as you would expect from such a noble little country. Little children would run out with cries, 'Vive la Americaine,' etc., and the village and town streets were decorated with many flags of the Allies. They did not have many flags of America, so, many of these were made with their own hands. Many were of amusing shapes with varying stripes, and stars of various shapes pinned on."

The greeting was no less warm in Luxembourg, A. R. Sunde wrote friends:

"In Luxemburg, the buildings were decorated with their own flag, and in one or two towns other decorations had been made, but nothing like Belgium. The people seemed very friendly and treated us real nice in the places where we were billeted, which was mostly in private homes. They even served us lunch of some kind and hot coffee from barley shortly after we were billeted."

The reception the Americans received in Germany was far more pleasant than they expected. "There were no triumphal arches at the new stations, but no display of ill feeling either," wrote Taber. "The men marched in, took the billets allotted them, and settled down for the night with the usual calmness." Some villages even received the Americans with apparent enthusiasm. Sergeant William Argall remembered a few months later:

"I'll never forget the morning we marched into that German town. . . . We expected the Germans to treat us with scorn and be utterly indifferent and even nasty with us but we surely got the surprise of our lives, when as we marched through the main street of the town we were greeted by the entire populace. Evidently they knew we were coming for the German girls marched ahead of us and strewed our path with wreaths of flowers of every description."

A Wyoming private declared:

"And say! Talk about receptions, those Germans simply couldn't do enough for us. They took us into their homes and we were wined and dined like kings. The Germans took to us like a duck to water and naturally we were all skeptical—didn't know what to make of it, and many of us became suspicious and began to steer shy. They the Germans would become all the more attentive. . . . We were billeted in their homes, two men being assigned to a residence. We got the best beds and the best eats. The old folks would even go without things to give us the best of it." Fraternizing was forbidden, but nevertheless, the Americans saw much of the Germans and got along surprisingly well.

Those Germans who did not cooperate were forced to do so. One young sergeant who looked like the Kaiser, running into trouble where he was billeted, smashed the picture of the Kaiser on the wall, substituted his own, and forced the occupants to salute it. Difficulties of this sort seem to have been the exception, but some friction was inevitable. A. F. Tingle of the 355th Infantry wrote realistically to a friend:

"After several weeks stringent orders became effective and civilian offenders faced arrest. Every soldier must be provided with a bed, even if male inhabitants from 12 to 60 years be required to sleep on the floor. Dissatisfaction and grumbling came from many. Our association with civilians was then forbidden. This was not pleasant to Germans, and some angry editor published in his paper that if women were seen talking to Americans they must suffer the loss of their hair.

"Even now there are great numbers in this country who are glad of the opportunity to favor or speak to us, which shows that certain classes only are hostile. There is scarcely a family who has not some one in the U.S.A., and so invariably asks: 'Do you know Hans so-and-so, in New York, Chicago, or St. Louis?' "

How genuine was the German cordiality? Even at the time, most of the soldiers were suspicious, but the feelings of their involuntary hosts seem to have ranged widely. Sergeant Elmer F. Straub, who spoke German, recorded a number of conversations in his diary. Most of those to whom he talked who had fought in the war were proud of their service, yet not hostile toward Americans. This was true of even one choleric sergeant with whom he was billeted on December 6:

"I asked him if he was not glad that the war was over, and he immediately turned around and looked me over and then said in a very stern tone 'NO'. Dick and the boys saw from the beginning that he was a little radical and when he got 'peeved' at the question I asked him they all wanted to know what he said but I was afraid they would start something and I would not tell them. They all walked over and got close to their guns while I happened to be wearing mine. The old boy was certainly bitter not so much against the Americans but bitter that they had lost the war, he said, 'four times have I gone forward with my company and never did I taste defeat, and then to have the Germans give up at this stage. No, I wish that they were still fighting.' "

Even those who continued suspicious of the Germans found it difficult to dislike their children. The fierce German sergeant had a "little girl . . . only about three or four, if that old with pretty white curls down her back." And Captain Arthur Hyde wrote his sister:

"It is next to impossible for me to scowl at the timid, pretty German children with their round eyes and yellow hair and shy 'Gute Tag's,' or to act haughty to the deferential grown-ups as they cringingly lift their hats as I pass."

The new enemies of the American troops were the stiffening army regulations, the continued training and maneuvering (with live ammunition), boredom, restlessness, and the growing desire to go home. There was plenty to drink, lots of dances (with a few Y.M.C.A. girls and no Frauleins), and Y.M.C.A. excursions up the Rhine. One lucky soldier even got to Berlin, and returned boasting he had written his name on the Kaiser's palace. These diversions did not suffice. Sergeant Aksel Olson wrote home:

"I trust we get back before this d__monotony, and consequent depression of spirits incident to the act of occupying Germany, get the best of us. I hate this life with all that is in me. There is nothing here to live for that I can see. While at war there was everything to live for, everything to die for—death, real death, is a part of right living—but now there is nothing here worth dying for, nothing to inspire living. Our job is ended and everyone wishes to go home. . . .

"I imagine that many people are envying us the privilege of being here, but, like most other things, it loses its romance when subject to close study; and, man! There is nothing in this world like old U.S.A. That is a lesson learned over and again by the soldiers in Europe. We know it by heart now."

Private Ernest Swift of the 58th Infantry put it more succinctly in writing a friend in Colorado: "I always said some day I'd leave that d—town, but when I get back, Durango is good enough for me."

These were equally the emphatic sentiments of those soldiers who, in November, marched not to the Rhine, but back to the training areas in France. Their feelings about the French were mixed. France was suffering inflation and prices were sky high. Mess sergeants to buy poultry for Christmas dinners had to pay 85 cents a pound for ducks and $1.20 for turkeys; many a restaurant proprietor near a rail center charged unmercifully for sandwiches. Many of the soldiers became hostile toward the French, and never in later years relinquished their hostility. Charles B. Hoyt wrote a few months later:

"It was better that the soldiers be returned as soon as possible. The breach between the Americans and the French had widened and in the chasm across which they gazed there was to be found no common interests and sympathy. Lafayette had been repaid, but the thanks of the French were expressed in increased prices to the soldiers. The mass of the soldiery never understood and never forgave. Between the inhabitants of some of the villages and the men billeted there the relationship trembled on the brink of racial clashes. The soldiers desired a quick return to America and the only love the French now held to stay their departure was for their money."

Undoubtedly many of the French were tired of having Americans in their midst. A woman Red Cross worker interviewed by Katherine Anne Porter in January 1919 strongly urged American girls not to head for Paris: "The country has been fairly bursting with alien humanity for more than four years; no matter how welcome or useful we were, we were a houseful of strangers, and France is tired."

Nevertheless, tired France did show unusual hospitality to most of the American soldiers during the months that remained. At least among those men who had been to the front there was far more appreciation than irritation. Thus, the experiences of the men of Battery C, 102nd Field Artillery.

In Salmagne: "Another feature which it had seldom been our unlucky lot to contend with was the inhospitable disposition of the peasants, in this village towards us. They were cold and hostile to all Americans, for some reasons or other and we were very thankful that the stay was a short one."

In Pouilly-Haute-Marne: "The people in this town were very hospitable and soon made friends with us. Many, in fact most of them, had spare rooms, with great big French beds and many of the boys hired these rooms, for the small sum of one franc (about twenty cents). They took us in as one of the family and all the privileges of their little homes were graciously extended to us. When we ate with the battery it became necessary to eat out in the cold and rain, as mess halls were a luxury unknown to us, but it was not often that we would eat outside, for we were almost always invited by the peasants to eat in their homes. . . . Quite often . . . we would have one of the grand old French Madames kill a chicken or a rabbit, cook up some 'French fries' and set a supper for us, for which we always paid them liberally."

Enlisted men and reserve officers alike were far more irritated with Army higher-ups who not only enforced strict discipline but also felt that this was the opportunity to provide the men with further training. The net result was less the production of a first-rate army reserve than an indoctrination against all things military. Captain L. Wardlaw Miles of the 308th Infantry wrote later:

"Very soon there began to descend from Division Headquarters countless memoranda and bulletins concerning drill schedules and programs to be followed. A long and intricate system of terrain exercises and maneuvers had been worked up and upon these all kinds of training were based. Innumerable pamphlets and booklets were showered on unsuspecting Company Commanders. "I Have Captured a Boche Machine Gun. What Shall I Do With It?" . . . Men who had fought in Lorraine, on the Vesle, Aisne, Meuse, and in the Argonne, were instructed by the pamphlets . . . how always to blacken one's face before going on a patrol. . . .

"Machine gun after machine gun was captured with unfailing regularity. Constant liaison was maintained with either flank, with the rear, with the artillery, with everybody. . . . And G.H.Q. expressed its pleasure at the success of the exercises and mentioned the 'remarkable interest displayed by all concerned.' "

Captain Tiebout of the 305th Infantry satirized an inspection:

" 'That underwear should not hang in the sleeping quarters.'

" 'It must dry somewhere, sir.'

" 'Don't dry it in the sleeping quarters. Set aside one of your rooms for a sort of laundry. Put a stove in it, and keep it hot.'

" 'Sir, every available room is used for sleeping purposes. This is a mighty poor town. The Mayor cannot give us another inch of space. Besides, no stoves have been issued. This is the only fireplace in the building; but then, the issue of fuel is so meagre that it all goes to the kitchen fires. These clothes dry out a little during the day, and are further dried by whatever sort of fire the men can scrape together at night.' (They steal the wood.)

" 'My boy,' begins the inspector, feeling that he approaches the point where he can pull the favorite old Army gag and pass the buck; 'don't say it can't be done. That word is not in our dictionary. Now, the real soldier, the real officer, is the one who utilizes every means at this disposal to accomplish his object. When the proper materials are not forthcoming, he must exercise his ingenuity and initiative. He takes even the old tin can from the—Have your men shower baths? Then take a number of tin cans, punch holes in the bottom and—' "

This sort of treatment left many of soldiers and their immediate officers with little respect for many of the top officers, except General Pershing himself, who, arriving for inspections and to bestow decorations, inspired undiminished awe. Lieutenants Bryant Wilson and Lamar Tooze wrote:

"We were off in motor trucks, at seven o'clock bound for a field. . . . After leaving the trucks and waiting at the village until 10 A.M., we moved off to the appointed place. Here we waited till shortly after 1 P.M. in the snow, eating some sandwiches we carried along for the occasion and stamping our feet to keep warm.

"Suddenly, several swift U.S.A. automobiles drew up and the Chief and his staff stepped out. Mounting a horse and accompanied by one other officer, he quickly made the rounds of the Division, drawn up in line of the regiments, mass formation, with the bands playing 'Hail to the Chief!' He then dismounted and began a careful rank to rank inspection, passing along each rank of every company of the Division. Questions such as, 'Where are you from?' or 'Where were you wounded?' were asked of doughboys as the General hurried on his rounds. Next, those to be decorated were drawn up in front of the Division, accompanied by the colors. . . .

"The whole Division stood at attention while the citations were read and General Pershing himself pinned on the medals and crosses and congratulated the recipients. His manly handgrasp was in keeping with the Big stalwart soldier that he is. . . .

"The Division next marched past the reviewing stand. As the column swung past the General, each man proudly squared his shoulders, for the appraising eyes of his Chief were upon him. After the last platoon had passed, the officers assembled before the reviewing stand to receive the General's message to the Division. He spoke with pride of the accomplishments and clean record of the Ninety-first and urged us to carry the same high ideals back with us into civil life. 'May you have a safe journey home. Good-bye!' "

A few soldiers participated in an equally impressive review before President Wilson on Christmas morning, 1918. Captain Hyde wrote:

"It was a chill cloudy day and the muddy plains near the town looked pretty drear. A grandstand with a long duck-board walk, was arranged for the Presidential party. They arrived, in a long train of automobiles, with 12 or 15 aeroplanes flying overhead. The troops were formed in a dense mass in front of the stand in line of companies. I was struck by the enthusiasm of the crowd, which was of course almost entirely military—only a few French civilians there (and they made most of the noise). The President looked well, in a long fur coat, as he walked to the stand with Gen. Pershing, who looked splendid. He was followed by Mrs. W., with Lt. Gen. Ligget,—then many civilians and officers. Gen. Pershing's little speech opened the proceedings and was good and well delivered, but I had difficulty hearing the President. He has aged and is quite bald. The review was impressive in spite of the muddy field, and the difficulty of neat manoeuvres, but I was certainly sorry for all those poor half-frozen soldiers. They all carried gas-masks, but many had no gloves. . . . But the event was an historical occasion and I am glad I was lucky enough to see it."

President Wilson's reception in Paris was tumultuous, Sergeant E. V. Arnold of the 158th Infantry, who was in charge of a platoon of the President's honor guard, wrote his mother:

"I saw him several times, but he didn't come over and shake hands or anything like that. . . . The town went wild the day he came and is still going. The people do nothing but walk, promenade they call it, and the crowds are so dense that cars can hardly get through. . . . The girls join hands forming a circle of about ten, they then get a soldier inside and he has to kiss them all before he can get out. They throw confetti in our faces and, of course, we kiss them then."

But how the American soldiers felt about President Wilson's ideals and his proposed League of Nations was less apparent in their letters home. These for the most part were strikingly apolitical. There were a few exceptions. S. A. Bush wrote from Bourges in July 1919:

"Everyone gets homesick and relieves his feeling by swearing. . . . But they can keep me here forever, and I will not grumble if they will just kill that league of nations. I am willing to protect America at any time, but to hell with these insects over here. I would like to see the whole eastern hemisphere sink into hell as soon as all the Americans get out of here."

A more typical political attitude was that Sergeant Neil W. Kimball expressed in March 1919:

"I have talked and discussed matters with A.E.F. men from the Rhine to Nice, and the feeling of these two million odd on vital questions facing our country . . . will surprise and dismay a lot of stay-at-homes. . . . The members of the A.E.F. are going to be the biggest little steam roller that ever hit American politics. . . . The only thing that is going to save the United States from Bolshevism of the worst sort is the fact that her young generation knows better."

All such talk was secondary, as Sergeant Kimball well knew. He had earlier written:

"The only thing that can break up a barracks room French lesson is a 'when are we going home' discussion. Every man in a company of 230 gets at least two rumors a day, and some have a much better average than that. A new dish at dinner, a headline in a month old paper from the States, a laughing remark from an officer, a word with a sailor fresh in port—it is all grist for the barracks room mill. . . .

" 'What I'm going to do when I get out' is another favorite topic. One thing sure—the soda fountains and restaurants are certainly going to be punished.

"Rear ranker says he wants to take his rifle with him when he is mustered out. He is going to stand it up under the drain spout and watch it rust."

Division by division, the men during the spring months began to undergo thorough delousing and physical examinations (leaving behind the handful with venereal disease). They then entrained for the ports of debarkation, most of them to Camp Pontanezen at Brest. There they underwent further waiting and were hampered with senseless regulations. Sergeant William L. Langer wrote of the morning of embarkation:

"When the company had been formed there began that long series of waits characteristic of all important moves. The packs were heavy, but at first we did not mind that so much. The worst of it was that we were 'at ease,' not permitted to speak or smoke. This was a camp regulation, and it further specified that we should march through the camp at attention. I hardly know whether we felt more jubilant at leaving or more indignant at the imposition of this and similar orders. But it could not be helped; it was a choice between asserting ourselves and going home. We unanimously chose the latter. So we marched out, units of a victorious army on their way home tramping through and out of the camp, along the hilly army on their way home through it to the docks. It was a hard hike, made of harder yet by the bitter feeling that we were obliged to leave like a pack of slinking, whipped curs the country to which we had come prepared to give gladly all we had in us."

When Colonel George C. Marshall visited the 27th Division, embarking upon the *Leviathan*, he was angered to find it being victimized, and went directly to the Chief of Staff of the Service of Supplies in order to cut some of the red tape.

At length division after division embarked for the United States. In May 1919 alone a third of a million men sailed, and by the end of August all but the five regular divisions on the Rhine had left for home. In September 1919 General Pershing himself sailed.

One last wisecrack went the rounds of the disbanding A.E.F. A returning soldier, at last seeing the Statue of Liberty looming through the mist in New York Harbor, declared fervently: "Old girl, if you ever want to look me in the face again, you'll have to turn around on your pedestal."

Photographing
the War

Literally thousands of photographers contributed to the amassing of an enormous photographic record of the First World War. By the time the United Sates entered the conflict, war photography had passed largely from the domain of the resourceful newspaper photographer of earlier, smaller wars, who roamed at will behind the lines, at the front, and sometimes even in the advance of the contending armies. Rather, each army had its official uniformed photographers, working under military orders. Photographers served in the United States Army as part of the Signal Corps; almost all of the great pictures are the work of these skillful, brave, and anonymous men.

Photographic technology had improved enormously, even in the few years since the Spanish-American War, and in a revolutionary fashion since the Civil War. The Chief Signal Officer in his report after the close of the First World War wrote:

"It is a grand stride from the methods employed by Matthew Brady, who during the Civil War made his wet plates in the field, drove through the lines of the Union Army, using camera with a lens made of spectacle glass, taking photographs, which later were developed in the shelter of some barn with uncertainty as to the results, to the present day photographer conveyed to points of vantage by motorcycle, automobile, or airplane equipped with his graphic camera containing a lens made from the finest of optical glass, high speed shutter dryplates, and cut film, which enable him to make both still and moving pictures of objects moving at high rates of speed, and with the aid of a portable dark room produce a finished print of a still photograph in the field within 15 minutes."

The Signal Corps trained men in both still and motion picture photography at Columbia University, and in aerial photography at a school in Rochester. It sent 38 divisional photographic units overseas, including 54 officers and 418 men. Some of these men, like their fellow soldiers, found themselves permanently assigned to the service areas. Leighton Davies of Parkersburg, West Virginia, attached to the Central Medical Laboratory, wrote his parents October 12, 1918:

"I go all over the country and in that way see a lot of it. I do all the photographic work of this unit and have everything to myself. I go to the hospitals and do photographic work quite often. Some of the boys are shot up pretty bad, but most of them are nervy and don't complain much. We have four artists and three moving picture men in our unit besides myself. We get a lot of auto rides, but strictly business. In our travels over the country we generally go in box cars, taking our baggage with us. . . . I suppose you are working hard. I would like to be there and help out in the studio during the Christmas rush, but no chance at present anyway."

Other photographers found themselves sharing the hazardous life of the infantrymen. The Chief Signal Officer reported:

"The record of the photographic service contains also its casualties and instances of wit and daring. First Lieutenant Edwin Ralph Estep on duty with an infantry patrol, 42nd

Division, near Sedan, on the night of November 7, 1918, was killed by shell fire, and the plates taken from his camera showed the last acts of his life. Corporal Daniel J. Sheehan, attached to the 2nd Division, listed as missing and presumed dead, was repatriated from a German prison camp in January, 1919. While accompanying a scouting party following the obliteration of the St. Mihiel salient, he was wounded by a gas shell. He succeeded in getting on his gas mask before losing consciousness and was taken prisoner by the Germans.

" 'What have you there?' demanded the Prussian officer before whom he was brought to be interrogated, indicating his camera.

" 'Just a camera,' the corporal answered. 'See,' and he quickly pulled out the plate magazine exposing the plates to the light and prevented the enemy from developing the negatives.

"Six other photographers of the Signal Corps units in the field were wounded in action."

ACKNOWLEDGMENTS

I am indebted to numerous people whose generosity made it possible for me to assemble the pictures and text. Most of the photographs are from the enormous and excellent collections in the Still Picture Branch, National Archives. I was aided especially by Forrest Williams, at that time Archivist in Charge, and by Josephine Cobb, who first introduced me to the collections. For several naval photographs I am grateful to Admiral E. M. Eller, Director of Naval History, Office of the Chief of Naval Operations. A large part of the letters published in newspapers are from the extensive file in the Western Historical Collections at the University of Colorado. I am especially indebted to Lucile Fry, Librarian, for her extraordinary kindness and helpfulness. For other manuscripts I wish to thank Gene M. Gressley, Archivist, University of Wyoming Library; the University of West Virginia Library, and the Alabama Archives. For providing me with heretofore unpublished materials I am grateful to my former teacher, Professor Chester V. Easum of the University of Wisconsin, and to Professor Harold G. Merriam of Montana State University.

Once again the photographic and circulation staffs of the Harvard University Library have performed invaluable services. For continued advice and encouragement I am indebted to Ned Bradford and Madeleine Freidel.

FOR FURTHER READING

A summary introduction to the war is *World War I: An Outline History* (1962) by Hanson W. Baldwin, the American authority; a British survey is Cyril Falls, *The Great War, 1914–1918* (1959). A dramatic account of the initial battles in 1914 is Barbara W. Tuchman, *The Guns of August* (1962). One of the most illuminating studies of the events in Europe as well as the United States leading to American entrance is Ernest R. May, *The World War and American Isolation* (1959). Laurence Stallings, *The Doughboys* (1963), is a vivid history of the American Expeditionary Forces. On the relations of the United States with the Allies see David F. Trask, *The United States in the Supreme War Council* (1961).

The contemporary and near-contemporary accounts that are quoted throughout this book are from collections cited in the Acknowledgments, from the books listed below, and from letters in the *Literary Digest* and the *New Republic*. Official reports,

both American and German, are to be found in the multivolume
United States Army in the World War 1917–1919 (1948) published
by the Historical Division, Department of the Army. Indis-
pensable for its summaries of American battles and its excellent
maps (a number of which are reproduced herein) is the volume
prepared by the American Battle Monuments Commission,
American Armies and Battlefields in Europe (1938). I have drawn upon
it extensively for factual information, especially the location of
troop units.

Soldiers' letters quoted throughout the book may well contain some exaggerations and inaccuracies. Sometimes boastful
letters printed in hometown newspapers caused embarrassment
to their authors when copies of the papers reached France. I
have not quoted a wounded hero's statement that in one day's
fighting at Chateau-Thierry, out of 250 men only one lieutenant
and one private were left. Nor have I quoted the letters of his
younger brother who had entered boot camp as an apprentice
seaman. He wrote home that he saved the commandant from
being murdered, and as a reward was sent to officers' school and
commissioned. Next through his quick thinking he saved a submarine from sinking, and was promoted to lieutenant, junior
grade. Alas, while en route to his admiring family, he was arrested for impersonating an officer. "We can't understand it," his sister lamented, "unless it's just because someone is jealous because
he was promoted so fast."

Those sensational accounts that appear are entirely verifi-
able—for example, the adventures of Lieutenant Issacs as a cap-
tive aboard a German submarine and later as a fugitive from
German prisons.

Americans Defending Democracy; Our Soldiers' Own Stories (1919)
Army Times, *A History of the U.S. Signal Corps* (1961)
Arnold, H. H., *Global Mission* (1949)
Atkinson, Minnie, *Newburyport in the World War* (1938)
Baker, H. L., *Argonne Days* (1927)
Baker, N. D., *Frontiers of Freedom* (1918)
Bakewell, C. M., *The Story of the Red Cross in Italy* (1920)

Bonsal, Stephen, *Unfinished Business* (1944)

Brown, E. S., *A History of Switzerland County's Part in the World War* (1919)

Brown, H. U., ed., *Hilton U. Brown, Jr.* (1920)

Bucher, Georg, *In the Line: 1914–1918* (1932)

Bullard, R. E., *Personalities and Reminiscences of the War* (1925)

Catlin, A. W., and W. A. Dyer, *"With the Help of God and a Few Marines"*

Chamberlin, J. E., *The Only Thing for a Man to Do* (1921)

Chastaine, Ben H., *Story of the 36th* (1920)

Coolidge, Hamilton, *Letters of an American Airman* (1919)

Crozier, Emmet, *American Reporters on the Western Front, 1914–1918* (1959)

Cushing, Harvey, *From a Surgeon's Journal, 1915–1918* (1936)

Cutchins, J. A., and G. S. Steward, Jr., *History of the Twenty-Ninth Division* (1921)

Daniels, Jonathan, *The Man of Independence* (1950)

Daniels, Josephus, *Our Navy at War* (1922)

Dawes, C. G., *A Journal of the Great War* (2 vols., 1921)

Dulles, F. R. *The American Red Cross, A History* (1950)

Elliott, P. B., ed., *On the Field of Honor* (1920)

English, G. H., *History of the 89th Division* (1920)

Frothingham, T. G., *The Naval History of the World War: The United States in the War, 1917–1918* (1926)

Gleaves, Albert, *A History of the Transport Service* (1921)

Graves, W. S., *America's Siberian Adventure, 1918–1920* (1931)

Hagood, Johnson, *The Services of Supply* (1927)

Hall, N. S., *The Balloon Buster: Frank Luke of Arizona* (1928)

Harbord, J. G., *The American Army in France, 1917–1919* (1936)

———, *Leaves from a War Diary* (1925)

Harris, Frederick, ed., *Service with Fighting Men: An Account of the Work of the American Young Men's Christian Associations in the World War* (2 vols., 1922)

History of the American Field Service in France (3 vols., 1920)

Hoehling, A. A., *The Fierce Lambs* (1960)

Howe, M. A. DeW., *Memoirs of the Harvard Dead in the War Against Germany* (vol. 2, 1921)

————, *Oliver Ames, Jr., 1895–1918* (1922)

Hoyt, C. B., *Heroes of the Argonne: An Authentic History of the 35th Division* (1919)

In Memoriam; Arthur Sewall Hyde, 1875–1920 (1920)

Janis, Elsie, *The Big Show* (1919)

Langer, W. L., and R. B. MacMullin, *With "E" of the First Gas* (1919)

Luby, James, *One Who Gave His Life: War Letters of Quincy Sharpe Mills* (1923)

McKeogh, Arthur, *The Victorious 77th Division in the Argonne Fight* (1919)

"Mademoiselle Miss": Letters from an American Girl Serving with the Rank of Lieutenant in a French Army Hospital at the Front (1916)

Mathews, William, and Dixon Wecter, *Our Soldiers Speak, 1775–1918* (1943)

Meehan, T. F., ed., *History of the Seventy-Eighth Division in the World War* (1921)

Miles, L. W., *History of the 308th Infantry, 1917–1919* (1927)

Mitchell, William, *Memoirs of World War I* (1960)

Morison, E. E., *Admiral Sims and the Modern American Navy* (1942)

New England Aviators, 1914–1918 (2 vols., 1919)

[O'Brien, H. V.], *Wine, Women and War: A Diary of Disillusionment* (1926)

Paine, R. D., *The Fighting Fleets* (1918)

Palmer, Frederick, *Newton D. Baker: America at War* (2 vols., 1931)

Paxson, F. L., *America at War, 1917–1918* (1939)

Pershing, J. J., *My Experiences in the World War* (2 vols., 1931)

Pogue, F. C., *George C. Marshall: Education of a General* (1963)

Reilly H. J., *Americans All: The Rainbow at War* (1936)

Rickenbacker, Edward, *Fighting the Flying Circus* (1919)

Roosevelt, Kermit, ed., *Quentin Roosevelt, A Sketch with Letters* (1921)

Russel, W. M., *A Happy Warrior: Letters of William Muir Russel* (1919)

Seeger, Alan, *Letters and Diary* (1917)

Sibley, F. P., *With the Yankee Division in France* (1919)

Sims, W. S., and B. J. Hendrick, *The Victory at Sea* (1920)

Sirois, E. D., and William McGinnis, *Smashing Through the World War with Fighting Battery C* (1919)

Straub, E. F., *A Sergeant's Diary in the World War* (1923)

Sweeney, D. J., ed., *History of Buffalo and Erie Country, 1914–1919* (1919)

Sweetser, Arthur, *The American Air Service* (1919)

Taber, J. H., *The Story of the 168th Infantry* (vol. 2, 1925)

Thomason, J. W., Jr., *Fix Bayonets!* (1926)

Tiebout, F. B., *A History of the 305th Infantry* (1919)

Toulmin, H. A., *Air Service American Expeditionary Force, 1918* (1927)

Treadwell, M. E., *The Women's Army Corps* (United States Army in World War II, Special Studies, 1954)

Wecter, Dixon, *When Johnny Comes Marching Home* (1944)

Williams, C. H., *Sidelights on Negro Soldiers* (1923)

Wilson, Bryant, and Lamar Tooze, *With the 364th Infantry in America, France, and Belgium* (1920)

INDEX